# Constructing
# Medieval Sexuality

# MEDIEVAL CULTURES

SERIES EDITORS
Rita Copeland
Barbara A. Hanawalt
David Wallace

*Sponsored by the Center for Medieval Studies
at the University of Minnesota*

Volumes in the series study the diversity of medieval cultural histories and practices, including such interrelated issues as gender, class, and social hierarchies; race and ethnicity; geographical relations; definitions of political space; discourses of authority and dissent; educational institutions; canonical and non-canonical literatures; and technologies of textual and visual literacies.

*For other books in the series, see p. 206*

# Constructing
# Medieval Sexuality

❖

Karma Lochrie, Peggy McCracken, and
James A. Schultz, editors

Medieval Cultures
Volume 11

University of Minnesota Press
Minneapolis
London

Published by the University of Minnesota Press
111 Third Avenue South, Suite 290
Minneapolis, MN 55401-2520

http://www.upress.umn.edu

**Library of Congress Cataloging-in-Publication Data**
Constructing medieval sexuality / Karma Lochrie, Peggy McCracken, and
James A. Schultz, editors.
    p.     cm. — (Medieval cultures ; v. 11)
    Includes bibliographical references and index.
    ISBN 0-8166-2828-9 (alk. paper). — ISBN 0-8166-2829-7 (pbk. :
alk. paper)
    1. Sex—Europe—History.   2. Social history—Medieval, 500–1500.
3. Civilization, Medieval.   4. Europe—Social life and customs.
I. Lochrie, Karma.   II. McCracken, Peggy.   III. Schultz, James A.
(James Alfred), 1947–   .   IV. Series.
HQ14.C66   1997
306.7'094—dc21                                                              97-9425
                                                                               CIP

Printed in the United States of America on acid-free paper

The University of Minnesota is an equal-opportunity educator and employer.

10 09 08 07 06 05 04 03 02 01 00 99 98      10 9 8 7 6 5 4 3 2 1

# Contents

✛

# Acknowledgments

❖

The impetus for this collection of essays on medieval sexuality came from a conference held at the Newberry Library in Chicago March 4–5, 1994. Of the essays published in this volume, those by Joan Cadden, Michael Camille, Dyan Elliott, Mark D. Jordan, and Karma Lochrie were first presented as papers at the Newberry conference. The conference was organized by Karma Lochrie, Peggy McCracken, James A. Schultz, and Karen Scott and was sponsored by the Center for Renaissance Studies at the Newberry Library; De Paul University; Loyola University, Chicago; and the University of Illinois at Chicago. The editors of this volume would like to take this opportunity to thank their co-organizer, Karen Scott, as well as the Center for Renaissance Studies and its director, Mary Beth Rose, and staff, Tonia Triggiano and Kim Giesel, for their invaluable help in making the conference possible. We would also like to acknowledge those scholars who participated in the conference but who, for one reason or another, were unable to contribute essays to this volume: James A. Brundage, Carolyn Dinshaw, Simon Gaunt, Kathryn Gravdal, and Ruth Mazo Karras. They are part of the conversation on medieval sexuality that made this collection possible. We thank Linda Vavra and the staff of the Institute for the Humanities at the University of Illinois, Chicago, for help with manuscript preparation.

# Introduction

❖

Explaining what motivated him to abandon his original plan and extend his history of sexuality back to ancient Greece, Michel Foucault cites the desire for a kind of knowledge that causes one to stray afield—from oneself, one's culture, and one's historical moment: "There are times in life when the question of knowing if one can think differently than one thinks, and perceive differently than one sees, is absolutely necessary if one is to go on looking and reflecting at all."[1] Few topics are more likely to challenge us to think differently than past sexualities, since we often assume what Peter Brown calls a "certain knowingness,"[2] a smug confidence that we already know "it." Yet if we hope to continue "looking and reflecting" on the Middle Ages, modernity, or ourselves, then we must attempt to think and perceive historical sexualities "differently." A medieval history of sexuality must take seriously Foucault's project of thinking and seeing differently without denying our participation in the present. The challenge is to look at the Middle Ages without presentist assumptions yet without forfeiting the tools of contemporary theories of sexuality and, at the same time, to remain attentive to how thinking differently about medieval sexuality may change the way we think about sexuality in the present.[3]

Such an undertaking inevitably risks anachronism. Like Foucault, we feel ambivalent about the term "sexuality," using it in our title, as he used it in his, "for want of anything better."[4] It indicates the pleasures of the sexual body as they are practiced, imagined, disciplined, and understood. As is well known, there is no medieval equivalent.[5] "Sexuality" designates a domain that is of interest to us today, and that interest has led us to look back to the Middle Ages to find phenomena that answer to it. In this sense, the object of study, medieval sexuality, is a modern construction. Like Foucault, we understand sexuality not as a natural category of human experience but as a "very real historical formation" produced by "our discourses, our customs, our institutions, our regulations, our knowledges."[6] Sexuality is a product of history. The medieval phenomena that answer to our interest in sexuality will also have been historical formations, produced by and embedded in specifically medieval discourses, customs, institutions, regulations, and knowledges. In this sense too, medieval sexuality is a construction, a medieval construction. And as such, Steven Kruger reminds us, medieval sexuality is implicated in other medieval constructions defined by the categories of race, gender, ethnicity, and religion.

As a practice invested with contested ideological values, medieval sexuality is not seamless, and it is far from constituting the transparent, "markedly unitary" discourse often attributed to the Middle Ages—by Foucault among others—in order to make a modern "explosion" of discursivities about sexuality seem all the more exhilarating.[7] This volume brings together essays from a variety of disciplinary perspectives—literary, theological, philosophical, medical, historical, and art historical—that demonstrate both the diversity of sources for reading medieval sexuality and the sometimes contradictory nature of the evidence offered by those sources. Even a single text may reveal startling contradictions: according to Mark Jordan, in the *Summa theologica* Aquinas "oscillates" between the view that sodomy is merely a "middling species of a subsidiary class of sins" and the position that it represents "the eponymous denial of the order of animal nature, hence of nature's God." Although Peter of Abano taught in Paris only a few decades after Aquinas's death, he takes a much different view. Joan Cadden shows that Peter judges the desire of some men for anal stimulation to be irregular but still natural. That two texts addressing related phenomena from within what is essentially the same intellectual milieu reveal such tensions and contradictions suggests the much greater complexity and diversity that one will find on venturing farther afield into the larger realm of medieval sexuality.

Although the medieval texts and images discussed in this volume represent varied and often contradictory constructions of sexuality and although the authors who discuss them come from a variety of academic disciplines, the essays are united by a number of shared commitments. First, when we address ourselves to sexuality we always consider it in relation to gender; second, we consider medieval constructions of the body as integral to the medieval construction of sexuality; third, we situate sexuality in relation to medieval constructions of identity and "otherness"; and finally, we acknowledge the effect of the present on our readings of the past and invite a consideration of the implications of medieval constructions for modern theories of sexuality.

## Gender

Thinking differently about the medieval past often requires one to think differently from Foucault. This is especially true with regard to gender, which many have criticized Foucault for ignoring. Others, however, have been inspired by his example as well as by Gayle Rubin's influential article calling for "an autonomous theory and politics specific to sexuality" to distinguish between the study of sexuality and that of gender, the latter the particular province of feminism.[8] Rubin herself has challenged such a reading of her essay,[9] and Judith Butler has noted its dangers: "The sexuality that is 'liberated' from feminism will be one which suspends the reference to masculine and feminine. . . . Such a 'liberation' dovetails with mainstream conservatism and with male dominance in its many and various forms."[10] The contributors to this volume do not suspend the reference to masculine and feminine. Instead, they show how the asymmetrical gender relations that arise from culturally specific meanings attached to sex difference constitute one of the most important matrices within which medieval sexuality was constructed.

Looking carefully at medieval texts and images, one discovers that gender is constructed according to a number of paradigms, that these entail different sorts of sexuality, and that neither the categories of gender nor the sexualities they entail are as stable as one might have expected. Michael Camille discusses images that are determined in large part by a medical model that grounds gender differences in the physiology of the organism itself. Because women's bodies are by nature cooler than men's, women's flesh must be painted whiter and bluer than men's. Other traditions represent gender as independent of the body. James Schultz shows that in Gottfried's *Tristan* the desirable body does not have any anatomical features that reveal its sex. Not grounded in the morphology of the body, gender difference is constructed instead by a semiotics of clothing and is elaborated in a structure of desire that distinguishes between desire for a man and desire for a woman. Although both Camille and Schultz discuss traditions in which gender definitions are relatively stable, as might be expected, the medically inspired illuminations are focused primarily on procreation, while in the vernacular romance, sexuality is focused on the satisfaction of a gendered desire completely indifferent to the medical-theological obsession with reproduction.

The French romance texts Jane Burns investigates are similar to Gottfried's *Tristan* in that they establish gender difference not through anatomy but through clothing. Here, however, the categories thus defined are not so reliable: the knight steps out of the armor that establishes his masculinity, dons the unisex *chemise* worn at court, and reveals his white flesh, the marker of femininity, while the lady in a love service relationship assumes the position of lord. In such a context, "gender cannot be made to signify monolithically," and such an instability undermines the heterosexual presumption of the ethic of courtly love, which depends on strictly defined gender roles. French romances betray no particular anxiety over the instability of gender, and this lack of anxiety is another unsettling factor for the heterosexual presumption of the courtly love ethic that ostensibly structures sexuality in these stories.

If the French romances allow a slippage of gender identities that may suggest a subversion of the heterosexual model of courtly love, other medieval discourses more anxiously resist the disruption of gender categories on which they stake definitions of privilege and hierarchy. Dyan

Elliott traces a theological concern with nocturnal emissions, which, although they might seem to mark the body as unmistakably male, could represent the danger of effeminization; their involuntary nature challenges clerical pretensions to rational (masculine) control of the (feminine) body; the priest who experiences such "pollution" can be likened to a menstruating woman. Faced with these dangers, clerical writers sought to "consolidate masculine identity" against the feminizing effects of nocturnal emissions. On the other hand, as Karma Lochrie argues, the blurring of gender identity is embraced by women mystics in their devotion to Christ's wounds. In images of the wounded, feminized body of Christ, gender becomes unstable, and sexuality begins to stray as a consequence. The stimulation of bodies, intensification of pleasures, and incitements to discourse found in medieval mysticism are a reminder that sexuality is never "exempt from the enmeshments and constraints of gender" or of the body.[11] Similar constraints and enmeshments condition courtly love, as well. Louise Fradenburg explains the "repetitively failed transactions, exchanges, and unions" that are so problematic in Chaucer's *Legend of Good Women* as symptomatic of a larger impossibility structured by the gendered demands of the courtly love ethos. The dynamic created by chivalric masculinity as rescue and femininity as "good woman" renders all courtly love futile, heroic, and tragic. Nor is the "lady" of courtly love a stably gendered object of desire, but one that dangerously invites the knight's "sodomitical encounter, *via* the *ascesis/jouissance* of shame."

The Middle Ages revealed by these essays is one in which there is a considerable tension between efforts to stabilize gender and tendencies that undermine fixed gender. At the same time, one encounters a considerable variety of strategies—physiological, vestimentary, theological—that engender bodies. Each of these strategies constitutes and is constituted by a particular, more or less stable, sexuality. Such evidence compels us to reconsider familiar narratives of the history of sexuality, according to which the "relative uniformity"[12] of the Middle Ages gives way to a modern "explosion" of discourses about sexuality, and reminds us that gender and sexuality are so inextricably linked that one cannot write usefully about the one without incorporating the other as well.

## Bodies

Near the end of the introduction to the *History of Sexuality* Foucault gives an example of how the kind of work he envisioned might cause us to think differently. He suggests that we challenge the modern regime of sexuality by rallying around "bodies and pleasures," calling for "a 'history of bodies' and the manner in which what is most material and vital in them has been invested."[13] This call has been abundantly answered by recent works in medieval studies, including those of Peter Brown, Caroline Walker Bynum, and Joan Cadden.[14] Feminism, queer theory, and writing about AIDS have provided us with theoretical matrices for reading the medieval body.[15] Medievalists are using these matrices to explore how a history of the body, with its economy of humors, sexual and reproductive faculties, sensations, somatic expressions, gender hierarchy, and exacting moral codes, might intersect with a history of sexuality, including its economy of desires, pleasures, incitements to discourse, and the regulatory regimes that govern it. By looking at a number of historically specific bodies and the sexualities they entail, the contributors to this volume negotiate this double intersection of modern theories and medieval texts and of bodies and sexualities in the effort to foster new ways of thinking and seeing.

If the bodies of courtly romance do not make a clear morphological distinction between male and female, then such distinctions can play no role in the articulation of sexual desire, and the "heterosexual" relations of such bodies must have a different meaning from the heterosexual relations with which we are familiar. Medical writers are more concerned with the anatomy of sex. In the text examined by Joan Cadden, Peter of Abano asks why certain men desire anal stimulation and answers that their seminal passageways do not lead to the penis but to the region around the anus. Thus Peter describes a historically specific body that explains a particular sexual desire. The images discussed by Michael Camille depend on theological as well as medical constructions of the body that are more prescriptive: they hold, for example, that intercourse might harm either the man or the fetus unless the partners have sex facing each other with the woman underneath the man. The inevitability with which visual representations of coitus reproduce this one position reinforces the construction of a very inflexible (hetero)sexuality and banishes all other forms of sexual relations to the margins of the unnatural, the unhealthy, and the sinful. The courtly romances, the medical text, and the manuscript images all construct a particular body inseparable from a particular construction of sexuality.

However, bodies are not always as reliable as the various doctors and illustrators would have wished. Dyan Elliott shows how the ideas of Augustine, who wrote of the "insubordination" of the flesh, are taken up with a vengeance in the High Middle Ages by clerics who agonize over the status of nocturnal emissions. They are troubled by "the unruly masculine body" and the challenge it represents to the dictates of the will. The demon incubi and succubi formed from spilled semen represent an even greater threat to bodily stability, since they can shift at will from seeming males to seeming females. This sort of instability is not always resisted. In her investigation of female devotion to the wounds of Christ, Karma Lochrie argues that the polymorphous body of Christ, "with its feminine genital wound and its simultaneous masculine properties, introduces confusion at a very foundational level of religious language." The desire for such a body, although it confuses heteronormative categories and is often deeply painful for the mystic herself, is neverthe-less embraced.

If one approaches medieval bodies willing to see differently, then one discovers that they are actually quite different from modern ones. While some are female and others male, while some desire anal stimulation and others have wet dreams, while some are unstable or polymorphous or queer, these properties and behaviors have specifically medieval causes and meanings. These specifically medieval bodies are the products of and the prerequisites for specifically medieval constructions of gender, identity, and sexuality.

## Identities

One of the best-known legacies of Foucault's effort to think differently about sexuality in the past is his distinction between the sodomite and the homosexual. The sodomite, defined by an act he committed, "had been a temporary aberration"; the homosexual, created by a nineteenth-century discourse that made sexuality an integral part of the person, "was now a species."[16] This distinction has been taken up with much passion by students of lesbian and gay history, who have disagreed about whether it is permissible to speak of homosexuals or gay people before the recent past. Those who deny the applicability of these terms to ear-lier periods often distinguish between an earlier classification of sexual-ity according to "acts" (sodomy) and a later classification according to "identities" or "persons" (the homosexual).[17] Recently, however, this tidy historical narrative has been called into question: classification by acts has not disappeared, as is revealed by the Supreme Court's reliance in *Bowers v. Hardwick* (1986) on a category of "homosexual sodomy," and material continues to be discovered suggesting that "identities" of some sort existed in the past.[18] The essays in this volume offer evidence that challenges both those who would discover homosexuals in the past and those who would restrict identities to the present. They show as well that "identities," however they are understood, are seldom simple and never single.

On the subject of same-sex relations, the evidence is resistant to sim-ple categorization. According to Mark Jordan, when Aquinas writes of the "sodomitic vice" he is talking about a vice that "is precisely not a physiological disposition or its behavioral consequences." As a result Aquinas "cannot responsibly be made even to speak in debates where 'homosexuality' and 'heterosexuality' serve as categories for personal iden-tity." When Joan Cadden studies the passage from Peter of Abano in which he discusses men who desire anal stimulation, she too finds "no serious analogue to the modern term 'homosexuality.'" And yet, Cadden ex-plains, Peter does isolate a *kind* of person, one whose seminal passage-ways lead to the area around the anus, who therefore *by nature* desires anal stimulation. This apparent clarity is undermined, however, by the isolation of a second class of men, whose passageways follow the orthodox route but whose delight in anal stimulation has become habit or *second* nature. Thus while Peter "clearly presents much more than particular sexual acts and desires," he just as clearly does not suggest a coherent sexual "identity" in the modern sense. He should serve as a warning that the continuing debate over acts and identities may well have posed two false alternatives.

Recently the debate over the history of homosexuality has been joined by one over heterosexuality. As Jonathan Ned Katz, Eve Kosofsky Sedgwick, and others have shown, the consolidation of heterosexuality since the end of the nineteenth century is inseparable from and dependent on the articulation of a recognizable homosexuality.[19] Burns, Schultz, and Fradenburg consider the undefined terrain of what Schultz calls "heterosexuality before heterosexuality." What they find is not a safe heteronormative regime but a troubled one. Studying Chaucer's *Legend of Good Women*, Fradenburg explores the paradox that only through obstacles to heterosexual union are the gender categories upon which heterosexuality depends reinforced and preserved. The securing of gender's boundaries through a rescue fantasy exposes the impossibility of heterosexual love and the chivalric lie of honor that depends on it. In different ways Burns and Schultz argue against the presence of a heterosexual imperative, as we know it, in medieval French and German romance, where bodies are gendered not according to heterosexual models of intelligibility but according to clothing and class. A tendency to stray afield from our modern constructions of heterosexuality is perhaps most marked in the visions of female mystics, as Lochrie argues, where cultural struggle ventures into the realm of the queer and heteronormativity is adrift. All of these essays force us to rethink medieval sexuality without the stable guidance of the concept of heteronormativity and, perhaps, to cut our own ideas about "other" medieval sexualities adrift, too.

As Steven Kruger argues, medieval sexual "identities" are never discrete or self-contained. They are always implicated in other categories of cultural differentiation and opposition, including race, gender, ethnicity, and religion. Yet, as he also argues, these categories are not parallel, nor are they even consistent in their representation as either "natural" or "moral." In conversion narratives, the intractability of each of these categories often leaves a "queer residue," marking the convert as still sexually, racially, and/or ethnically different. Kruger finds sexuality not in its own place, per se, but somewhere between the categories of race and religious conversion. This position resists the efforts of modern scholars to identify it within the homo-hetero divide where it is expected to reside. His essay urges us to look elsewhere, as well as differently, in order to elaborate fully the workings of sociocultural exclusions and individual identity formations.

The essays in this collection suggest that the Middle Ages did recognize that some people, at least, can be grouped on the basis of their sexual practice but that these groups do not correspond to their modern identity categories either in definition or status. The class of men that Peter of Abano distinguishes who desire anal stimulation "by nature" is in no way commensurate with the class-specific but sexually undefined groups of courtly men and women who desire each other. And while medieval sexual categories sustain mutually constitutive relations with categories of class, gender, religion, and ethnicity, they are not neatly congruent with these categories either. The medieval texts and images provide powerful evidence of the dangers that beset any attempt to isolate sexual "identities" in the past or in the present.

## Medieval and Modern

Foucault's desire to think differently than one thinks — to stray afield of oneself — has a larger analogue in this volume, the desire to stray afield of medieval studies in order to rethink contemporary theory and histories of sexuality. How can constructing medieval sexuality urge us to think differently than we currently think about ourselves and our culture? How can we as moderns learn to stray afield from that which makes us intelligible to ourselves and to tolerate the unsettling illegibility that the study of others inevitably brings to us?

In Tony Kushner's *Angels in America,* a gay man named Prior Walter is living with AIDS.[20] In the first part of the play, his ancestor, Prior I, who died of pestilence in the thirteenth century, visits him and gets him to dance with a fantasy of his estranged lover, Louis — a dance of death — before Prior I, snickering over the sodomitic scene, exits with the parting comment, "I don't like it here." The inhospitability of modernity to the medieval past is ironically represented not only in Prior I's parting observation, but in the play's depiction of him as primally medieval, or as another character calls him, a "medieval gnome." The legibility of sexual identity and suffering in this otherwise moving play relies here upon an alienation of the medieval from the modern, or the sodomitic from the queer, of the plague victim from the AIDS sufferer. By banishing the medieval from modern discussions of sexuality, by assuming that the medieval subject "would not like it here," we attempt to reassure ourselves with a "myth of a heteronormative past and a queer modernity."[21]

Stripped of this comfortable reassurance, we must confront the strangeness not only of our past but also in ourselves. The immense and immensely varied domain of medieval sexuality compels us to acknowledge articulations of sexuality that may at first seem familiar but that are actually quite different from our own. Such an exercise defamiliarizes the present and makes the natural strange. In this way it helps us, in Foucault's eloquent formulation, "to learn to what extent the effort to think one's own history can free thought from what it silently thinks, and so enable it to think differently."[22] The freeing of thought—and its academic disciplines—from what it silently thinks is not possible without a dialogue between medieval and modern studies. The study of medieval sexuality provides a crucial reminder that sexuality cannot be meaningfully analyzed apart from other categories of identity, including gender, race, and religion. Our awareness of how these categories are mutually reinforcing as well as differentiating in the Middle Ages helps us to resist the exclusionary politics of a contemporary conservative era even as it forces us to rethink the isolation of sexuality as an object of investigation. The study of medieval sexuality also challenges the widespread assumption that both homosexuality and heterosexuality are ahistorical categories, and it suggests that the more academic debate between acts and identities may have posed two unrealistically simple alternatives. It shows that the sexual instabilities and transgressions often held up as distinctive elements of the modern are not by any means the sole province of the contemporary world. At the same time the study of medieval sexuality reminds us that sexuality is normative or queer only in relation to historically specific genders, bodies, and identities. We will recognize the strangeness of medieval sexuality only if we attend to its historical specificity, and we will think differently about ourselves only if we acknowledge the strange and very recent structures of gender, bodies, and desires that construct our own sexuality.

## Notes

1. Michel Foucault, *The Use of Pleasure*, trans. Robert Hurley (New York: Vintage Books, 1990), 8.

2. Peter Brown, drawing on Foucault (ibid). Brown cites this passage in warning against such a sense of entitlement regarding "the sexual concerns of men and women in a distant age" (Peter Brown, *The Body and Society: Men, Women, and Sexual Renunciation in Early Christianity* [New York: Columbia University Press, 1988], xviii).

3. For a recent discussion of some of these methodological issues, see Louise Fradenburg and Carla Freccero, "Introduction: Caxton, Foucault, and the Pleasures of History," *Premodern Sexualities* (New York: Routledge, 1996), xiii–xxiv; and an earlier version of this essay, "The Pleasures of History," *GLQ: A Journal of Lesbian and Gay Studies* 1, no. 4 (1995): 371–84.

4. Michel Foucault, "Confessions of the Flesh," in *Power/Knowledge: Selected Interviews and Other Writings, 1972–1977* (New York: Pantheon Books, 1980), 209.

5. Joan Cadden, *Meanings of Sex Difference in the Middle Ages: Medicine, Science, and Culture* (Cambridge: Cambridge University Press, 1993), 7; Pierre J. Payer, *Sex and the Penitentials: The Development of a Sexual Code, 550–1150* (Toronto: University of Toronto Press, 1984), 14.

6. Michel Foucault, *History of Sexuality*, vol. 1: *An Introduction*, trans. Robert Hurley (New York: Vintage, 1990), 157, 158.

7. Ibid., 33.

8. Gayle S. Rubin, "Thinking Sex: Notes for a Radical Theory of the Politics of Sexuality," in *The Lesbian and Gay Studies Reader*, ed. Henry Abelove, Michèle Aina Barale, and David M. Halperin (New York and London: Routledge, 1993), 34.

9. In a recent interview with Judith Butler, Rubin argues that she never meant to suggest that gender should be limited to feminism and sexuality to gay and lesbian studies, only that feminism "should not be seen as the privileged site for work on sexuality" (Gayle Rubin with Judith Butler, "Interview: Sexual Traffic," *differences* 6, nos. 2–3 [1994]: 88).

10. Judith Butler, "Against Proper Objects," *differences* 6, nos. 2–3 (1994): 20.

11. The phrase comes from Biddy Martin's critique of sexuality studies that exclude gender from their theoretical fields of vision ("Sexualities without Genders and Other Queer Utopias," *diacritics* 24, nos. 2–3 [1994]: 107).

12. Foucault, *History of Sexuality,* 1:33.

13. Ibid., 157, 152.

14. See Brown, *The Body and Society;* Carolyn Walker Bynum, *Holy Feast and Holy Fast: The Religious Significance of Food to Medieval Women* (Berkeley and Los Angeles: University of California Press, 1987); Bynum, *Fragmentation and Redemption: Essays on Gender and the Human Body in Medieval Religion* (New York: Urzone, 1991), and *The Resurrection of the Body in Western Christianity, 200–1336* (New York: Columbia University Press, 1995); Cadden, *Meanings of Sex Difference in the Middle Ages;* Linda Lomperis and Sarah Stanbury, eds., *Feminist Approaches to the Body in Medieval Literature* (Philadelphia: University of Pennsylvania Press, 1993); and Miri Rubin and Sarah Kay, eds., *Framing Medieval Bodies* (Manchester and New York: Manchester University Press, 1994).

15. For examples of feminism and the body, see Judith Butler, *Bodies That Matter: On the Discursive Limits of "Sex"* (New York and London: Routledge, 1993). A complete list of feminist work on the body would be too long to provide here. For writing on AIDS and the body, see the following essays in *Discourses of Sexuality: From Aristotle to AIDS,* ed. Domna C. Stanton (Ann Arbor: University of Michigan Press, 1992): Judith Butler, "Sexual Perversions," 344–61; Douglas Crimp, "Portraits of People with AIDS," 362–88; and Jeffrey Weeks, "Values in the Age of Uncertainty," 389–412.

16. Foucault, *History of Sexuality,* 1:43.

17. The debate has often been polarized between John Boswell's "essentialist" argument in *Christianity, Social Tolerance, and Homosexuality: Gay People in Western Europe from the Beginning of the Christian Era to the Fourteenth Century* (Chicago and London: University of Chicago Press, 1980) and the social constructionist camp of David Halperin, *One Hundred Years of Homosexuality and Other Essays on Greek Love* (New York and London: Routledge, 1990); Jeffrey Weeks, *Coming Out: Homosexual Politics in Britain, from the Nineteenth Century to the Present* (London: Quartet, 1977); and Robert A. Padgug, "Sexual Matters: On Conceptualizing Sexuality in History," in *Hidden from History: Reclaiming the Gay and Lesbian Past,* ed. Martin Bauml Duberman, Martha Vicinus, and George Chauncey Jr. (New York: New American Library, 1989).

18. For an excellent argument about the slippage of sodomy in this ruling, see Janet E. Halley, "*Bowers v. Hardwick* in the Renaissance," in *Queering the Renaissance,* ed. Jonathan Goldberg (Durham, N.C.: Duke University Press, 1994), 15–39. On our contradictory belief in both acts and identities, see Eve Kosofsky Sedgwick, *Epistemology of the Closet* (Berkeley and Los Angeles: University of California Press, 1990), 85–90.

19. Halperin, *One Hundred Years of Homosexuality,* 15–18; Jonathan Ned Katz, *The Invention of Heterosexuality* (New York: Dutton, 1995), 1–56; Sedgwick, *Epistemology of the Closet,* 1–63.

20. Tony Kushner, *Angels in America: A Gay Fantasia on National Themes. Part One: Millennium Approaches* (New York: Theatre Communications Group, 1993), 3.6, p. 114.

21. Fradenburg and Freccero, "The Pleasures of History," 380.

22. Foucault, *The Use of Pleasure,* 9.

CHAPTER 1

✣

# Pollution, Illusion, and Masculine Disarray:
## Nocturnal Emissions and the Sexuality of the Clergy

*Dyan Elliott*

*A box full of clothes—if left for long—will putrefy. So it is with our thoughts if we don't perform them corporeally.*
—Evagrius of Pontus[1]

In his *Moralia* Gregory the Great discusses some of the more insidious ways in which the devil afflicts God's holy people. Although making little headway during their waking hours, the devil is nevertheless permitted to fill the minds of the saints with filthy thoughts in sleep. But Gregory also prescribes a remedy, one that precociously anticipates Freud's theory of sublimation. A person must overcome these anxieties by raising the mind to higher things. Thus he glosses the biblical verse "So that my soul rather chooseth hanging and my bones death" (Job 7:15):

> What is designated by the soul except intention of the mind, what by the bones except the strength of the flesh? Everything which is hung is beyond a doubt raised from lower things. The soul therefore chooses hanging so that the bones die, because when the intention of the mind raises itself to the heights, all strength of the outer life dies within.[2]

To stay with Freud for a moment, it is safe to say that Christian ascetics may have longed for sexual sublimation, but they generally had to settle for repression, with the attendant problems suggested in the epigraph. The presence or absence of erotic dreams, especially those culminating in ejaculation or "pollution" (to use the medieval term) represented for the would-be ascetic the sad distance between aspiration and actuality, providing a sensitive gauge for clocking the relative success or failure of disciplinary efforts to gain mastery over the body. The problem of such emissions also provided one of the rare occasions for theologians and pastoral counselors to speak frankly about the male's sexuality and body, by which I mean that these discussions could and did occur divorced from any reproductive telos. Here I should add that despite efforts of doctors and the occasional theologian to make pollution an equal-opportunity offense for men and women, the discourse was inescapably framed around masculine embarrassments, particularly those of the would-be celibate ascetics and priests who were preoccupied with the way in which physical impurity impinged on ritual activities.[3]

Autoeroticism, whether voluntary or involuntary, often frustrates attempts at historicization. Hence, Eve Sedgwick's article "Jane Austen and the Masturbating Girl" argues that masturbation "seems to have an affinity with amnesia, repetition or the repetition compulsion, and ahistorical or history-rupturing rhetorics of sublimity."[4] Likewise with nocturnal emissions; even the external disciplinary ramparts erected against such shadowy occurrences seem to argue for a transhistorical dimension. For example, the unflagging presence of prayers warding off pollution in the Compline service is an indication that at least on the ritualistic level, pollution never ceased to be a concern throughout the Middle Ages. But the level of intellectual and probably emotional engagement with this subject was temporally uneven. Nocturnal emission was a matter of considerable concern until the time of Gregory the Great, received only the most routine treatment (mainly in penitential literature) from the seventh until the twelfth century, and thereafter commanded increased attention until the end of the Middle Ages. The intensification of discourse in pastoral and theological circles in the later period is the primary focus of this study. However, the urgency of the later discourse was predicated on the all-too-effective efforts at repression in the early Middle Ages. And to this "first wave" of concern I must first briefly turn.

The patristic age set the stage for later discussions of nocturnal emissions by framing three interlocking problems: the extent to which such emissions inhibited participation in ritual, the way in which pollution could be transformed into an occasion for self-examination, and the determination of the degree of culpability of the individual. Ritualistic interests could be said to constitute the "seminal" category. Attention to ritual purity raised the question as to whether a person so stained should abstain from the Eucharist — as a recipient, of course, but especially as a celebrant. This was a very real concern in the early church, when pollution taboos ran high. Both the *Didascalia* and the *Apostolic Constitutions*, for example, were reacting against this level of rigor in the Syrian church.[5]

Although a potential liability from a sacramental standpoint, such emissions had possibilites from the perspective of ascetical training, which developed into a second nexus of concern. Spiritual directors turned to pollution and its attendant circumstances as a possible index to the relative strength of the passions and, conversely, to the progress of the soul's ascent. This stratagem is especially clear in the symptomologies of John Cassian in the West or John Climacus in the East. Cassian, for example, posited an ascending scale of chastity with six gradations. In the first stage, the monk does not succumb to the assaults of the flesh while waking; in the second his mind does not linger over voluptuous thoughts; in the third, the sight of a woman no longer inspires lust; in the fourth, the waking body is immune to even the most simple movements of the flesh; in the fifth, the mind is no longer flustered by writings that discuss reproduction. By the sixth and final stage, a monk is impervious to sexual temptation while asleep. To demonstrate the last stage, which is extremely rare, Cassian invokes the exceptional purity of a singularly graced monk with the appropriate name of Serenus. His stable and enduring purity was the result of a visionary evisceration in answer to his earnest prayers for perfect chastity.[6] Cassian also proffers practical advice against pollution. The diet must be strictly regulated and the intake of water reduced so that the bodily humors become sluggish and slow.[7] He also recommends that one cover the kidneys with lead, as the touch of metal inhibits the "obscene humors."[8] Occasionally the devil's malice will stimulate gratuitous pollution just prior to communion to forestall the reception of the sacrament, as was the case of one monk. In this instance, the only way of breaking the vicious cycle was the reception of the Host.[9] But to play it safe, the monk should never go to sleep after evening services, as the devil, ever jealous of purity, would almost inevitably sully him with pollution.[10]

The third discursive strand that bridges both questions of ritual purity and the impetus to self-examination concerns the degree of culpability inherent in nocturnal emissions. Athanasius, hostile to the overscrupulousness of monastic culture, was the first to argue that such experiences were sinless since they were involuntary and required by nature, pragmatically enlisting the support of medical authorities to buttress his contention.[11] Clearly, Athanasius was advocating a much more forgiving approach than either the impersonal taboo that had governed many early eucharistic discussions or the ascetic program of self-examination. But Athanasius's resolution only addressed the raw physicality of ejaculation—an occurrence that was, in fact, merely an epiphenomenon of a much more complex process: the dream.[12] Augustine, on the other hand, was less willing, or less able, to divorce orgasm from its dream context, thus offering one of the more nuanced contributions to the issue of culpability. Book 10 of the *Confessions* reviews classical theory regarding the way in which the mind stores in the memory various images that have been abstracted by the senses.[13] This leads to a frank but angst-ridden discussion concerning the problems arising from memories of his sexual past. By pondering the vexed relations between sexual memory, erotic dreams, culpability, and selfhood, Augustine offers an arresting instance of the link between shame and identity formation that has been posited by developmental psychologists:[14]

3

When I am awake [these memories] obtrude themselves upon me, though with little strength. But when I dream, they not only give me pleasure but are very much like acquiescence in the act. The power which these illusory images have over my soul and my body is so great that what is no more than a vision can influence me in sleep in a way that reality cannot do when I am awake. Surely it cannot be that when I am asleep I am not myself, O Lord my God? . . . And why is it that even in sleep I often resist the attractions of these images, for I remember my chaste resolutions and abide by them and give no consent to temptations of this sort? Yet the difference between waking and sleeping is so great that when, during sleep, it happens otherwise, I return to a clear conscience when I wake and realize that, because of this difference, I was not responsible for the act, although I am sorry that by some means or other it happened to me.[15]

Augustine would seem to be at least partially enacting what one theorist describes as the "Thank God, it was only a dream" syndrome, wherein the awakened dreamer feels authorized to dismiss the content and certainly the outcome of fantasies as an interruption in the regular program rather than an expression of real desire.[16] But one would assume that, with Augustine's solicitude for his defamiliarized sleeping self ("I am sorry that by some means or other it happened to me"), he would have more consideration for what we now term the unconscious.

Yet, as becomes clear from his other works, Augustine raised these questions in order to suppress them once and for all.[17] Master of the interior that he was, Augustine mobilized his full theological genius around the problem of disowning the realm of dream-fantasy, thence forestalling the examination of its contents. In so doing, Augustine definitively broke with the classical tradition of oneirocriticism, which subjected every aspect of dreams to painstaking analysis. Indeed, if the dream book of Artemidorus is any indication, erotic dreams elicited particular scrutiny.[18]

Augustine first distanced the realm of unconscious fantasy by his invocation of concupiscence—the inevitable and unruly consequence of original sin, operating as an impersonal chaos theory but affecting the individual in a deeply personal manner. Concupiscence created a tragic estrangement between the spirit and the body: "Through the justice of God, who is our master and to whom we his subjects refused service, our flesh, which had been subject to us, is troublesome by its insubordination." Like static interfering with a clear transmission, concupiscence inhibited the body's reception of and ready compliance with the commands of the higher spirit. Not surprisingly, the genitals were the site of greatest affliction: "It is reasonable then that we should feel very much ashamed of such lust, and reasonable too that those members which it

4

moves or does not move by its own right, so to speak, and not in full subjection to our will, should be called pudenda or shameful parts."[19]

Second, Augustine's *Literal Meaning of Genesis* points to the necessary symbiosis of image, thought, and speech, suggesting the ways in which these could lead to "no-fault arousal" in sleep: "Now if the images of these corporeal things, which I have necessarily thought of in order to say what I have said, were to appear in sleep as vividly as do real bodies to those who are awake, there would follow that which in waking hours could not happen without sin."[20] The dreamer is free from sin, however, since the will is immobilized or bound during sleep.

Third, and finally, Augustine exculpates the sleeping state by pointing to the realm of the demonic, an area that already loomed large in the *Sayings* of the desert fathers and from this font had made considerable inroads into Cassian's work.[21] Augustine provided lurid and compelling descriptions of the body's susceptibility to demonic infiltration: "This evil thing creeps stealthily through all the entrances of the senses: it gives itself over to forms, it adapts itself to colors, it sticks to sounds, it lurks hidden in anger and in the deception of speech, it appends itself to odors, it infuses taste."[22] On at least one occasion, Augustine even enhanced demonic power considerably by arguing that the devil actually read minds, supplementing the more common view (to which he also subscribed) that the devil's perspicacity was predicated on his grasp of subtle body language that was imperceptible to mere mortals.[23] Thus, for Augustine and his successors,[24] unwelcome sexual fantasies were the unsolicited and unwilled work of demons who penetrated the human senses, accessed the images stored in the memory, and came up with illusions so potent, so familiar, yet so diabolically vitiated that not only was the dreamer without guilt (provided he did not consent to these images), but the actual content of these dreams did not warrant scrutiny.[25]

The suppression of the dream landscape was confirmed in the celebrated letter attributed to Gregory the Great written in response to a series of questions posed by the later Augustine of Canterbury. This is a key text for the West, uniting the three strains of inquiry discussed above. Thus "Gregory" uses culpability, determined through careful self-examination, as a touchstone for resolving questions of ritual purity. The ninth and last question is "Can anyone receive the Body of the Lord after an illusion such as is wont to occur in a dream; and if he is a priest can he celebrate the holy mysteries?" In his response, "Gregory" discerns between three types of nocturnal emissions. Two of them are relatively innocuous: those occurring "through a natural superfluity or weakness" are pronounced guiltless and thus not considered impediments to ritual; those resulting from a superfluity brought on by gluttony do carry a taint, but do not absolutely bar participation in or celebration of communion if it is an important occasion, such as a feast day—provided that

5

the individual was not entirely overwhelmed by evil imaginings (*turpi imaginatione*). If a substitute celebrant could be found, however, the author advises the besmirched priest to abstain from celebrating, although not from receiving. However, emissions resulting from evil waking thoughts are more serious and need to be broken into their several stages to be understood adequately:

> For all sin is committed in three ways, namely by suggestion, pleasure and consent. The devil makes the suggestion, the flesh delights in it and the spirit consents. It was the serpent who suggested the first sin, Eve representing the flesh was delighted by it, and Adam representing the spirit consented to it: and when the mind sits in judgement on itself it is necessary to make careful distinction between suggestion and delight, between delight and consent.[26]

It is only the consent of the spirit that constitutes a completed sin, which would be an absolute bar to the Eucharist.

The Augustinian-flavored focus on the will reduced dream imagery to depersonalized figments produced by the devil. Analysis, never leveled at the dream proper, is reserved for determining the degree of the dreamer's complicity or resistance. Significantly, by Gregory the Great's time, the word "illusion," designating demonic interference in a dream, becomes intrinsically linked with erotic subject matter and probable pollution, an association that invariably cast a pall over efforts to analyze any dream.[27] This elision resulted in what Jacques Le Goff has designated a "repression of dreams," associated with the repression of sexuality.[28] We can see this dual repression at work in multiple liturgical contexts. The famous "Ambrosian" prayer at Compline beseeches: "Let dreams and the fantasies of the enemy recede far away; and suppress our enemy, lest we pollute our bodies."[29] Evening prayers, dubiously attributed to Alcuin, ask that fantasies and beautiful apparitions be held at bay and that the supplicant's chaste members, timorously entrusted to bed each evening, rise as clean temples of the Holy Spirit, prepared to do God's work.[30] Likewise, the celebrating priest prays for the "humor libidinis" to be extinguished in him.[31]

The positive side to this repression was that the potential for individual responsibility, and thus guilt, was greatly reduced. There was a tendency to see all emissions as practically interchangeable pollutions (in the generic sense of the word) that could be scrubbed away in much the same way as the dirt in a room. And, in point of fact, the ritual to reconcile a church defiled by various unsavory emissions like the shedding of blood or the spilling of seed, treats the church much like a person in need of scrubbing. Thus the priest and the congregation pray: "Take away from us, Lord, we beseech, all our iniquities, that we may merit to approach purified spots with pure minds." The consecration, said by the bishop, asks God to restore "anything polluted through negligence, or committed by anger, or stimulated by drunkeness, or subverted by passion [*libido*]," all of which are attributed to the "jealousy of the ancient serpent."[32] Occasionally, the penitentials do impose greater penalties on a nocturnal emission abetted by consent: hence a passage from *Excerpts from a Book of David* isolates "he who willfully has become polluted in sleep," which Pierre Payer takes to mean someone who went to sleep desirous of such an experience.[33] Similarly, Rudolph, bishop of Bourges, in his disciplinary *capitula* of 866, slaps on extra penance for the priest that knowingly abetted his fantasy life by dwelling on filthy thoughts while awake.[34] But the provoking fantasy no more necessitated analysis than the "obscene humor" that issued from the unwitting cleric's loins.

Although the patristic period successfully repressed the full complexity of the problem of pollution, the High Middle Ages saw the repressed return, trailing six hundred years of symptoms. If we are to believe Jacques Lacan, the repressed always returns retroactively, in conjunction with the historical perspective requisite for interpretation. Hence, in the words of Lacanian interpreter Slavoj Žižek:

> The Lacanian answer to the question: From where does the repressed return? is therefore, paradoxically, From the future. Symptoms are meaningless traces, their meaning is not discovered, excavated from the hidden depth of the past, but constructed retroactively—the analysis produces the truth; that is, the signifying frame which gives the symptoms their symbolic place and meaning.[35]

In the High Middle Ages a new set of historically defined circumstances renders previously repressed phenomena impossible to ignore. The first of these new circumstances is the effort to reform the church by developing a ritually pure clergy.[36] Intrinsically linked to this reform was the development of a formal sacramental system, enhanced by a new emphasis on the Eucharist. And thus, despite the fact that Cassian's association between the malice of the devil and unwarranted pollution just prior to communion had become something of a commonplace by the High Middle Ages,[37] the heightened premium placed upon the Eucharist worked to exacerbate concerns about pollution. The official promulgation of the term "transubstantiation" at Lateran IV in 1215 is in many ways a veritable celebration of the wonder-working powers of a newly purified—and hence newly vulnerable—clergy.[38]

The second circumstance is the rise of the penitential forum. Through the mandatory imposition of auricular confession on the laity—also an innovation of Lateran IV—pollution fear was transmitted like a virus from the clergy to the laity.[39] The potential for the laity's progressive sensitivity to such matters becomes apparent when comparing two English confessors' manuals. Robert of Flamborough's twelfth-century manual seems to regard nocturnal emissions as undifferentiated stains that can be erased by sufficient penance. Thus a person who receives the sacrament after such an occurrence is assigned seven days on bread and water.[40] Thomas of Chobham's *Summa confessorum*, however, written shortly after Lateran IV, discerns between seven kinds of nocturnal emissions with varying degrees of culpability, hence calling for a higher level of self-examination.[41] Pastoral sources would continue to encourage this heightened awareness. The late-thirteenth-century John of Freiburg, who incorporated many of the sophisticated insights of Dominican theologians into confessional discourse, reaffirms that nothing is sinful when reason is bound. Yet he introduces the sobering notion that a nocturnal emission might be symptomatic of mortal sin if the waking thought that led up to it was mortally sinful.[42] By the fifteenth century, the Dominican theologian John Nider further refines analysis of this issue by applying scholastic discussions of interpretative consent: when the will's exercise of rational judgment is suspended due to delectation, such deliberate suspension is nevertheless tantamount to a mortal sin.[43]

But the fifteenth-century Jean Gerson's contribution is most notable, since he saw fit to devote several treatises to this and related problems. Indeed, his introduction to the work *On the Knowledge of Chastity* suggests that the preoccupation with seminal emissions eddied out beyond men to women, beyond the privileged zone of the confessional to alternative discursive venues, and beyond the sleeping to the waking state:

> I wrote a few things earlier about preparation for the mass under ten considerations, the occasion taken principally from the subject of nocturnal pollution. Lately, however, I've been asked about pollution that seems to occur while one is awake—something that especially disturbs timorous consciences. Individuals of both sexes have asked me—in confession and out.[44]

The contagious viscosity of this paranoia is in many ways a tribute to the inquisitional tactics of the confessors. Gerson was himself something of a virtuoso in this respect. Stategically advising the confessor to move from the general to the specific, Gerson directs the priest to begin with matters involving little or no blame, "because if the sinner wishes to lie or flee, he will often be overtaken by such things that naturally happen to all . . . ; if he immediately denies those things it is clear that he is afraid to speak of more serious matters."[45] The priest, who is cautioned not to make a stern face, might then proceed to a more direct inquisition:

> "Friend, do you remember ever in your childhood, around ten or twelve years, that your penis or shameful member was erect?" If he says no, he's immediately convicted of a lie because he wishes

to flee and fears to be caught. ... If he should confess that it is so, again the confessor should say, especially if the [penitent] is young: "Friend, was that indecent? What therefore did you do so it would not be erect?" ... If he does not want to answer, it should consequently be asked more plainly: "Friend, did you not stroke and rub your penis in the way boys do?"[46]

Nor should the confessor be deterred by the fear of putting wicked thoughts in the innocent penitent's head, a misgiving often expressed in earlier confessors' manuals. Because of the "corruption of nature," boys of three or four are already inclined toward masturbation because of a certain unfamiliar itch that accompanies erections.[47]

Yet the therapeutic effort to discover and diagnose sins was not without danger to the practitioner. As Gerson was aware, the penitent-patient's sexual confessions could infect the priest-doctor sufficiently to provoke pollution. Hence Gerson reassured the potentially abject priest that pollutions resulting from spiritual responsibilities were sinless, although he does volunteer directions for hearing confession that were designed to keep sexual arousal at a minimum. The confessor, averting his gaze from the speaker, should assume a posture least conducive to stimulation—be this standing, kneeling, or even full prostration. He should limit himself to terse and controlled speech, which was more easily accomplished the better prepared the penitent was for confession. If the sinner was ready "to vomit forth the entire virus willingly," fine and good. If, however, the penitent was excessively inhibited by shame and the sin required painstaking extortion, this put the confessor at greater risk. But it was always safer to hear confessions *after* one had celebrated Mass.[48]

Female penitents presented a particular challenge. So anxious was Gerson to spare the priest the anguish of pollution that in one vernacular sermon he saw fit to alert women to their possible role as passive temptresses. Thus he raises the delicate question: if a woman was certain that her confession would arouse the priest—particularly if she was guilty of erotic thoughts involving him—should she confess elsewhere?[49] Gerson reluctantly resolves this problem with an affirmative answer: she should go to another confessor even if her usual priest refuses to grant her leave. A similar awareness of the dangers of the female penitent doubtlessly directed Robert of Flamborough's much earlier prophylactic reticence. Operating under the assumption that the average priest had not attained Cassian's fifth stage of chastity (wherein reading about sex was a matter of indifference), Robert anticipates and blocks the potential eroticism of the written word. He urges that "sins against nature" should be extorted from female penitents with extreme caution, "but the way of extorting should not be written down."[50]

Despite its attendant dangers, the confessional nevertheless had the potential for providing Christendom with a forum in which its fantasy life might be scrutinized, as confessors trained the analytical spotlight inward. Such introspection would be in keeping with the contemporary revival of interest in dreams especially apparent in secular letters.[51] However, the clergy limited culpability to conscious intention, which corresponded with the Augustinian identification of self with consciousness and will. This led to renewed efforts to exculpate the polluted individual and to put distance between the dreamer and what Freud would call the work of the dream. There were exceptions: the twelfth-century Hildegard of Bingen, for instance, regarded the erotic movements of the sleeping body as implying consent of the soul—a perception that might be psychologically damaging in its own way, but one that augurs well for the examination of fantasy.[52] But the Dominican John of Freiburg was much more typical: as we have already seen, John urged that nothing should count as sin if reason is bound. Following Thomas Aquinas, he asserts that a pollution that begins and ends in sleep by no means constitutes a sin. Indeed, he points out that Thomas was prepared to disregard a waking pollution provided that the fantasy began in sleep.[53] Jean Gerson similarly advanced that since fantasies are produced without our consent, they are sinless. Although granting that some bodily fluids can pollute the spirit, others only simulate corruption, "just as in sordid or impure dreams, when it is not a sin but a similitude of sin."[54] This approach authorized most theologians to discount the content of the dream. Matthew of Cracow's *Concerning the Manner of Confession and Purity of Conscience*—a late-thirteenth-century treatise that enjoyed considerable authority since it circulated under Aquinas's name—was typical. It advised that in the course of confession "nothing ought to be said about the dream itself because there is no fault there." He did, however, concede that thoughts leading up to a dream or the delight inspired by the dream after the fact were potentially culpable.[55]

Gerson would initially appear to be something of an exception in this respect, in one sermon actually encouraging the penitent to reveal the content of dreams. Moreover, in another context he uses the *visio* (one of several subgenres of a dream, according to the various schemata for classification) to talk about pollution.[56] Yet these avenues for fuller investigation—for better or for worse—are limited in their effect and basically consistent with the principle of denial enunciated earlier. Thus he argues that the revelation of the dream's contents might direct the confessor to the sin that preceded the dream. The dream itself, however, is of no intrinsic interest.[57]

Gerson's evocation of dreams for the purpose of discussing the problem of pollution in his *On Preparation for the Mass*, while on the surface more analytically promising still, is ultimately symptomatic of even greater repression. The ninth consideration he cites is that, in the event that one fails in his preparations for the Eucharist, God will help him rise. To demonstrate this principle, Gerson evokes a nameless man's dream of being cast in a toilet (*in cloaca*). The man clings to the supporting stick lest he be cast further in the excrement, but loses hold due to the terrible stench. When he prays to God, however, he again catches hold of the stick. Gerson explains: our conscience is a clean toilet filled with daily excrement. The stick is our own industry in rising upward. The more we raise our eyes to God, the more successful we are in distancing ourselves from the excrement. Excrement also plays a central role in the second exemplary dream. The tenth consideration of the same treatise features a dream of Celestine V, originating in his autobiographical writings.[58] According to Gerson's version, which retains the basic contours of the original, Celestine ascended to a marvelous royal court, only to be humiliated when the ass he was riding voided its bowels on the road: "The most pure man was horrified and detested not this iniquity but this pollution [*hanc non iniquitatem sed unquinationem*]." But a voice from the throne assured Celestine that the court could not be contaminated by his irrational and fat ass (*suus asellus corpulentus et irrationalis*), which voided itself unconsciously and by necessity.[59] Celestine's dream was in response to a specific appeal to God about his own worthiness to celebrate the Eucharist after experiencing a pollution, even as Gerson's rendition was specifically prompted by certain priests' scruples over performing Mass after being polluted by a "night dream."[60] In either case, the ready substitution of infantile dreams of defecation for the erotic dreams of adults—of excrement for semen—is disturbing. And it is with this anecdote that Gerson concludes his treatise.[61]

But, if the content of the fantasy was frequently unexamined and unexaminable, its consequences could not be ignored. Even if the sinful potential of nocturnal emission could be neutralized by insisting on the absence of intention, clerical purity was still at a premium. Thus most authorities continued to abide by the counsel against celebrating Mass after nocturnal emissions unless so required by some compelling reason such as danger of scandal—the position articulated in the letter to Augustine of Canterbury and attributed to Gregory the Great.[62] Moreover, as seen above, this same letter demonstrated the extent to which masculine identity was overinvested in the will and its exercise of reason: "It was the serpent who suggested the first sin, Eve representing the flesh was delighted by it, and Adam representing the spirit consented to it." Thus the occurrence of involuntary pollution posed a severe challenge to masculine pretensions. Gerson is sensitive to the limits of the will, and warns against the dangers of overscrupulosity, arguing that excessive abstinence and attention can be counterproductive, and can in fact stimulate pollution. Thus he urges the superior to "be not too overjust" (Ecclesiastes 7:17) because "he that violently bloweth his nose bringeth out blood" (Proverbs 30:33).[63] He also evokes the analogy of someone obsessed with not properly attending to the recitation of the hours who finds that this concern issues in useless and inattentive repetition. Gerson advises that the confessor *not* permit this recalcitrant penitent to repeat his hours as penance.[64]

Even as efforts to consolidate masculine identity through emphasis on rationality lapse into irrational obsession, likewise too rigorous a focus on the unruly masculine body has the undesired effect of dissolving it into a feminine one. In keeping with the discursive idealization of sexual "apatheia" and perhaps even the androgyny current in some early Christian circles, past authors had made moves toward validating a passionless expulsion of masculine seed that might well be described as "quasi-menstrual." In Cassian's sixth and most auspicious degree of chastity, for example, a person would purge himself of extra humors without titillation. But the total lack of affect in this description was rather disconcerting: the perfect individual was just as likely to ejaculate while waking as while sleeping, in prayer as in bed, in a crowd as alone, nor would he perceive it as the kind of secret that he would hide from other men or would make him blush.[65] Although Cassian was frequently utilized in various theological treatments of pollution and chastity in the High Middle Ages, this passage was rarely invoked. With the revival of medical discourse, and the quasi-medical expertise of confessors such as Gerson (who frequently consulted doctors for information about bodily emissions),[66] cognoscenti would have found too many similarities between Cassian's notion of perfect chastity and the involuntary emissions and general effeminacy associated with physical conditions like gonorrhea. According to the classical physician Soranus, whose influence continued into the later Middle Ages, gonorrhea entailed frequent emissions without sexual arousal. He also prescribes the same remedy for this ailment that Cassian had advised for nocturnal emissions—a leaden plate.[67]

But the danger of slippage into femaleness remained uneasily at the margins of the discourse. Medieval medical authorities, such as the eleventh-century Constantine the African, explicitly link frequent nocturnal emissions with a colder, moister, and hence weaker, more feminized seed. Not surprisingly, the sower of such seed tends to engender daughters.[68] Likewise, Gerson's *On Preparation for the Mass* cannot avoid an onslaught of female images and analogies in its discussion of whether a priest who has experienced a nocturnal emission should perform Mass. Sifting carefully through the various levels of consent, Gerson's basic intention was, as suggested above, to allay the fears of the overscrupulous and exculpate any but the most complicit dreamers—an old agenda, employing familiar material. Gerson draws on the exegetical tradition, so extensively employed by Gregory the Great, in which the menstruous woman is seen as a type of sinner.[69] But by explicitly associating this imagery with masculine pollutions, Gerson seems to take greater liberties with conventional gender boundaries. He initially compares the dreamer to the menstruous rags of sin referred to in Isaiah 64:6, sending him, as did Gregory in the case of sinners or unclean women, to the fountain of the house of David (Zechariah 13:1). The celebrating priest is then likened to the woman with flux:

> You suffer bleeding and cannot be cured by doctors, namely by your exercises; touch with complete faith along with the hemorrhaging woman—Martha, according to Ambrose—the fiber of Jesus' clothing. Namely touch the most holy host so that you will be purged.[70]

Gerson thus offers a cure similar in nature to the one that Cassian reported as successful for the monk who was consistently prevented from receiving the sacrament by untimely pollutions: to put this demonic perturbance to flight by receiving the sacrament. Although there is nothing remarkable or new about this counsel, it was nevertheless being proferred in a very different religious culture than that of Cassian. Hence Gerson's already rather transgressive use of conventional imagery leads directly into a discussion of the mystery of transubstantiation. He first ventriloquizes the complaints of those who think it revolting that Christ's body should enter our "stinking stomachs," and then counters with the fact that Christ consented to be preserved in the maternal viscera for nine months and endured the skin of afterbirth—a material of unrivaled powers for pollution, inspiring unparalleled horror.[71]

To recapitulate Gerson's thought: the priest is first likened to a menstruating woman through his contact with the Christ/host; then, more obliquely, to the Virgin Mary for harboring Christ in his stomach. (The first time Gerson touches on this subject he uses the word *venter*, which can be translated as stomach or womb.) He also argues that Nature will find a way to expel its filthy liquid (*foedum humorem*), using the example of a lactating mother: "It is evident in women who have recently given birth whose paps are dry when milk is not elicited but otherwise [milk] is always ready to flow."[72] But Gerson was not content simply to vindicate nocturnal pollution by virtue of its inevitability. Argumentatively salvaging as much as he can from an unpropitious situation, Gerson maintains that pollution wins merit for whoever suffers it unwillingly. The image he uses to emphasize this point is striking. He compares the resisting victim of pollution to Saint Lucy, who assures her would-be violator: "If you corrupt me against my will, my chastity will be double-crowned."[73]

The many-gendered crossings of Gerson's torturously feminized clergy give new meaning to Augustine's initial portrait of the divided self, vitiated by demonic interpolations and unpredictable fluxes. Yet one final dimension to the discourse on pollution remains to be discussed. In the High Middle Ages the intimate enemy (namely, erotic thoughts and their physiological consequences), unexamined and repressed internally, is ultimately externalized and begins to walk abroad. This eventuates in the dramatic emergence of the demon lover in ecclesiastical culture, a figure that was probably never absent from folk tradition and would now enjoy an extended life in venues as disparate as the witch trials and romantic fiction. The learned preoccupation with demons was in many ways a by-product of the scholastic methodology: as Jeffrey Burton Russell has suggested, efforts to contend rationally with the natural world had the effect of forcing more and more inexplicable phenomena into the realm of the demonic. The concurrence of such beliefs with the pollution fears generated by the scholastic discourse on transubstantiation was probably no mean accident. Both sets of beliefs convey a new preoccupation with tangibility and embodiment. The emphasis on the "real presence" of Christ in the sacrament of the altar might be seen as reinforcing the insistence on the real presence of demons polluting the minister of the altar. Certainly by the thirteenth century the conviction that demons sexually consorted with humans was generally maintained in learned circles—a position that sharply contrasted with the marked incredulity of past centuries.[74]

From the standpoint of a preoccupation with demonic love as well as a heightened degree of credulity in these matters, the thirteenth-century Caesarius of Heisterbach's *Dialogue on Miracles* is representative of the age. Caesarius is a Cistercian monk; most of his anecdotes portraying men beset by amorous succubi (or women beset by their male counterparts, incubi) concern celibates of various stripes. Although Caesarius's fascination with the realm of the demonic is manifest, the nature of his investment is, I would argue, often inflected or even concealed. For example, Caesarius tells of a scholar of Prüm who, upon learning that he had slept with a succubus, "replied with a strange word, which modesty forbids me to repeat, scoffing at the devil, and no whit disturbed."[75] Thus Caesarius ends his anecdote: abruptly and rather opaquely, resisting any possible impulse to interpret or moralize. This might suggest that demons were more a locus of entertainment than of anxiety. Likewise, the rather clipped account of an incident involving a nocturnal emission might be interpreted as indicating a parallel detachment. A monk in Caesarius's house developed an embarrassing itch after he had forgotten to say the single psalm that had been assigned to him as penance for a wet dream. The itch disappeared the moment he said the psalm.[76]

These two relatively truncated anecdotes never name repressed and volatile material directly, nor should we expect them to do so. Their presentational strategy is to treat such materials as unexceptional and uncontroversial, and the reader becomes complicit with this strategy by accepting the story's surface reassurances. A third and more narratively suggestive anecdote, however, offers the conflation of demon lover and wet dream within a single frame. It demonstrates the way these two phenomena, united by repression, are situated at the crossroads of desire and fear. The lay brothers of the Cistercian order were taking a midday rest in the dormitory one summer. A certain brother saw the devil in the shape of a Benedictine nun making the rounds of the various beds until she stopped at a particular one. She placed her arms around the neck of the bed's sleeping occupant, kissed him, and then vanished. When the onlooking brother rushed to his confrere, "he found [him] fast asleep indeed, but lying in a fashion that was both immodest and exposed."[77] The violated brother died within three days.

The illusion is distorted by a dramatic but purposeful fracturing. The person who actually experiences the illusion is not the sleeper but the waking, watching brother. Yet the nun is clearly an interpretative elaboration of what the sleeping brother is experiencing. She is literally a dream come true and on the most obvious level represents the rejected heterosexual alternative implicit in clerical celibacy. But if we were going to subject this material phantasm to more rigorous analysis, any semblance of a heterosexual matrix suddenly dissolves. We soon learn that such figures are not just the object of fantasy, but are themselves the materialization of fantasy. They are constituted entirely from surplus semen. Elsewhere, when speculating on the demonic paternity of the Huns, the magician Merlin, or the English kings and whether such individuals will rise on the day of judgment, Caesarius volunteers: "I have heard about this question from a very learned man; he says that demons collect all wasted human seed, and from it fashion for themselves human bodies, both of men and women, in which they become tangible and visible to men."[78] Nor is Caesarius completely unjustified in his assessment. More sophisticated thinkers, such as Aquinas, also argue that demons can present certain natural effects to the human senses because of their diabolical collection of seeds.[79] The authors of *Malleus maleficarum*, the notorious fifteenth-century inquisitorial manual directed against witchcraft, will dangerously narrow this inquiry by asking explicitly whether the seeds gathered from nocturnal emissions can be used by a demonic incubus to impregnate a human woman. Their answer is probably not, unless the devil knew that there was sufficient generative virtue in the seed. Our inquisitors are more inclined to follow a different but equally invasive line, probably first enunciated by Aquinas. Thus a demon would first pose as a succubus, garnering the unsuspecting human male's seed, next would transport it at dizzying speed (so none of the heat of its generative virtue would be lost), and then would shapeshift into a male-seeming incubus. In this form it would impregnate a woman.[80]

And so the succubi and incubi of the High Middle Ages possess no fixed sexual identity. The prefixes of the words are the key to their situational gendering: the incubus lies on top; the succubus lies underneath. This etymology is implicit in John Nider's discussion of demonic paternity in his *Formicarium*, the first significant work on witchcraft: "[A demon] is not able to generate offspring of its own but of the man for whom it made itself a demon succubus." The same message hovers as a damaging subtext to the inflected comment in Nider's confessor's manual when he compares a husband having sex on the bottom to a "demon succubus."[81]

Ironically, however, it is precisely the unstable sexual identity of the predatory demon stalking the cleric that makes this scenario a compelling *figura* for the cleric subjected to unwelcome emissions.

The occasion of involuntary ejaculation, and its phantasmic accompaniments, opens the way to anxious acknowledgment of gender turmoils held at bay by original and inadequate acts of stabilization and exclusion. The clergy had attempted to create a female-free zone premised on a body that was hermetically sealed by ascendant male reason. Women reentered through the fissures in body and soul. The fantasy women that return to our sleeping clerics are masculinized monsters that lure the clerical world toward the witchhunts. Family and lineage are repressed, and the sleeping cleric—menstrual in his weakness and preyed upon by quasi women constituted from wasted seed—dreams of a possible better human future for the wasted seed at the end of this illusion. Demonic seed-swapping also attacks the very core of paternity and even identity in so lineage-conscious a patriarchy. The mutating gender of the demon lover signals the clergy's bewildered sexual orientation. Finally, the dissolution of the priest's gender identity in the course of demonic illusions elevates pollution fears surrounding the Eucharist to an entirely different plane by challenging not simply the purity of the clergy, but also its claims to unalloyed masculine ascendancy. This is a critical anxiety, since transubstantiation was fast becoming the central mystery of the faith, threatening to displace the Incarnation and its heterosexual core. For transubstantiation was based on the ineluctable stability of gender identity—a male cleric handling the body of a male God.[82]

## Notes

An earlier version of this essay was presented at the conference "Constructing Medieval Sexualities," sponsored by the Newberry Library's Center for Renaissance Studies in Chicago, March 4–5, 1994. I would like to thank Peter Brown for several valuable suggestions about sources. I am also grateful to David Brakke for allowing me to read his paper on nocturnal emissions in the early church prior to its publication.

1. Cited by Vincent of Beauvais, *Speculum historiale* 15.100, vol. 4 of *Speculum quadruplex; sive Speculum maius* (Douai: Belleri, 1624), col. 617.

2. Gregory the Great, *Moralia in Iob* 8.25.4, ed. Marcus Adriaen, Corpus Christianorum, Series Latina (hereafter CCSL), vol. 153 (Turnhout: Brepols, 1979), 415. Cf. Freud's definition of sublimation: "the process...through which the excessive excitations from individual sexual sources are discharged and utilized in other spheres, so that no small enhancement of mental capacity results from a predisposition which is dangerous as such" (*Three Contributions to the Theory of Sex*, in *The Basic Writings of Sigmund Freud*, trans. and ed. A. A. Brill [New York: Modern Library, 1938], 625). All biblical translations are from the Douai translation of the Vulgate.

3. The effort to realign female sexuality in accordance with the male "norm" accords with the unisex model of the body discussed by Thomas Laqueur in *Making Sex: Body and Gender from the Greeks to Freud* (Cambridge, Mass.: Harvard University Press, 1990), 25–62. Despite these attempts at realignment, however, authorities like Albert the Great had to concede that women were less prone to nocturnal emissions than men. See *Animalium libri XXVI* 9.1.1, in *Opera omnia*, ed. A. Borgnet (Paris: Vivès, 1891), 11:498.

4. Eve Kosofsky Sedgwick, "Jane Austen and the Masturbating Girl," in *Tendencies* (Durham, N.C.: Duke University Press, 1993), 111.

5. See David Brakke's discussion in "The Problematization of Nocturnal Emissions in Early Christian Syria, Egypt, and Gaul," *Journal of Early Christian Studies* 3, no. 4 (Fall 1995): 419–60.

6. John Cassian, *Conférences* 12.7, ed. and trans. E. Pichery, Sources Chrétiennes (hereafter SC), no. 54 (Paris: Editions du Cerf, 1958), 2:131–33. For Serenus's spiritual mutilation, see *Conférences* 7.2, SC, no. 42, 1:245. Alardus Gazaeus notes the analogues to Serenus's castration in Gregory the Great's account of Equitius (*Dialogues* 1.4) and in the life of Thomas Aquinas; see Gazaeus's commentary on Cassian's *Collationes* 7.2, *Patrologiae: Cursus completus... series latina* [*Patrologia Latina*] (hereafter PL), ed. J.-P. Migne, vol. 49 (Paris: J.-P. Migne, 1874), cols. 669–70, n. c. Also see Michel Foucault's discussion of Cassian, "The Battle for Chastity," in *Western Sexuality: Practice and Precept in Past and Present Times*, ed. P. Ariès and A. Béjin; trans. A. Forster (Oxford: Blackwell, 1985), 14–25.

7. Cassian, *Conférences* 12.11, SC, no. 54, 2:139.

8. Cassian, *Institutions cénobitiques* 6.7.2, ed. and trans. Jean-Claude Guy, SC, no. 109 (Paris: Editions du Cerf, 1965), 270–72.

9. Cassian, *Conférences* 22.3, SC, no. 64, 3:118. John Climacus envisages a similar program to Cassian's: "The beginning of chastity is a refusal to consent to evil thoughts and occasional dreamless emissions; the middle stage is to be free of dreams and emissions even when there are natural movements of the body brought on by eating too much; the completion of chastity comes when mortified thoughts are followed by a mortified body." To his mind, the best strategy against pollution is to fall asleep while saying the "Jesus Prayer" (*The Ladder of Divine Ascent*, step 15, trans. Colm Luibheid and Norman Russell [New York: Paulist Press, 1982], 172, 178).

10. Cassian, *Institutions* 2.13.1–2, SC, no. 109, p. 82; cf. his discouragement of sleep after Matins (3.5.1, p. 106).

11. See Athanasius, Ep. 48 to Amun, trans. A. Robertson, in *St. Athanasius: Select Works and Letters*, ed. P. Schaff and Henry Wace, A Select Library of Nicene and Post-Nicene Fathers of the Church (hereafter LNPNFC), 2d ser., vol. 4 (Edinburgh: T. and T. Clark, 1891; reprint, Eerdman's, 1987), 556–57. Also see Brakke's discussion of Athanasius ("Problematization," 442–44).

12. For an overview of early Christian attitudes to dreams, see Jacques Le Goff, "Christianity and Dreams (Second to Seventh Century)," in *The Medieval Imagination*, trans. Arthur Goldhammer (Chicago: University of Chicago Press, 1988), 193–231; and Steven F. Kruger, *Dreaming in the Middle Ages* (Cambridge: Cambridge University Press, 1992), 35–56.

13. Augustine, *Confessions* 10.8 ff., trans. R. S. Pine-Coffin (Harmondsworth, Middlesex: Penguin, 1961; reprint, 1979), 214ff. Also see Mary Carruthers, *The Book of Memory: A Study of Memory in Medieval Culture* (Cambridge: Cambridge University Press, 1990), 46–71, regarding the nature of the memorial phantasm and the twofold process of storage and recollection.

14. See Eve Kosofsky Sedgwick's citation of Francis Broucek, in "Queer Performativity: Henry James's *The Art of the Novel*," *GLQ* 1, no. 1 (1993): 5.

15. Augustine, *Confessions* 10.30, pp. 233–34; see Peter Brown, *The Body and Society: Men, Women, and Sexual Renunciation in Early Christianity* (New York: Columbia University Press, 1988), 404–8.

16. Slavoj Žižek, *Looking Awry: An Introduction to Jacques Lacan through Popular Culture* (Cambridge: MIT Press, 1991), p. 16.

17. On Augustine's progressive mistrust of dreams, see Le Goff, *The Medieval Imagination*, 216–18.

18. See Michel Foucault's analysis of Artemidorus in *The Care of the Self*, vol. 3 of *The History of Sexuality*, trans. Robert Hurley (New York: Vintage, 1986), 3–36.

19. Augustine, *City of God* 14.15; 14.17, trans. Philip Levine, Loeb Classical Library (London: William Heinemann; Cambridge, Mass.: Harvard University Press, 1966 ), 4:349, 355. See Brown, *Body and Society,* 416–18; Dyan Elliott, *Spiritual Marriage: Sexual Abstinence in Medieval Wedlock* (Princeton, N.J.: Princeton University Press, 1993), 46–50.

20. Augustine, *The Literal Meaning of Genesis* 12.15, trans. John Hammond Taylor, Ancient Christian Writers (hereafter ACW), no. 42 (Newman Press: New York, 1982), 2:198. Also see Kruger, *Dreaming,* 43–45.

21. See Pelagius's and John's translation from the Greek, *Verba seniorum,* especially the section entitled "De fornicatione" (bk. 5), *PL* 73, cols. 873–88. Cassian's *Collationes* were allegedly based on conversations with such desert ascetics.

22. Augustine, *Eighty-Three Different Questions* c. 12, trans. David L. Mosher, Fathers of the Church (hereafter FC), vol. 7 (Washington, D.C.: Catholic University Press, 1982), 43. Cf. his parallel description: "They persuade them [men], however, in marvellous and unseen ways, entering by means of that subtlety of their own bodies into the bodies of men who are unaware, and through certain imaginary visions mingling themselves with men's thoughts, whether they are awake or asleep" (*The Divination of Demons* 5.9, trans. R. W. Brown, in *Saint Augustine: Treatises on Marriage and Other Subjects,* ed. R. J. Deferrari, FC, vol. 27 [New York: Fathers of the Church, 1955], 430). Also see Cassian's similar view, attributed to the monk Serenus (*Conférences* 7.10–15, SC, no. 42, 1:255–59).

23. See Augustine, *On the Literal Reading of Genesis* 12.17, p. 201 and p. 309 n. 81. The conception of a quasi-omniscient devil, who could read human hearts as God does, was altogether too threatening a notion, and was accordingly dropped. Thus Aquinas argues that angels and demons are only capable of reading the mental images of an individual's intellect; they cannot know precisely how these images will be utilized in thought (Aquinas, *De malo* q. 16, art. 8, resp. ad obj. 3 and 4, in *Opera,* ed. S. E. Fretté [Paris: Vivès, 1875], 13:606). Cf. *Summa theologiae* 1a, q. 57, art. 4, resp. (London: Blackfriars, in conjunction with Eyre and Spottiswoode; New York: McGraw Hill, 1968], 9:137.

24. Eight centuries later, when Aquinas alleges that demons can change the cognitive part of the soul, it is Augustine's graphic description, cited above, to which he turns (*De malo* q. 16, art. 11, resp., in *Opera,* 13:613). Also see the thirteenth-century encyclopedist Vincent of Beauvais's parallel use of the same passage (*Speculum naturale* 2.115, vol. 1 of *Speculum quadruplex,* col. 151).

25. My view of Augustine's reliance on demonic interpolation differs from that of Le Goff, who argues that Augustine places little emphasis on demons as originators of dreams, viewing dreams as an essentially "psychological phenomenon" (*The Medieval Imagination,* 217–18). This difference may be owing to my focus on Augustine's view of erotic dreams. Note, however, that even in *On Care to Be Had for the Dead,* wherein Augustine expresses his most profound scepticism regarding dreams (likening some to the waking ravings of the mad), he still thinks that the truth quotient of dreams is a result of angelic intervention — the flip side of the demonic (in *St. Augustin: On the Holy Trinity, Doctrinal Treatises, Moral Treatises,* LNPNFC, vol. 3 [Eerdmans: Grand Rapids, Mich., reprint, 1978], c. 12–18, pp. 544–48).

26. Bede, *Bede's Ecclesiastical History of the English People* 1.27, ed. Bertram Colgrave and R. A. B. Mynors (Oxford: Clarendon, 1967), 101; cf. Cassian, *Conférences* 22.3, SC, no. 64, 3:116–18.

27. Gregory the Great, *Dialogues* 4.50, ed. Adalbert de Vogué, trans. Paul Antin, SC, no. 265 (Paris: Editions du Cerf, 1980), 3:172–74; idem, *Moralia* 8.24.43, p. 414. Also see the pseudo-Gregory's response in Bede, *Ecclesiastical History* 1.27, p. 100. Cassian was probably responsible for this set of associations, as the entry for *illusio* in the *Thesaurus linguae latinae* (Leipzig: B. G. Teubner, 1934–64), vol. 7,i, col. 393, seems to suggest. Note especially the rubric "De nocturnis inlusionibus" (*Conférences* 22, SC, no. 64, 3:113). Also see *Institutions* 2.13.1 (SC, no. 109, p. 82), where he addresses the jealous enemy's contamination of a monk's purity through the illusion of a dream (*somni inlusione*).

28. Le Goff, *The Medieval Imagination,* 228.

29. See Aquinas's citation in *Summa theologiae* 2a 2ae, q. 154, art. 5, resp., 43:224. Also see Le Goff, *The Medieval Imagination*, 225, and Alardus Gazaeus's Commentary on Cassian's *Collationes* 22.3, *PL* 49, cols. 1219–20, n. e.

30. *Preces nocturnae*, *PL* 101, col. 726.

31. See Alardus Gazaeus's Commentary on Cassian's *Collationes* 7.2, *PL* 49, cols. 669–70, n. c.

32. See, for example, the ritual for *Reconciliatio violatae ecclesiae*, Cyrille Vogel and Reinhard Elze, eds., *Le Pontifical romano-germanique du dixième siècle*, Studi e Testi, 226 (Vatican City: Biblioteca Apostolica Vaticana, 1963), 182–85.

33. Pierre J. Payer, *Sex and the Penitentials: The Development of a Sexual Code, 550–1150* (Toronto: University of Toronto Press, 1984), 50; see 49–52 generally for a discussion of nocturnal pollutions in the penitentials.

34. Rudolph of Bourges, *Capitula* c. 45, *PL* 119, col. 726. The greater part of his discussion is drawn from the letter to Augustine of Canterbury, attributed to Gregory the Great.

35. Slavoj Žižek, *The Sublime Object of Ideology* (London and New York: Verso, 1989), 55–56. Cf. Ned Lukacher's discussion of Freud's primal scene, which is to be found not in the past, but in the future "in the projective repetition of the origin as it is elaborated through transference" (*The Primal Scenes: Literature, Philosophy and Psychoanalysis* [Ithaca, N.Y.: Cornell University Press, 1986], 42).

36. See Elliott, *Spiritual Marriage*, 98–104.

37. See Matthew of Cracow's confessor's manual, *De modo confitendi et de puritate conscientie* c. 14 (Paris: Guy Marchant for Denis Roce[?], before 1501); cf. Jean Gerson's *De praeparatione ad missam*, in *Oeuvres complètes*, ed. Mgr. Glorieux (Paris: Desclée & Cie, 1973), 9:42. Also note Thomas Aquinas's citation of Cassian's monk, who was cured of his precommunion pollutions by receiving the sacrament (*Summa theologiae* 2a 2ae, q. 154, art. 5, resp., 43:224–26). John of Freiburg also tells this story, citing Aquinas's invocation (*Summa confessorum* bk. 3, tit. 24, q. 73 [Rome, 1518], fol. 123v).

38. For the official pronouncement, see G. D. Mansi, *Sacrorum concilium nova et amplissima collectio* (Venice: Antonius Zatta, 1778), c. 1, 22:981–82. For pre–Lateran IV discussions bearing on this doctrine, see Gary Macy, *Theologies of the Eucharist in the Early Scholastic Period* (Oxford: Clarendon, 1984). For the first usage of this term, see Joseph Goering, "The Invention of Transubstantiation," *Traditio* 46 (1991): 147–70. Regarding the lack of consensus over what transubstantiation actually implied, see Macy, "The Dogma of Transubstantiation in the Middle Ages," *Journal of Ecclesiastical History* 45 (1994): 11–41. On the rise in clerical prestige incumbent on the doctrine, see Caroline Walker Bynum, *Holy Feast and Holy Fast: The Religious Significance of Food to Medieval Women* (Berkeley and Los Angeles: University of California Press, 1987), 56–60; Miri Rubin, *Corpus Christi: The Eucharist in Late Medieval Culture* (Cambridge: Cambridge University Press, 1991), 49ff. Cf. Peter Brown's discussion of transubstantiation in "Society and the Supernatural: A Medieval Change," in *Society and the Holy in Late Antiquity* (London: Faber and Faber, 1982), 326–27.

39. See Mansi, *Sacrorum concilia* c. 21, 22:1007–1010. Also see Michel Foucault's stimulating discussion of the impact that this legislated compulsion to confess had on western conceptions of sexuality in *Introduction*, vol. 1 of *The History of Sexuality*, trans. Robert Hurley (New York: Vintage, 1978), 58–67. Cf. Nicole Bériou, "La Confession dans les écrits théologiques et pastoraux du XIIIe siècle: Médication de l'âme ou démarche judiciaire?" in *L'Aveu: Antiquité et moyen-âge*, Actes de la table ronde organisée par l'Ecole Française de Rome avec le concours du CNRS et l'Université de Trieste, Rome, 28–30 Mars 1984; Collection de l'Ecole Française de Rome, 88 (Rome: Ecole Française de Rome, Palais Farnèse, 1986), 261–82. For the laity's initiation into heightened concerns over pollution, see Dyan Elliott, "Sex in Holy Places: An Exploration of a Medieval Anxiety," *Journal of Women's History* 6, no. 3 (Fall 1994): 13ff.

40. Robert of Flamborough, *Liber poenitentialis* 4.340, ed. J. J. Firth (Toronto: Pontifical Institute of Mediaeval Studies, 1971), 268.

41. Thomas of Chobham, *Summa confessorum* 7.2.1.1.1, ed. F. Broomfield (Louvain and Paris: Nauwelaerts, 1968), 330–33.

42. John of Freiburg, *Summa confessorum* bk. 3, tit. 24, q. 73, fol. 123r; cf. Thomas Aquinas, *Summa theologiae* 2a 2ae, q. 154, art. 5, resp., 43:223, and 1a, q. 84, art. 8, resp., 12:44–47.

43. John Nider, *De morali lepra* c. 4 (Louvain: Johann von Paderborn, 1481), fols. 21v-22r.

44. Gerson, *De cognitione castitatis*, in *Oeuvres complètes*, 9:50; cf. Matthew of Cracow, *De modo confitendi et de puritate conscientie* c. 16.

45. Gerson, *De arte audiendi confessiones*, in *Oeuvres complètes*, 8:13–14.

46. Gerson, *De confessione mollitei*, in *Oeuvres complètes*, 8:71.

47. Gerson, *De confessione mollitei*, in *Oeuvres complètes*, 8:72–73.

48. Gerson, *De cognitione castitatis*, in *Oeuvres complètes*, 9:61, 63. Cf. Aquinas's recognition that a person could experience a nocturnal emission as a result of pondering these matters in an exclusively theoretical manner (*Summa theologiae* 2a 2ae, q. 154, art. 5, resp., 43:224).

49. Gerson, *Poetimini: Contre la luxure*, in *Oeuvres complètes*, 7, ii:827; cf. *De cognitione castitatis*, 9:61. See Caesarius of Heisterbach's anecdote about a noblewoman who told her aged confessor that she was burning with love for him. The confessor managed to dissuade her from her folly. But his immediate reaction was to cross himself—a gesture that was traditionally held to be effective against diabolical illusion. Caesarius may have been implying that the priest's first response was to regard her as a demonic succubus (*Dialogue on Miracles* 3.43, trans. H. von E. Scott and C. C. Swinton Bland [London: George Routledge, 1929], 1:182–83). On the efficacy of the sign of the cross against demons, see Thomas of Cantimpré, *Bonum universale de apibus* 2.57. 33-4 (Douai: Belleri, 1627), 562–63.

50. Robert of Flamborough, *Liber poenitentialis* 4.224, p. 197. Robert is also representative of the more traditional school of circumspection, arguing that confessors should be careful not to put ideas in their penitents' heads (196).

51. This is apparent not only in the revival of the genre of dream vision (e.g., Alan of Lille's *Plaint of Nature*, or the *Romance of the Rose*), but particularly in the intense interest in classical authors like Macrobius. See, for example, Chaucer's *Parliament of Fowls*.

52. Hildegard of Bingen, *Causae et curae*, ed. Paul Kaiser (Leipzig: B. G. Teubner, 1903), 83.

53. John of Freiburg, *Summa confessorum* bk. 3, tit. 24, q. 73–74, fol. 123r-v.

54. Gerson, *De praeparatione ad missam*, in *Oeuvres complètes*, 9:44. Also see his short treatise, *De primis motibus et consensu*, 9:167. Cf. Vincent of Beauvais's use of Augustine in this context to assert that it is impossible to think of certain things in sleep without becoming aroused (*Speculum naturale* 26.79, vol. 1 of *Speculum quadruplex*, cols. 1887–88). Elsewhere Vincent, inspired by Aristotle's treatise *De somno et vigilia*, demonstrates that nocturnal emissions occur "non ad animae imperium" (26.1, cols. 1841–42). For a discussion of consent and sin in the later Middle Ages, see Thomas N. Tentler, *Sin and Confession on the Eve of the Reformation* (Princeton, N.J.: Princeton University Press, 1977), 148–56.

55. Matthew of Cracow, *De modo confitendi et de puritate conscientie* c. 13.

56. According to Macrobius's fivefold classification, the *visio* is one of the most reliable types of dreams with respect to its basic quotient of truth. See his *Commentary on the Dream of Scipio* 1.3, trans. William Harris Stahl (New York: Columbia University Press, 1952), 87–92. Gregory the Great's classification seems to treat the word *visio* more loosely (see *Dialogues* 4.50, SC, no. 265, 3:172–76).

57. Gerson, *Poetimini: Contre la luxure*, in *Oeuvres complètes* 7, ii:832.

58. For Celestine's various sexual temptations, which culminate in the dream, see *Acta sanctorum* (Paris and Rome: Victor Palmé, 1866), May, 4:423–24. Celestine's candor generated considerable work for his hagiographer, Pierre d'Ailly. After a learned exposition of the dream-parable, differentiating between the rational and the irrational soul,

Pierre warns that the average person has not achieved Celestine's perfection and thus must interrogate the character of his or her pollution closely before participating in communion. He then offers an excursus on the various kinds of pollution and their attendant degrees of culpability (see *Acta sanctorum*, May, 4:488–89). According to the Bollandists, Pierre's *vita* was written between 1378 and 1408, while Glorieux situates Gerson's treatise in either 1408 or 1412. As the two clerics were close friends, Gerson may have been directed to this anecdote by Pierre.

59. Gerson, *De praeparatione ad missam*, in *Oeuvres complètes*, 9:46, 50. Celestine's description of defilement is somewhat more graphic, however. He struggles to convey his disgust by alluding to the wet texture of the excrement ("Ille malus asellus coepit turpiter eijecere de corpore stercus, quasi manducasset herbas teneras," *Acta sanctorum*, May, 4:424). Gerson, on the other hand, euphemistically relates that the ass paid the tribute of its belly ("Hic asinus tributum ventris per viam solvit").

60. Gerson, *De praeparatione ad missam*, in *Oeuvres complètes*, 9:35–36.

61. Note that earlier in the treatise, under the fifth consideration, Gerson compares nocturnal emissions to urination (*De praeparatione ad missam*, in *Oeuvres complètes*, 9:41).

62. Thomas of Chobham, *Summa confessorum* 7.2.1.1.1, p. 331; Gerson, *De praeparatione ad missam*, in *Oeuvres complètes*, 9:44.

63. Gerson, *De cognitione castitatis*, in *Oeuvres complètes*, 9:62.

64. Gerson, *De praeparatione ad missam*, in *Oeuvres complètes*, 9:43.

65. Cassian, *Conférences* 12.8, SC, no. 54, 2:135.

66. Vincent of Beauvais, however, does include Cassian's challenging description of the passionless sixth stage in his encyclopedic *Speculum naturae* 31.19, vol. 1 of *Speculum quadruplex*, col. 2307. For Gerson's appeals to medical expertise, see *De praeparatione ad missam*, in *Oeuvres complètes*, 9:42, 43; *De cognitione castitatis*, 9:51.

67. Soranus, *Gynecology* 3.12.45, trans. Owsi Temkin (Baltimore, Md.: Johns Hopkins University Press, 1956; reprint, 1991), 168–69. According to Soranus, the lead plate should be placed under the loins, while Cassian recommended placement above. For discussions of gonorrhea, see Joan Cadden, *The Meanings of Sex Difference in the Middle Ages: Medicine, Science and Culture* (Cambridge: Cambridge University Press, 1993), 26–27, and Danielle Jacquart and Claude Thomasset, *Sexuality and Medicine in the Middle Ages*, trans. Matthew Adamson (Polity Press: Oxford, 1988), 147–51.

68. Constantine the African, *De coitu*, trans. Paul Delany, *Chaucer Review* 4 (1970): 58. Also see Cadden, *The Meanings of Sex Difference*, 65 and n. 25.

69. Drawing inspiration from Zechariah 13:1, Gregory points to the fountain open to the house of David and the inhabitants of Jerusalem for the washing of both sinners and unclean women (*menstruatae*). Sinners as diverse as King David, Mary Magdalene, Peter (in his denial of Christ), and the repentant thief can all be understood to have washed in this fountain. But in Gregory's hands, the unclean woman is a still more subtle imagistic tool than is an active sinner since she need not be guilty of explicit deeds; she is equally implicated by evil thoughts (*in prava cogitatione*). Thus she pollutes her own flesh and the flesh of all she comes in contact with. Again with respect to the lines, "All that seek her shall not fail; in her monthly filth [*menstruis*] they shall find her" (Jeremiah 2:24), Gregory associates the beasts stalking a female in heat with evil spirits stalking the polluted soul (*Homiliae in Hiezechihelem prophetam* bk. 2, hom. 8, c. 19–20, ed. Marcus Adriaen, CCSL, vol. 143 [Turnhout: Brepols, 1971], 350–52).

70. Gerson, *De praeparatione ad missam*, in *Oeuvres complètes*, 9:48.

71. Gerson, *De praeparatione ad missam*, in *Oeuvres complètes*, 9:49. Regarding the revulsion over the polluting aspects of afterbirth, see Thomas of Chobham, *Summa confessorum* 7.2.2.3, pp. 338–39.

72. Gerson, *De cognitione castitatis*, in *Oeuvres complètes*, 9:63. On the essential sameness of blood, semen, and breast milk, see Charles T. Wood, "The Doctor's Dilemma: Sin, Salvation, and the Menstrual Cycle in Medieval Thought," in *Speculum* 56 (1981): 710–27.

73. Gerson, *De cognitione castitatis*, in *Oeuvres complètes*, 9:63; cf. Aquinas, *Commentum in libris IV sententiarum* 4.33.2.3.3, resp., in *Opera*, 30:154. For more on emissions and merit, see *De praeparatione ad missam*, 9:44–45. Also see Gerson's analogy between Augustine's exculpation of a consecrated virgin raped against her will (*City of God* 1.25) and a sleeping cleric who experiences a pollution (9:41). This assimilation was already latent in Augustine, who argued that a violated virgin is no more responsible for the pleasure inadvertently enjoyed in the course of an assault than is a sleeper.

74. Regarding the healthy incredulity of previous centuries (extending to major figures, such as Gratian, in the twelfth century), see Jeffrey Burton Russell, *Witchcraft in the Middle Ages* (Ithaca, N.Y.: Cornell University Press, 1972), 75–80. The Carolingian *Canon episcopi* is the most important document for the official statement of skepticism; see Russell's appendix for the text of *Canon episcopi* and its variations (291–93). For the importance of scholasticism in validating many folkloric beliefs, see Russell, *Witchcraft*, 115–20, 142–47; Nicolas Kiessling, *The Incubus in English Literature: Provenance and Progeny* (Pullman: Washington State University Press, 1977), 21–23. For widespread belief in demon lovers, see H. C. Lea, *Materials toward a History of Witchcraft*, ed. Arthur C. Howland (Philadelphia: University of Pennsylvania, 1939), 1:145–62. On the literary tradition, see Peter D. Grudin's 1971 dissertation, *The Demon-Lover: The Theme of Demoniality in English and Continental Fiction of the Late Eighteenth and Early Nineteenth Centuries* (New York: Garland, 1987), and Kiessling, *Incubus*, 43ff. For various efforts to refine the doctrine of transubstantiation, see n. 38 above.

75. Caesarius of Heisterbach, *Dialogue on Miracles* 3.10, 1:138. For other instances of demon lovers see 3.6, 1:130–32; 3.7, 1:134; 3.8, 1:136; 3.9, 1:136–37; 3.11, 1:138; 3.13, 1:140–42. Cf. the profuse treatment by Caesarius's more learned contemporary—scholastic theologian and bishop of Paris, William of Auvergne (d. 1249), in *De universo* pt. 2,3, c. 25, *Opera omnia* (Paris: A. Pralard, 1674; reprint, Frankfurt am Main: Minerva, 1963), 1: 1070–73.

76. Caesarius of Heisterbach, *Dialogue on Miracles* 3.4, 1:128. Also see Thomas of Cantimpré's anecdote about a monk who was publicly humiliated when his unconfessed erotic dream was exposed by a demoniac (*Bonum universale* 2.57.6, p. 541).

77. Caesarius of Heisterbach, *Dialogue on Miracles* 5.33, 1:363. Note that the novice who plays the stooge in the dialogue was shocked that such a heavy punishment be exacted over an incident occurring in one's sleep, since "God is exceeding merciful, and a sleeping man differs but little from one who is dead." The older monk suggests that the lay brother may have been negligent with regard to seemly demeanor (hence his exposed state), or was purposefully lingering over erotic thoughts while awake, or had overindulged in alcohol (1:363). The fact that this occurred at midday is clearly meant to evoke the noonday demon of Psalm 90:6, a figure associated with sloth (see Penelope B. R. Doob, *Nebuchadnezzar's Children: Conventions of Madness in Middle English Literature* [New Haven: Yale University Press, 1974], 29–30, 178–79, 197). Thomas of Cantimpré relates a similar tale about a relative of his who was lying in the dormitory before Prime when the demon in the shape of a beautiful woman lay down beside him. But when he began to shout and kick, she disappeared (*Bonum universale* 2.57.37, pp. 564–65). The fear of women implicit in these tales is self-evident. Cf. the more visceral misogyny of William of Auvergne: a man dreamed he was having sex with a beautiful woman only to awake in the midst of a carcass of a rotting cow (*De universo* pt. 2,3, c. 23, in *Opera*, 1:1065).

78. Caesarius of Heisterbach, *Dialogue on Miracles* 3.11, 1:139–40. One wonders if this less than perfect fabrication is in any way linked to Caesarius's bizarre revelation that demons will not turn around. As one incubus reports: "We are allowed to take the human form, nevertheless we have no backs" (1:132).

79. Thomas Aquinas, *De potentia* q. 6, art. 7, resp. ad obj. 6, in *Opera*, 13:206; *De malo* q. 16, art. 9, resp. ad obj. 10, in *Opera*, 13:609–11, 613. Cf. Thomas of Cantimpré's account, *Bonum universale* 2.57.16, p. 548. Also see Lea, *Materials toward a History of Witchcraft*, 1:153–57.

80. Heinrich Institoris and Jakob Sprenger, *Malleus maleficarum* pt. 1, q. 3; pt. 2, q. 1, c. 4, trans. Montague Summers (London: John Rodker, 1928), 21–28, 110–13; Aquinas, *De potentia* q. 6, art. 8, obj. 6, and resp. ad obj. 6, in *Opera*, 13:205, 206; cf. *Summa theologiae* 1a, q. 51, art. 3, resp. ad obj. 6, 9:43. Note that Aquinas had earlier addressed the possibility of an incubus stealing the semen from a nocturnal emission in a quodlibetal question asking if a man can be both virgin and father. His treatment was fleeting and oblique, however. He did not comment on the probability of so disturbing a paternity (*Quaestiones quodlibetales*, ed. Raymond Spiazzi, 8th ed., rev. [Turin and Rome: Marietti, 1949], quod. 6, q. 10, art. un., ad 2 and resp. c, pp. 129, 130).

81. John Nider, *Formicarium* 5.10 (Douai: Belleri, 1602), 401; *De morali lepra* c. 16, fol. 80r.

82. I am here distinguishing between the practical protocols required by ritual and the fluid use of female imagery in devotional tradition, as discussed by Caroline Walker Bynum (see *Jesus as Mother: Studies in the Spirituality of the High Middle Ages* [University of California Press: Berkeley and Los Angeles, 1982]). Canon law continued to discuss castration as a possible impediment to the ministry of the altar (see Gratian's *Decretum* Dist. 55 c. 4; also see X.1.20.4. Cf. John of Freiburg's discussion of castration as an impediment to the ministry of the altar and promotion in orders, *Summa confessorum* bk. 2, tit. 1, q. 6, fols. 52v-53r). Gratian also cites canons forbidding women to approach the altar, implying that their presence is polluting (see Dist. 23 c. 25; Dist. 23 c. 34 dpc; cf. X.3.2.1). Also see Aquinas's preemptory discussion of "Whether the female sex impedes the reception of ordination," wherein he argues that a male is necessitated both according to the requirement of the sacrament and according to precept (*Commentum in libris IV sententiarum* 4.25.2.1, in *Opera*, 11:52–53).

CHAPTER 2

✣

# Homosexuality, *Luxuria*, and Textual Abuse

### *Mark D. Jordan*

To begin, titles—and *our* title first: *Constructing Medieval Sexuality* means, at least, that a sexuality is the kind of thing that must be constructed; that the medievals, if they had such a thing, had to construct it for themselves; that we have to (re)construct their constructions; that we (re)construct what they constructed as a "sexuality"—our word, not theirs; that our word "sexuality" is itself endlessly under construction somewhere between "sex" and "gender" or "pleasure" and "power" or "fate" and "identity"; and that we construct their sexuality as "medieval," itself a term of construction, of contempt and nostalgia.

Next the dangerous puns in my title, where "textual abuse" calls up "sexual abuse" and is linked to "homosexuality." Constructions of medieval homosexuality regularly contain allegations of textual abuse. There are allegations that medieval texts are abused to authorize continued repression of lesbians and gays, then counterallegations that revisionist scholars try to distort the plain meaning of authoritative theological texts so as to condone homosexual activity. The term "homosexuality" itself often seems an abusive construction when applied to medieval texts and, indeed, an essentially abusive term, so far as it records juridico-medical efforts to punish or cure adults who have erotic relations with adults of the same genital configuration. Textual abuse as prelude to sexual abuse. But then many medieval texts regard genital relations between members of the same sex as an abuse of the natures of the sexed bodies and the unsexual persons inhabiting them.

I trust that you are losing your way. I think that we have to begin by losing our way in order to discover the conflicts of motives and the surplus of stories that beset us whenever we approach these topics. Conflicting motives of historical accuracy, political advocacy, personal enunciation. Surplus stories of misreadings corrected, repressions overcome, sufferings redeemed. The motives and stories cannot be reconciled or reduced in advance. We can begin only by displaying the conflicts and enacting the stories. I know no better way to do this than by attending self-consciously to how we see or fail to see the very different multiplicities of motives and surpluses of stories in the medieval texts before us.

In what follows, I propose to attend to a trio of terms in a microscopic network of medieval texts. These are the terms *luxuria, vitium sodo-*

*miticum,* and *peccatum* (or *vitium*) *contra naturam;* the texts are some passages by Thomas Aquinas and his principal interlocutors. I will not translate those terms, although I will transliterate the last two as "sodomitic vice" and "sin (or vice) against nature." *Luxuria,* the root term, cannot even be transliterated. We have reasons for thinking that the terms are referentially and genetically connected to some terms that we use, such as "homosexual activity" or "sodomy." I mean, we have reasons for thinking that the writers of these medieval texts would have used the term *vitium sodomiticum* to refer to actions or events that we would call "homosexual," and we have historical narratives that lead us to believe that their application of terms became remote ancestors to ours. I hope to show that these reasons mislead us.

### *Luxuria* and Unnatural Vice

The target terms appear in the *secunda secundae* of Thomas's *Summa theologiae* within two questions on the vice of *luxuria* (2–2.153–154), which is to say, in the middle of Thomas's rereading of the confusion of theological instruction in morals. The first question, in five articles, begins by restricting received notions of *luxuria,* next defends an authoritative teaching about how *luxuria* causes other sins. *Luxuria* is, Thomas says, properly a vice of excess in "venereal pleasures" (*voluptates venerei*), although it is secondarily applied to a number of self-indulgent excesses such as drinking too much wine (153.1 ad 1, ad 2). The restriction is meant to discipline lax uses of a term that ranged in contemporary Dominican pastoral discourse and in many antecedent texts over a host of pleasures, from soft clothing to hot baths.[1] For Thomas, *luxuria* is to be understood as principally concerned with venereal pleasures. It is a vice so far as it is an excess of pleasure. There is no sin in the "use of venereal things" (*usus venereorum*) according to proper manner and order, that is, as directed to the end of human generation (153.2 corp). There are qualifications here, of course. The "use of woman" (*usus feminae*) is a lesser good that bars one from complete virtue (153.2 ad 1). (Beyond underscoring the quoted phrase, I will not insist further that Thomas's texts speak only and always with a male voice.) The present intensity of venereal pleasure is a penalty for the Fall (153.2 ad 2, ad 3). These explicit qualifications belong to the evidently dialectical structure of the question. Having said that *luxuria* is an excess of venereal pleasure, Thomas argues that a "venereal act" (*actus venereus*) is not always sinful, but that it often is — and, indeed, that excess in this kind of act is an important cause of other sins. The question ends by defending Gregory the Great's teaching that *luxuria* is a capital sin with a number of "daughters," including hatred of God and despair (153.5 corp).

Thomas's next question, the center of our target, proposes a division of *luxuria* into six kinds: simple fornication, adultery, incest, deflowering (*stuprum*), abduction (*raptus*), and vice against nature. Thomas cites as his authority for this division a text from Gratian. Gratian there distinguishes, not six kinds of *luxuria*, but five kinds of "illicit intercourse" (*illicitus coitus*), and he does so in a different order and without mention of a vice against nature. Thomas is in fact choosing a variation on several divisions of *luxuria* current in the Parisian faculty of theology,[2] which divisions themselves had derived from Gratian through Peter Lombard.[3] Here and elsewhere Thomas defends the accuracy of the list of six against authoritative alternatives, including four passages from Paul.[4] Thomas also follows the received order of the list, although it conforms neither to his own logical derivation of the species (154.1) nor to his assessment of their gravity (cf. 154.12).[5]

The body of question 154 runs through the six species of Thomas's list in the received order.[6] The only significant addition to the taxonomy is the subdivision of the vice against nature. This vice comprises procuring pollution without "sleeping together" (*concubitus*), doing so by sleeping with a member of another species, doing so by sleeping with someone not of the proper sex (*sexus*), and doing so in other than the natural way, either by using an improper instrument or by using certain "monstrous and bestial manners" (154.11 corp).[7] The question ends with an article on the relative seriousness of the kinds of *luxuria*. The most serious is the vice against nature; the least serious, simple fornication (154.12 corp). Of vices against nature, the worst is bestiality; the least serious, solitary uncleanness (154.12 ad 4).

If you recall scholarly narratives about Thomas's importance in the history of Christian intolerance,[8] you may be surprised to learn that the article on vice against nature is one of the shortest in these two questions. Indeed, it is about a quarter of the length of the longest article, which is the article that argues for the sinfulness of simple fornication. This crude, quantitative comparison would seem to suggest that the matter of the article on vice against nature is either not particularly important or not particularly difficult for Thomas. It does not require a complex set of distinctions or the defusing of difficult authorities. Hence there is no reason, on the surface of the text, to think that the discussion is tense or that particular importance attaches to vice against nature.

Nor is there any reason on the surface of the text to think that emphasis is being put on the sleeping together of persons of the same sex. The language used to describe it is colorless. Indeed, the very term "sleeping together" (*concubitus*) is rather prim.[9] The only phrase of invective in the whole article is used to describe improper manners by which members of different sexes lie together. These manners are "monstrous and bestial"; the others are merely practices of an unemphatically named "sodomitic vice." The derogatory Pauline term "softness" (*mollities*) is used for what we would call masturbation (154.11 corp).[10] Nor, as I have said, is the sodomitic vice singled out for its gravity: if the whole class of vices against nature is the most serious in the category of *luxuria,* the sodomitic vice is not the worst of that class.

This impression that Thomas fails to emphasize sodomitic vice is strengthened by looking to the larger structure, which is the conclusion and the means for Thomas's rereading of moral traditions. Within that rereading, *luxuria* is given no particular prominence. One of the best-calculated effects of Thomas's organization of the *secunda secundae* of the *Summa* is to push the seven capital vices to the margin.[11] They appear, each in turn, but without obvious connection or special importance.[12] Now this might seem odd, because Thomas himself uses the list of seven in arranging his disputed questions *De malo.* But a study of either text will show that Thomas wants to correct misreadings that magnify the distinct gravity of these seven. Thomas insists that they are neither the "roots" nor the "starting points" of all other sins. They are, in *De malo,* the ends to which desire is ordered "principally" or "for the most part."[13] They are, in the *Summa,* the vices from which others arise "most frequently," but not exclusively.[14] For Thomas, then, *luxuria* is not emphasized just so far as it is one of the seven sins.

It might be argued, even so, that *luxuria* remains most prominent among the seven once they are dispersed throughout the *Summa.* It merits two questions, after all, and by far the most extended discussion. But that is due, I think, to the number of species and "daughters" of *luxuria.* Sloth and envy have neither species nor daughters. Avarice and vainglory have daughters, not species. Gluttony and wrathfulness have both daughters and species, but their species are fewer and less confusing than those of *luxuria.* The extent of the treatment of *luxuria* is determined by taxonomy, not by gravity. Nor is the presence of an article on whether *luxuria* is the greatest of sins particularly significant. The same issue is raised with respect to three other of the capital vices.[15] The determination in each case is negative. None of the capital vices is the gravest or greatest sin. That distinction is reserved, even within Gregory's scheme, for pride, which is the gravest sin, the first sin, and the ruler of the capital sins.[16]

With all of this contextual reinforcement for the relative unimportance of *luxuria* and any of its species, the attentive reader of Thomas will be puzzled to recall one remark in the question on *luxuria*—a remark connected to other, much more emphatic references to the sodomitic vice, although it is not elsewhere called by that name.[17] The remark is this: "Just as the order of right reason is from man, so the order of nature is from God himself. And so in sins against nature, in which the very order of nature is violated, an injury is done to God himself, the orderer of nature" (2–2.154.12 ad 1). What is peculiar about the remark is that the same syllogism can be constructed for any sin whatever. Every vice or sin is against nature, hence against God.[18] More superficially, Thomas himself uses sins of *luxuria* as a clear example of "sins against self" when these are to be contrasted, according to a different schema, with "sins against God."[19]

Now Thomas does explain in what way it is justified to single out one vice as "the vice against nature." He notes, in an article on the inclusiveness of natural law, that "the sleeping together of men" (*concubitus masculorum*) is said especially to be a vice against nature because it controverts the "commingling" (*commixtio*) of men and women that is natural to human beings and animals (1–2.94.3 ad 2). This is not an admission, frank or otherwise, that the terminology "is a concession to popular sentiment and parlance."[20] It resonates too strongly with other passages where the "vice against nature" is seen as a violation of a fundamental teleology. In *De malo*, for example, every act of *luxuria* other than the commixture of men and women is said to be against the nature of any animal as such (15.1 ad 7). Again, in the *Contra Gentiles*, sins against nature are coupled with murder so far as they prevent human conception.[21] Thomas also follows Aristotle in using desire for such copulation as an example of an unnatural desire—as unnatural as the desire to eat coal or dirt.[22] In these and related texts, Thomas seems to undo the terminological precision of the *Summa*, where the sin against nature is subdvided equally into four species. Elsewhere Thomas himself will mean by "sin against nature" only one of those species—same-sex copulation. It becomes the sin against nature, simply speaking.

On the one hand, then, Thomas's rereading of the moral traditions places the sodomitic vice as a middling species of a subsidiary class of sins, which cannot, as carnal, be among the gravest. On the other hand, the vice against nature is the eponymous denial of the order of animal nature, hence of nature's God. What is it that makes this vice at once a circumscribed self-indulgence and a radical denial of human purposes? What makes it, to pervert Eve Sedgwick's categories, at once minoritizing and universalizing?[23]

## Carnal, Bestial, Unnameable Vice

Three descriptions of the vice enact this oscillation with great energy: they teach that it is a carnal vice, a bestial vice, and a vice that cannot be named. Each of these descriptions is justified by what I will begin by calling a "misreading" of an authoritative passage.

A carnal sin is, says Thomas, a sin that is consummated in a turning toward, a cleaving to some bodily good.[24] It arises from and is partly mitigated by the violence of our "concupiscence of flesh." Sins of *luxuria* are eminently the carnal sins in part because of the violence of concupiscence evident in them.[25] On Thomas's account, *luxuria* is a sin because it permits concupiscence to command what is against the common good, that is, against the conservation of the human species. But this account oscillates between two diagnoses of *luxuria.* The first diagnosis discovers a sin of self-indulgence that issues immediately in the dissolution of the soul. The second discovers a sin that imperils the future of the species by misusing its powers of reproduction.

The resulting instability can be seen quite plainly in Thomas's misreading of a quotation from Augustine's *Confessions.* Augustine says this:

> Disgraceful acts [*flagitia*] against nature are everywhere and always to be detested and punished, as those of the Sodomites were; if all people did these, all would be held guilty of the same crime by the divine law, which did not make human beings that they should use each other in this way. Indeed the society that we ought to have with God is violated when the nature of which He is the author is polluted by perversity of lust.[26]

Thomas quotes this whole passage, rather unusually, in replying to an objection that sins against nature are less serious than adultery, deflowering, or abduction because they do not harm one's neighbor. He replies through the quotation that sins against nature are the more serious because done against God.

The Augustinian *auctoritas* becomes pertinent only after two misreadings. The first misreading, the explicit one, moves the accent in the passage from the perversity of lust—*libido,* the great word of Augustinian spiritual diagnosis—to the misuse of created bodies. The second misreading, the implicit one, changes the allusion to the Sodomites from the ferocity of their punishment to the (presumed) species of their crime. With the Old Testament prophets, and much patristic exegesis, Augustine takes the destruction of Sodom as a type for the ferocity of divine judgment. Aquinas, with much medieval exegesis, takes it as a type for a certain kind of sin.

There is nothing in the *Confessions* to make clear what Augustine has in mind when he speaks of the *flagitia contra naturam.* Augustine has here fallen into the hissing cauldron of lust, but not, it would seem, into acts that we would call "homosexual." Moreover, the immediate context for the passage is an argument against the Manichaean charge that the God of the Old Testament changes his laws. Augustine is seeking to distinguish crimes that are always punished by the divine law from crimes that can be punished or not depending on particular historical circumstances. The "disgraceful acts against nature" are everywhere and always to be punished in the way that the Sodomites were punished. What are these disgraces? They are specified only by the remark that human beings were not intended to use one another in such a way. There is no reference to the thwarting of reproduction or to the teleology of reproductive organs. Indeed, the Augustinian sense of "use" as the counterpoint for "enjoyment," and the teaching that all creatures are only to be used, would lead one to conclude that the passage in the *Confessions* is not about physical *usus* at all. Yet Thomas's argument will go through only if the passage refers to sins against nature understood as misuse of reproductive powers. He specifies this reference by relying on the now traditional misunderstanding of "Sodomites." That misunderstanding permits the transfer of Augustine's opprobrium—indeed, the full force of prophetic invective—to a particular set of acts, which it then understands as a misuse of the natural power of reproduction.

Another kind of misreading supports Thomas's description of the sodomitic vice as a bestial vice. In the explicit taxonomy of the *Summa*, it is by no means the only one. Every carnal sin is bestial so far as it privileges the bodily delights that we share with other animals, thus rendering us "in some way...animal-like" (*"quodammodo...brutalis,"* 1–2.73.5 ad 3). But the explicit taxonomy is again broken here by particular associations between sodomitic vice and animality. On the one hand, the vice is consistently linked with cannibalism and what we still call "bestiality."[27] On the other, it is inserted into an Aristotelian discussion of bestial vice, namely, vice that falls below the level of the human. Both associations are misreadings.

The association of an erotic desire for members of the same sex with cannibalism seems to come by misremembering Aristotle's discussion of unnatural desire. As Thomas tells it in his literal exposition of the *Ethics*, Aristotle distinguishes brutish desires from unnatural desires that arise from illness or custom.[28] Examples of the brutish states are atrocities that include cannibalism. The examples of morbid desire resulting from custom include erotic activity between men.[29] It is Thomas who collapses Aristotle's distinctions by connecting cannibalism, bestiality, and same-sex copulation under the notion of bestial desire.[30] He makes this clear in letting stand an objection according to which "the vice against nature is not contained under malice, but under bestiality, as is clear from the Philosopher in *Ethics* 7."[31] The impulse toward this misreading is so strong that it pushes Thomas to intervene untypically in the text of Aristotle's *Politics* as he expounds its letter. In reviewing Lacedaemonian and Cretan legislation, Thomas cannot stop himself from twice inserting the adjective "wicked" (*turpis*) when naming sexual acts between men.[32]

Transferring the erotic acts between men into the Aristotelian category of bestial vice yields both a rhetorical and a conceptual advantage. The rhetorical advantage lies in being able to reinforce the shame produced by Aristotle's having stigmatized, earlier in the *Ethics*, certain kinds of physical pleasures as "slavish" and "bestial."[33] The sodomitic vice is not merely ridiculous and shameful in the way that gluttony is, it is also disgusting and horrifying in the way that atrocities are. The conceptual advantage comes in pushing this vice outside the boundaries of the conversation of ethics. The horrors enumerated by Aristotle in the discussion of bestial desire lie beyond the realm of rational inquiry. So too, for him, do the exaggerated diseases of desire. These acts are outside correction, hence outside ethical discussion. Thomas's conflation of the Aristotelian categories places the sodomitic vice as such in this inhuman beyond.

A more dramatic displacement occurs when Thomas appropriates the tradition according to which vice against nature is a vice that cannot be named. He does so explicitly not in the *Summa,* but in his first *Scriptum* on the *Sentences.* "The species of *luxuria* are divided first into lying together according to nature and against nature. But since *luxuria* against nature is unnameable, it will be set aside."[34] The authority for this prohibition is a misreading of Ephesians 5:3.[35] In commenting on that passage, Thomas explains that the idiom "are not to be named" means that the Ephesians are "to abstain from deeds, thoughts, and sayings" about a list of sins.[36] But in the *Scriptum* he appropriates the tradition that makes the precept dictate silence with regard to a certain class of sins against nature. If the precept is not explicitly recalled in the *Summa,* it seems to be practiced. The descriptions of sins against nature are remarkably vague. One may contrast Thomas's reticence, for example, with the enumeration of four kinds of sodomy by Peter Damian,[37] or even with the anatomical distinctions in William Peraldus.[38] Of course, Peraldus himself immediately inserts the pastoral caution that would seem to explain the Pauline prohibition: "This vice is to be spoken of with great caution both in preaching and in confessional questioning, that nothing be revealed to men that might give them occasion to sin."[39] Why this caution? If the sodomitic vice is the eponymous sin against nature, desire for which can be acquired only by long distortion of what is most innate, how can it be so easy to suggest?

The contradiction is a familiar one. It is enacted with particular clarity by Peter Damian in the few lines of his preface, which hesitates melodramatically to name a vice that it then likens to a raging epidemic. There is nothing so obvious in Thomas, and his aversion to gross contradictions may explain the omission of reference to Ephesians in the *Summa.* But in writings contemporary with the *Summa,* Thomas paraphrases and augments Aristotelian accounts of the genesis of the vice that suggest that it is much easier to acquire and perhaps to inculcate than the hypothesis of long abuse would allow. Thomas seems to agree with the *Politics* that the vice accompanies warlikeness and that it can be caused or exacerbated by the physiological effects of too much horseback riding.[40] Hence the vagueness of the *Summa* and its emphasis on the rare conditions under which the vice is generated would seem to indicate something of the traditional reserve.

31

In these three descriptions of the vice as carnal, bestial, and unnameable, Thomas misreads just in the way that produces the duality of the sodomitic vice as self-indulgence and eponymous crime against nature. But we cannot stop with calling them "misreadings." Misreadings are questions, not answers. Why do the oscillations enacted by the category "sodomitic vice" require such misreadings?

It may be part of an answer to say that the misreadings are justified by appeal to Thomas's largest judgments about the circumstances of moral teaching. These assumptions can be represented compendiously as a master narrative about the history of human learning. The master narrative is the double story of the deepening silence of natural law, caused by sin, and the growing articulateness of divine teaching, the work of grace. The narrative goes something like this: Original sin obscures our access to natural law, which was, in any case, never meant to serve as a guide apart from divine laws and human laws in conformity with them. As the effects of sin accumulate, the natural law speaks less and less clearly. Indeed, it can become so inarticulate that whole peoples forget one or another of its basic teachings. Thomas mentions, famously, Caesar's claim that the Germans did not regard theft as an evil.[41] The silences of natural law can be filled in only by divine revelation, by the articulation of divine laws of the Old and New Testaments. They make explicit and practicable what the natural law only suggested, when it spoke at all. The progress of Christian moral theology aids the work of articulation, not by adding new laws, but by specifying applications and correcting misunderstandings. Later theologians speak "more cautiously" and "as if selectively" in view of the history of misunderstandings and controversies that is the history of heresy.[42]

So far the narrative. It is easier to tell than to imitate. It requires of Thomas both that he speak what is silent in natural law and that he speak most judiciously about matters likely to cause scandal. He must both strengthen the voice of nature and conceal how often the voice has been unheard. Most particularly, since the *Summa* teaches "Christian religion" to those who would learn it in the school of religious life, he must present these sins as remote ones, beyond the border of nature—hence, much more, outside the cloister. He must omit to mention that the history of the Church has shown this vice to be a peculiarly clerical "contagion"—I use one of the recurring metaphors for it.

This narrative about the circumstances of Thomas's teaching justifies the misreadings of sodomitic vice as carnal, bestial, and unnameable by presenting them as corrective rereadings. It would be easy to show that Thomas regards this kind of correction as an essential part of the theologian's work. But in doing so we would lose the specific problematic of the sodomitic vice in a general account of theological procedure. We have not yet got what it is about the category of this vice that causes it to oscillate. We have not, because it is here that our conflicts of motives and surplus of stories diverge irremediably from Thomas's. I will end by trying to say how this is so.

## Oscillating Categories and Moral Teaching

I suggested above that the oscillation in the category of sodomitic vice, by which it swings from a middling sin of *luxuria* to the eponymous sin against natural teleology, was somewhat like Sedgwick's dialectic of minoritizing and universalizing accounts of homosexuality. But whatever the cause of the oscillation of Thomas's category might be, it cannot be the dialectic that Sedgwick describes. It cannot, because there is nothing resembling the categories homosexual/heterosexual in Thomas. Thomas cannot responsibly be made even to speak in debates where "homosexuality" and "heterosexuality" serve as categories for personal identity. When Thomas talks about the sodomitic vice, he is talking about a vice. The vice is precisely not a physiological disposition or its behavioral consequences. Neither is it an identity determining the whole of a person's action. Nor does the vice have anything specifically to do with gender inversions or exaggerations.[43] So far as I can see, there are no references to effeminacy, for example, in Thomas's passages on same-sex copulation. If Thomas speaks always in a male voice, he does not describe the sodomite as unmasculine.

It does not follow that Thomas regards nothing beyond acts of copulation. A vice is never the sum of acts. It is their cause and ground. The sodomitic vice is meant to explain why certain people do acts that are against their natures as reasonable animals. Part of the explanation reaches downward to particular circumstances. Part runs backward to personal history or physiology. Part spreads out into the network of the person's other vices and virtues, into passions, dispositions, character. But these explanations cannot be mapped onto the theories embedded in the term "homosexuality."

If the dialectic of homosexual/heterosexual cannot be the deep cause of the conceptual oscillation that we have traced through textual anomalies and acts of misreading, what is the cause? I am not content to answer that it is stupidity or a mere sloppiness in the use of basic terms — as if the matter could be solved by "being clear" about the meanings of "nature." Nor do I want to conclude that the oscillations are the most visible effects of an ideological abuse of discrepant conceptual schemes. I want to say, rather, that the oscillations of the category of sodomitic vice arise from what must appear to us as a paradox in the notion of unnatural pleasure — a paradox glimpsed in the category of *luxuria,* but observed most strikingly in the persistent fact that some people derive pleasure from unteleological copulation.

The paradox is this: For Thomas, true pleasure is the effect of natural completion, of the fulfillment of natural teleology. The sodomitic vice radically disrupts the most obvious continuities of animal nature. Yet the cause of this violently antinatural sin is the intensity of pleasure it yields—a pleasure so intense that it "dissolves the soul." It is not only the intensity that is troubling: Thomas here confronts a kind of pleasure that cannot be divided without remainder into teleological sequences. He confronts a pleasure without end. He names the possibility of this pleasure as the antithesis of nature. Much more than thieving Germans, the fact of sodomitic pleasures threatens to assert that a large group of moral arguments from natural teleology is specious.

Just here we are prevented from pursuing the paradox further. Indeed, we must wonder whether the paradox isn't our misapprehension. We are up against what seems to me the most startling divergence between our stories and Thomas's, his motives and ours. For Thomas, the assertion that venereal pleasures are for the sake of reproduction is not an assumption, but a tautology. It is the way of picking out certain pleasures as venereal. The category of *luxuria* is constituted by its relation to the teleology of reproduction. There is no other way of distinguishing the class of acts, pleasures, and sins as venereal. For us, on the contrary, the category of the "erotic" or even the "sexual" is constituted by the assertion that there is a distinctive class of pleasures whose members exceed—indeed, precede—the relation of the pleasuring organs to reproduction. For us, the restriction of "sexual" or "erotic" activity to procreation seems at best quaint, at worse tyrannical. For Thomas, there is no category of the sexual apart from animal teleology.

This divergence between our terms and Thomas's does confirm, in a small way, Foucault's assertion that our category of "sexuality" is itself a fairly recent invention. It also and immediately provokes another question: What was there before the category of "sexuality"? In Thomas, there is *sexus,* the complex of anatomical and physiological features that distinguish male and female. There is the right *usus* of procreative power, of copulation and any necessarily connected acts, for the reproduction of the species. And then there is *delectatio,* dangerous pleasure, with its threats to the soul's rational order. The terms are not independent. In Thomas's theology, the reason for both *sexus* and *delectatio* is reproduction. There are two sexes because man needed a helpmate for "the work of generation," which is made pleasurable so that the species will be safeguarded from extinction.[44] Precisely because they depend on each other in these ways, they do not map onto the objects or reasons implied by our term "sexuality." We begin again to diverge from Thomas.

Is there another way forward? Texts, like traditions of inquiry, carry unactualized possibilities. Might there be in Thomas's compositions principles or procedures or materials for constructing something more like the modern notion of "sexuality"? More specifically, might there be a potency for something akin to one of the modern notions of "homosexuality"?

The question demands three different answers. The first is that no exegetical strategy has done more violence to Thomas's texts than the strategy of trying to guess what he might have said to some modern dilemma. Thomas ends up saying what his readers wanted to say before turning to him.

The second answer is that Thomas's teaching on human *sexus* is one of the thinnest and least reflective parts of his moral doctrine. He worked much harder to clarify or to construct other moral teachings. What he did achieve by giving the sins of *luxuria* a reasoned placed within the structure of the *Summa* was undone by the kind of oscillations already described.

The third answer, the most interesting, is that there are in Thomas at least two principles that might have been used to great effect in constructing Christian discourses about same-sex desire. One principle holds that a virtue infused by God can require different actions than the corresponding natural virtue. Divine law can overrule any limited calculation of human goods or ends. Thomas uses the example of fasting. Natural temperance condemns severe fasting as a denial of the mean in nutrition. Infused temperance, the temperance of divine law, commands us to chastise and subjugate the body.[45] The principle is applied by Thomas repeatedly in his defense of virginity. The physical teleology of reproduction is suspended in particular cases by the higher call of divine law, which proclaims that there is something more than the imperatives of the body.[46] So Thomas argues in the pages of the *Summa* immediately before the questions on *luxuria*. Why not extend the principle to the consideration of human sex generally and to same-sex copulation in particular?

The other latent principle is one that Thomas invokes rarely if at all in moral matters, although it is his chief principle in the rest of theology. It is the principle of apophansis or negation: we speak more truly about God and divine things when we negate human categories than when we apply them. Theological discourse ought to be—and is, in much of the *Summa*—the precise arrangement of strings of negations. These strings lead the reader, again and again, to the point at which human language fails to capture divine truth. They lead the reader back to the decisive questions on the "divine names," that is, on the possibilities for speaking about God by negation. There is no stricter theological principle for recognizing the "other" as other.

Imagine, then, the principle of negative theology applied to the teaching on *luxuria*. Wouldn't it require that the Christian theologian suspect easy applications of prevailing categories for human actions? That she examine attentively any proposed deductions from comprehensive accounts of "nature"? That she wonder whether the divine teaching about human things might not be as offensive to societal prejudices as the doctrine of the Trinity is offensive to prevailing human logics?

I do not find that Thomas considers these injunctions or the possibilities of the apophantic principle in dealing with the morality of human sexes. He is not alone. I can find no application of negative theology to moral teaching about sexual activity before the fourteenth century, when it begins to seem really possible that God might suspend some or all of the ten commandments. Even this is not so much negative theology as the dialectical consideration of God's absolute power to separate whatever is logically distinct. The check on negative moral theology is not doctrinal. It is social. It arises not from the logic of Christian theology, but from the accommodations that Christian theology made to the various societies in which it found itself. A devoted reader of Thomas might well want to reject these accommodations in the name of Thomas's own best principles — say, in the name of pseudo-Dionysius and Aristotle. By its very terms, this rewriting of Thomas would go beyond any correction from Thomas's texts. It would no longer be the scholarly reading of a medieval theologian. It would be the writing of Christian theology in the present. And that might be the only reading of his texts that Thomas would recognize as adequate.

Thomas himself intends by his *Summa* to produce, not historians, but theologians. His best readers will not be mimics of his texts; they will be teachers of the things that his texts want to make present. He thus rejects the ideal of philological imitation with which I began. In so doing, he suggests that the best genre for writing on his texts will not be the genre of transparent commentary so much as the genre of engaged dispute. To read Thomas's teaching on same-sex copulation must, on Thomas's own account, lead beyond the assiduous interpretation of his texts to the redoing of moral theology in the reader's present — since it is only in the present that we have together Thomas's teaching, our questions, and the rule of Christian faith according to which every theology is judged.

## Notes

1. William Peraldus, *Summae de vitiis et de virtutibus* tractatus de luxuria pars 1 (Venice, 1497), fol. 203$^{va}$. For some Roman texts on *luxuria* and a reading of them, see Catharine Edwards, *The Politics of Immorality in Ancient Rome* (Cambridge: Cambridge University Press, 1993), 176–206. There is no detailed treatment of the term's fates in later Latin.

2. See the order *fornicatio, adulterium, stuprum, sacrilegium, incestus, peccatum contra naturam* in the prologue to *Summa Halensis* 2/2.3.4.2.2.1.7.9, as in *Alexandri de Hales... Summa theologica*, ed. Collegium S. Bonaventurae (Quaracchi: C.S.B., 1924–30), 3:604; the order *simplex fornicatio, stuprum, adulterium, incestus, peccatum contra naturam* in Peraldus, *Summae* tract. de luxuria pars 1 (fol. 203$^{vb}$).

3. Peter Lombard, *Sententiae* 4.41.5–9 is a close paraphrase of Gratian. Compare *Sententiae in IV libris distinctae*, ed. Collegium S. Bonaventurae (Grottaferrata: C.S.B., 1981), 2:500 no. 2, with Gratian's *Decretum* 2.36.1.2, as in *Corpus iuris canonici*, ed. Æ. L. Richter and Æ. Friedberg (Leipzig: Tauschnitz, 1922), 1:1289. Thomas knows both texts directly, of course.

4. The Pauline passages are 2 Corinthians 12:21, Ephesians 5:3, Colossians 3:5, and Galatians 5:19, on which see Thomas Aquinas, *Summa theologiae* 2–2.154.1 arg. 5, arg. 6,

ad 5, ad 6 (Ottawa: Studium Generale O. Pr., 1941–44), vol. 3, columns 2173a, 2174b–2175a., especially in comparison with his *Scriptum super Sent.* 4.41.1.4b arg. 1–3 and ad 1–3, as in *Opera omnia,* ed. Roberto Busa (Stuttgart-Bad Canstatt: Frommann-Holzboog, 1980), 1:625a–b.

5. Earlier Thomas had argued that the traditional list is in order of gravity, although he added even then that the order could be much varied by various circumstances. See *Scriptum super Sent.* 4.41.1.4c corp (Busa *Opera omnia* 1:625b).

6. There are two articles on simple fornication, two interjected articles on noncoital pleasures, then one each on the remaining species, with an interjected article against taking sacrilege as a separate species—as it is in the *Summa Halensis* 2/2.3.5.2.1.7 (C.S.B. 3:648–53).

7. It seems to me that Thomas does not mean to use *concubitus* as a synonym for *coitus.* He reserves *coitus* for penile-vaginal intercourse between humans, as would be suggested by Gratian and the Lombard. He is authorized in using *concubitus* for illicit sexual activity by the Vulgate, which uses *concubitores* only in the phrase "concubitores masculorum" (1 Corinthians 6:19, 1 Timothy 1:10). Thus the Latin renders Paul's *arsenokoitai,* for which see John Boswell, *Christianity, Social Tolerance and Homosexuality* (Chicago: University of Chicago Press, 1980), 341–53. The Vulgate uses *concubitus* twice neutrally (Genesis 38:16, Romans 9:10), twice in contexts of excess ("concubitus concupiscentiae" at Sirach 23:6, "insanivit libidine...super concubitu eorum" at Ezekiel 23:20).

8. Signally, Boswell, *Christianity,* 318–30.

9. Thomas could have used *contubernium,* for example. Originally used to designate cohabitation by slaves, who could not marry, the term was adopted in anti-Manichaean ecclesiastical legislation of the twelfth century with a strongly pejorative sense. See, for example, J. D. Mansi, *Sacrorum conciliorum nova et amplissima collectio* (Florence and Venice, 1759–98), 21:843.

10. On the difficulties of translating the Pauline *malakoi* (1 Corinthians 6:9), see Boswell, *Christianity,* 338–41.

11. Thomas is not unique in this regard. See Siegfried Wenzel, "The Seven Deadly Sins: Some Problems of Research," *Speculum* 43 (1968): 1–22, at 14. One instance of a return to old ways after Thomas's innovations is the compiling from the *Summa theol.* of a treatise on the seven capital sins, e.g., Bamberg, Staatlich Bibliothek MS patr. 122 (Q. V. 12), fols. 220r-225v, as in H. F. Dondaine and H. V. Shooner, *Codices manuscripti operum Thomae de Aquino* (Rome: Commissio Leonina, Sancta Sabina, 1967–), 1:48, no. 113.

12. *Acedia* and *invidia* appear together as vices opposed to *gaudium* (*Summa theol.* 2–2.35–36), which is one of the acts or effects of charity. *Avaritia* is one of two vices opposed to liberality (118), which is itself a quasi-integral part of justice. *Inanis gloria* is one of the vices opposed to magnanimity (132), itself a part of fortitude. The other three sins are listed among the vices opposed to subjective and potential parts of temperance. *Gula* is opposed to abstinence (148), *luxuria* and its species to chastity (153), *iracundia* to mercy (158). Thomas asks in each case whether the sin is a capital vice (35.4, 36.4, 118.7, 132.4, 148.5, 153.4, 158.6). In each case, the *sed contra* is a citation to Gregory's *Moralia.* Thomas is well aware that there are other authorities with other lists (36.4), but is willing to follow Gregory. Indeed, he follows him so faithfully that he refuses to identify *superbia* with *inanis gloria* or to call *superbia* a capital vice (162.8). Thomas defends Gregory's list as a suitable classification of these final causes (1–2.84.3–4), but he explicitly denies that the classification by final causes—or any causes—ought to count as an essential classification (1–2.72.3.corp & ad 3).

13. Thomas Aquinas, *De malo* 8.1 ad 1, "principaliter," as in *Opera omnia iussu impensaque Leonis XIII. P. M.* (Rome: Various imprints, 1882–), 23:195.370; 8.1 ad 6, "in pluribus" (195.402); 8.1 ad 8, "in pluribus" (196.432).

14. *Summa theol.* 1–2.84.4 ad 5: "ista vita dicuntur capitalia, qui ex eis ut frequentius alia oriuntur. Unde nihil prohibet aliqua peccata interdum ex aliis causis oriri."

15. With respect to *avaritia* (*Summa theol.* 2–2.118.5), *gula* (148.3), and *iracundia* (158.4).

16. See *Summa theol.* 2–2.162.6, 162.7, and 162.8, respectively.

17. Thomas speaks of *"vitium sodomiticum"* only in the *Summa*'s Question on the species of *luxuria* (2–2.154.11 corp, 154.12 ad 4) and in the commentary on Isaiah 4 (Leonine *Opera omnia* 28:33.43). In the latter, it is used as an example of an act that can never be ordered to the end of generation.

18. This is the principal argument of *Summa theol.* 1–2.71.2.

19. *Summa theol.* 1–2.72.4 corp: "Et quando in his peccatur, dicitur homo peccare in seipsum, sicut patet de guloso, luxurioso et prodigo."

20. Boswell, *Christianity*, 328.

21. Thomas Aquinas, *Summa contra Gentiles* 3.122, ed. Ceslao Pera, Pierre Marc, and Pietro Caramello, *Liber de veritate catholicae fidei contra errores infidelium* (Turin and Rome: Marietti; Paris: Lethielleux, 1961–67), sect. no. 2955.

22. *Summa theol.* 1–2.31.7 corp, 2–2.142.4 ad 3, to which compare Aristotle, *Nicomachean Ethics* 7.4 (1148b26), and Thomas Aquinas, *Sent. libri Ethicorum* 7.5 (Leonine *Opera omnia* 47:400.80–82). I will come back to Thomas's transposition of cannibalism in these contexts.

23. Eve Kosofsky Sedgwick, *Epistemology of the Closet* (Berkeley: University of California Press, 1990), 40, 41, and the review in her *Tendencies* (Durham, N.C.: Duke University Press, 1993), xii-xiii.

24. *Summa theol.* 1–2.73.5 corp.

25. *Summa theol.* 2–2.153.1 corp: "Maxime autem voluptates venereae animum hominis solvunt"; ad 1, "luxuria principaliter quidem est in voluptatibus venereis, quae maxime et praecipue animum hominis resolvunt."

26. Augustine, *Confessiones* 3.8.15, ed. M. Skutella and L. Verheijen, Corpus Christianorum, Series Latina 27 (Turnhout: Brepols, 1981), 35.3–9. Thomas's version (as in the Leonine) differs only in punctuation and in reading "omnes eodem" for "eodem." A truncated version of the passage is used by Peraldus in the parallel discussion. See his *Summae* tract. de luxuria 1 (fol. 204^va).

27. *Summa theol.* 1–2.31.7 corp, "in coitu bestiarum aut masculorum"; 2–2.142.4 ad 3, "in coitu bestiarum aut masculorum"; 2–2.154.11 corp, "Alio modo, . . . bestialitas. Tertio, . . . sodomiticum vitium"; 2–2.154.12 ad 4, "Post hoc [*scil.* bestialitas] autem est vitium sodomiticum. . . ."

28. Aristotle, *Nic. Ethics* 7.5 (1148b15–30).

29. Aristotle speaks of "hē tōn aphrodisiōn tois arresin," which Thomas's Latin renders quite literally as "quae venereorum masculis"; Aristotle, *Nic. Ethics* 7.5 (1148b29) = Aquinas, *Sent. lib. Ethic.* 7.5 (Leonine *Opera omnia* 47:398). In Grosseteste's version of the anonymous commentary on *Ethics* 7, the commentator has the same reading for the Aristotelian lemma, but goes on to speak of "abusing" or "corrupting" men ("masculis . . . abuti," "masculos corrumpere"). See H. Paul F. Mecken, *The Greek Commentaries on the Nicomachean Ethics of Aristotle* 3, Corpus Latinum Commentariorum in Aristotelem Graecorum 6/3 (Leuven: University Press, 1991), 41.95–05.

30. Albert, with whom Thomas studied the *Ethics* intensively, is more careful to distinguish the causality of long habit when raising questions about this passage. He also counts "concubitus masculorum" as less unnatural than some of the other Aristotelian instances. See Albertus Magnus, *Super Ethica, Commentum et quaestiones* 7.5, as in his *Opera omnia* 14, ed. Wilhelm Kübel (Münster: Aschendorff, 1987), 545, lines 37–40.

31. *Summa theol.* 2–2.154.11 arg. 2 and ad 2, to which compare *Scriptum super Sent.* 4.41.1.4b ad 4 (Busa *Opera omnia* 1:625b). Recall also the way in which Aristotle's remarks about the scope of temperance in *Ethics* 3.10 are taken as referring to *peccata carnalia* in 1–2.73.5 ad 3.

32. Thomas Aquinas, *Sententia libri Politicorum* 2.13 (Leonine *Opera omnia* 48:A164. 140–49), 2.15 (A174.117–23).

33. Aristotle, *Nic. Ethics* 3.10 (1118b1–8).

34. *Scriptum super Sent.* 4.41.1 4b corp (Busa *Opera omnia* 1:625a).

35. In the Vulgate, "Fornicatio autem et omnis inmunditia aut avaritia nec nominetur in vobis sicut decet sanctos. . . ." Note that the list extends considerably beyond *luxuria contra naturam,* and that the sense in the idiom is that these are not even to be mentioned among Christians, much less practiced.

36. Thomas Aquinas, *Super ad Ephes.* 5.2 (Busa *Opera omnia* 6:460c).

37. Peter Damian, *Liber Gomorrhianus,* printed as *Epistola* 31 in *Die Briefe des Petrus Damiani* 1, ed. Kurt Reindel, Monumenta Germaniae Historica (MGH): Die Briefe der deutschen Kaiserzeit, 4 (Munich: MGH, 1983), 287, lines 19–21. The corresponding passage in Migne's edition (*Patrologia Latina,* vol. 54 [Paris: J.-P. Migne, 1874], 161C) has been thoroughly bowdlerized. Among other changes, Peter's rather explicit *fornicatio in terga* becomes an unspecified "consummatus actus."

38. Peraldus, *Summae* tract. de luxuria pars 1 (fol. 203$^{vb}$).

39. Peraldus, *Summae* tract. de luxuria pars 1 (fol. 203$^{vb}$): "de quo vitio cum magna cautela loquendum est: et predicando: et interrogationes in confessionibus faciendo: ut nihil hominibus reveletur: quod eis prebet occasionem peccandi."

40. *Sent. lib. Politic.* 2.13 (Leonine *Opera omnia* 48:A164.140–53), with the inserted reference to the pseudo-Aristotelian *De problematibus.*

41. *Summa theol.* 1–2.94.4 corp.

42. Thomas Aquinas, *Contra errores Graecorum* pars prior prol. (Leonine *Opera omnia* 40:A71.39–40).

43. Thomas does follow old traditions, both pagan and Judeo-Christian, in associating all *luxuria* with effeminacy. Thus, following Hosea 4:11, he holds that fornication and drunkenness make a man effeminate (2–2.153.5 ad 2). On Thomas's view, the adulterer or rapist is just as likely to be effeminate as a man who copulates with other men.

44. For the distinction of sexes, *Summa theol.* 1.92.1 corp; for the pleasure of intercourse, *Super Sent.* 4.33.1.3a.

45. *Summa theol.* 1–2.63.4 corp.

46. *Summa theol.* 2–2.152.2 corp.

## CHAPTER 3

✛

# Sciences/Silences:
## The Natures and Languages of "Sodomy" in Peter of Abano's *Problemata* Commentary

*Joan Cadden*

### Origins and Meanings of Silence

Eloquent on the anatomy, physiology, and psychology of heterosexual coitus and the desire and pleasure associated with it, medieval medicine and natural philosophy are, for the most part, silent on feelings and contacts between women and women, men and men. The results of recent research remind us, however, that historical silences are often the result of the questions we have failed to ask — of our own taboos. Now that the history of sexuality has become an acceptable, indeed fashionable, subject, relevant texts have begun to come to light.[1] Among these is a section of Peter of Abano's early fourteenth-century commentary on Aristotle's *Problemata*.[2] Nevertheless, the clues are few and fragmentary: modern neglect only partly explains the limits of our knowledge.

A second source of silence inheres in the past itself. Mark Jordan has shown in the context of ethics and theology that there was something unspeakable about "sodomy" as Thomas Aquinas construed it (see chapter 2 in this volume); some medical authors, whose notions about licit speech did not differ entirely from those of their learned contemporaries,[3] found reasons to evade the issue in a condemnatory tone:

> It would be possible . . . to relate several types of sodomite coitus, which men and women abusively indulge in, and establish between them comparisons on their advantages and disadvantages, but I judge it better to keep silence, so that human nature, inclined towards evil and towards the exercise of new lusts, may not attempt, on hearing them, to put them into practice, and thus prejudice one's honor and one's soul.[4]

The words of Jacques Despars, a fifteenth-century medical commentator, suggest a set of ideological reasons for a naturalist to pass over these subjects. He calls attention to his omission, thus highlighting his audience's consciousness of what is proper and decorous; he elevates the avoidance of moral and spiritual harm above the communication of medical knowledge.

The apparent contagiousness of such impulses is not the only reason for reticence. Despars is commenting on Avicenna's *Canon of Medicine,* an Arabic work translated into Latin in the twelfth century, which came to occupy a significant place in the medical curriculum.[5] Avicenna mentions men who are accustomed to having other men throw themselves on them, to whose condition he applies a name, *al-liwat,* which is transliterated rather than translated in the Latin version as *halubuathi, halubnathi,* or *alguagi.*[6] He says that it is stupid to seek a cure for them, since "the origin of their disease is meditative, not natural."[7] Western readers, Despars among them, gave "meditative" a moral and religious gloss — "sodomite," "evil," "lust" — to suggest that the subject was beyond the disciplinary boundaries of medicine. Taken in conjunction with Aquinas's implication that it did not belong in the domain of ethics,[8] this foreign label and this systematic exclusion suggest a coherent if not unbreachable silence originating with medieval authors themselves.

In the face of these impediments, the existence of the early fourteenth-century text presented here, which discusses the desire of certain men for anal stimulation, may encourage scholars seeking to reconstitute an invisible past. But, although artifacts uncovered in the course of such a quest may be authentic, as in the case of Peter of Abano's text, their interpretation, as Mark Jordan demonstrates, will be fraught with difficulties. Thus, in addition to the practical limits of our research and the ideological constraints on medieval discussions, the silence poses a set of epistemological questions. Is it anachronistic to speak of "homosexuality" as a construct in the context of medieval medicine and natural philosophy? Did "homosexuals" exist in the Middle Ages; that is, did medieval culture name or otherwise give substance to a type of person associated with identities, desires, or behavior?

Like their theoretical and political dimensions, the empirical dimensions of these questions are likely to be complicated. If, for example, as a practical matter, secular women were seldom able to avoid their heterosexual responsibilities and medical authors regarded women's pleasure with women as a side effect of temporary and remediable dissatisfaction with a male partner and if men's pleasure with men were ascribed to different and more enduring causes, we might conclude that, in some sense, "gay men" existed in the Middle Ages but "lesbians" did not.[9] Similarly, if male authors entertained specific anxieties about the masculine body, rationality, and will, as Dyan Elliott suggests they did in the case of nocturnal emissions (see chapter 1 in this volume), their silences and discourses on same-sex relations would undoubtedly be gendered. Such effects would be independent of, if compounded by, the dominance of the male voice in the Latin record.[10] Furthermore, evidence might indicate that a construct suggesting some dimensions of our notion of "homosexual" was operating in medicine, but not in law or literature. Thus any historical finding, whether of silence or of positive evidence, must be evaluated not only in the context of general medieval mentalities and conceptual frameworks but also in the context of the specific cultural site in which it was generated.

Indeed, Peter of Abano accords clearer conceptual status to attractions and contacts between men than do theologians or philosophers like Aquinas. Nothing Peter says could reasonably be construed to correspond to modern notions of "homosexuality" or "homosexual identity." Yet, by speaking in the language of natural philosophy and by offering a rich scientific account of some men's appetite for anal sexual stimulation, Peter naturalizes inclinations and behaviors that point simultaneously to the medieval notion of sodomy and the modern notion of homosexual desire. In relation to the former, his account invokes the language of culpability; in relation to the latter, it deploys the language of nature. The congruences are only partial: for example, the specific focus on the anatomy, physiology, and psychology of a particular sexual practice is much too narrow to encompass either the medieval doctrines concerning sodomy or the modern identities of gay men. Nevertheless, this matter-of-fact text allows us to reevaluate what we have gleaned from theology, canon law and penitentials about learned medieval views of sexual relationships between men and men or (to a much lesser extent) women and women. While this scientific text reflects many of the paradoxes that Jordan has identified in his discussion of Aquinas, its creation of natural categories of men and its integrated explanation of male desire separate the medical model from the religious focus on the will and the individual. By the same token, Peter's naturalistic explanations suggest the difficulty of asserting that homosexuals had no conceptual existence in premodern times. Rather than directly answering modern questions about whether "homosexuals" simply did or simply did not "exist," the evidence of this text serves to broaden and complicate our ideas of how medieval intellectuals dealt with urgent dimensions of their experience.

## Peter of Abano's Voice

Peter of Abano was among the most prominent writers and teachers on natural philosophy and medicine at the turn of the fourteenth century. Originally from northern Italy, he was in Paris when he produced his huge, influential *Conciliator*, an encyclopedic work that discussed and resolved a long list of medical and scientific questions on which the established authorities disagreed. Peter's approach was persistently naturalistic, as he looked to anatomy or physiology, to the elements or the stars to explain the causes of natural phenomena.[11] Indeed, the operations of celestial bodies upon the lower world were a particular interest of his.[12] He was in trouble with the Inquisition three times: perhaps his extension of astrological determinism to sacred history or, more generally, his penchant for physical explanations had seemed to the authorities to encroach upon matters of faith.[13]

Peter was teaching at the University of Paris when he began his commentary on the work attributed to Aristotle known as the *Problemata*; he finished it in 1310 at Padua, where he taught for the latter part of his career. A sprawling collection of natural questions, or "problems," accompanied by sketchy suggestions for scientific answers, the ancient work's tone and character tended to encourage consideration of immediate natural causes and thus to reinforce Peter's interest in the mechanisms of the physical world. Part 4 of the *Problemata* deals with many sexual questions, such as whether baldness is a symptom of lust and why melancholics desire intercourse.[14] Part 4, Problem 26, asks about men who enjoy intercourse with men and suggests some answers that center on susceptibility to anal sexual stimulation.

Peter's breach of the prevailing silence of natural philosophy on the subject of sexual contacts between men may thus be attributed in part to its presence in the classical text on which he is commenting, but the conventions of academic expositions in no way required him to confront it. As Jacques Despars's frankly evasive treatment of the passage in Avicenna shows, the commentary form afforded medieval scholars considerable autonomy. A late Greek commentary on the *Problemata*, which Peter himself had translated into Latin, omits the passage in question (among others).[15] Like many of his contemporaries, Peter himself exercised this freedom to include, omit, elaborate, digress, and otherwise control his own text. Furthermore, since his commentary on the *Problemata* appears to have been the first produced in Latin, he was unburdened by an accretion of medieval textual traditions.

Of particular importance for understanding how Peter established his authority to give a scientific account, where Jacques Despars and others declined to do so, are (1) his practice of normalizing the subject by citing accepted authorities and using conventional scholastic methods to compare and associate the subject with the familiar and mainstream; (2) his persistent application of naturalistic explanations at the anatomical, physiological, and psychological levels; and (3) his evasive and unstable use of language, especially of names for the types of men he is discussing. He deploys these strategies from the outset, even before allowing the controversial nature of his subject to come to light.

## Opening Gambit: Normalizing the Unspoken

About the first quarter of the commentary on Problem 26 is an exercise in silence.[16] The ancient text asks about men's sexual pleasure. Its phrasing suggests that the subject is penile-anal intercourse, and by the end of his commentary Peter explicitly reads Aristotle in this sense. At the opening of his treatment, however, he chooses a vaguer and less likely reading, according to which Aristotle is asking why some people, "such as women or those analogous to them," derive pleasure from intercourse.[17] This move allows him to hint at sexual marginality without confronting its particulars. The characterization of the men to be discussed as "analogous to women" is to prove both useful and inadequate to Peter's task; it also prepares for a significant dimension of his later ethical arguments, which offer the men in question some protection from opprobrium. At the same time, the vagueness of this opening section deflects the discussion away from specific groups of men, permitting him to take full advantage of Aristotle's general explanation of sexual desire as a purposeful and comprehensible natural phenomenon.

The Aristotelian text introduces its suggestions about disordered sexual impulses with a brief allusion to the pattern by which physiological superfluities are produced by the body and collected in their respective anatomical receptacles. Peter takes advantage of the opportunity to give the standard general account of male sexual response: the buildup of superfluities, the accumulation of spirit or windiness, the pleasure associated with expelling what needs to be expelled at the place natural for its evacuation, and the ensuing feeling of harmony. He permits himself to digress to give an obvious answer to an easy question about the text, and pauses to treat in conventional terms a question that would have been familiar to his audience from commentaries on another work of Aristotle's: Why the expulsion of the seed is more pleasurable than the expulsion of other physiological superfluities.[18] In the course of this exercise, Peter makes sure to cite a number of works of unimpeachable medical authority: Avicenna's *Canon of Medicine,* Galen's treatise on the uses of the parts of the body, and a commentary on Galen's work *The Art of Medicine* by Ali ibn Abbas. In addition, on the relationship between pleasure and things that are good, he makes reference to Aristotle's *Ethics.*

Peter has given a standard account of male sexual response, he has cited a number of authorities, and he has said nothing controversial. Indeed, his only allusion to the central subject of the Problem, an oblique one at that, is the reference to "women and men who are analogous to them." He has, however, accomplished a great deal: first, he has placed on display his magisterial command of the sources and methods of scholastic philosophy and medicine; second, he has established the naturalistic tone that he deploys in the rest of the commentary; and finally, he has introduced specific elements of the argument that he will follow, including the anatomical and physiological mechanisms of desire and pleasure. He has done all this without any explicit mention of heterosexual intercourse and with only one indirect reference to reproduction, concentrating rather on the processes of buildup and release in the male. Unlike Aquinas, for whom the final cause of sexual desire and pleasure resided unambiguously in reproduction, Peter and his medical colleagues entertained individual health at least as prominently as the perpetuation of the species in their teleology.[19]

## Natural/Unnatural by Birth

Lurking over this monument of respectability and finesse is the specter of the problem without a name, to which Peter now turns, starting with the question why some men derive pleasure from both "acting" and "being acted upon," while others only from being acted upon. Activity being an essential feature of the male principle, men who enjoy the "active" role alone require no special explanation. The subject here is very limited: male susceptibility to anal stimulation. Modifying what the Aristotelian text suggested and adopting a position that Avicenna had rejected,[20] Peter explains that in some of those who enjoy the "passive" role only, the cause is anatomical: the pores and passages that would naturally convey the spermatic moisture and spirit to the penis are ill formed, blocked, or severed. Just as, in people who have been blinded, the fluids associated with sight fall short of the eye, so in these men the seminal fluid does not reach its destination in the penis, but rather accumulates at the base of the penis or around the anus. The cause may be anatomical but manifest itself physiologically, as happens, for example, with effeminate men who have small weak testicles or with eunuchs who lack them altogether and thus may have complexions so cool that they are reduced to the nature and behavior of women. Peter has picked up from the text the nouns "eunuchs" and "effeminates," words that are certainly not value neutral, especially given the comparison to blindness and the contrast between blocked pathways and natural ones. Thus begins the association of anal stimulation with sexual irregularity and defect. Yet their significance is circumscribed. Eunuchs and effeminates may manifest the anatomical traits and their symptoms, but are only some of the men thus affected. Elsewhere Peter uses these two groups neither as labels nor even as descriptions but only as heuristic examples. Whereas the Aristotelian text associates effeminacy with blocked pores, Peter's commentary declines to explicate its phrase "the acts and mores of women."[21] Furthermore, whatever other implications the terms "eunuch" and "effeminate" may bear, including the evocation of feminine behavior, they do not here engage the vocabulary of blame or sin, but rather suggest specific physical states. The anatomical picture Peter creates, as well as the rhetoric he employs, blurs gender boundaries to highlight the problematic nature of these sexual inclinations but avoids the radical confounding of gender that Dyan Elliott has detected in the context of theologians' consideration of nocturnal emissions.[22]

The explanation of what happens in those who enjoy both the "active" and the "passive" roles is a variation on the same anatomical and physiological arrangement: these men's passageways are not entirely blocked, so seminal substances may accumulate and be released both through the penis and around the anus. The result is that in those with either partially or wholly blocked passages, the accumulation of all or some spermatic moisture and spirit will cause desire for release that can be accomplished by rubbing around the anus, where subtle spirit and even a certain spermatic fluid may be expelled through the pores.[23]

The active-passive distinction had wide cultural currency, resonating with penitentials and polemics as well as with Aristotelian metaphysics, and it is directly suggested by the text on which Peter is commenting.[24] Thus it is all the more surprising to find Peter of Abano slighting this issue in favor of what was for him a more pressing question embedded in the text: Is the susceptibility to anal stimulation natural and, if so, in what sense? He devotes the rest of the commentary on Problem 26 to the natural causes of some men's desire to be rubbed around the anus.

At the most general level, "these men" (*illi*) or "such men" (*tales*), as Peter repeatedly and elusively calls them, are not in conformity with nature. He says, for example, that their pores "are not naturally formed"[25] and that "in them little or no [spermatic] moisture is evacuated or expelled from the place in which it is expelled in those who have those pores naturally and according to nature."[26] He even says that their experience is "the contrary of what is supposed to happen in natural intercourse."[27]

Sexual acts between men were often qualified as unnatural or against nature,[28] which might suggest their exclusion from the authority of science. But Peter's individual commitment to naturalistic explanations, as well as general scientific views about irregularities in nature, provided the occasion and context for the naturalization of these unnatural desires. His exposition follows two paths suggested by the text: in some men, the malformed pores and passages and the resultant susceptibility to anal stimulation occur naturally, in the sense that they are innate; in others, the inclination is instilled by habitual practices that create what is a kind of acquired nature, what we would refer to as "second nature." Elaboration of these two senses of "nature"—innate and acquired, material and psychological—displaces the permutations of passivity and activity as the central distinction in Peter's commentary.

At the physical level, Peter's interest is in the particular nature of those with irregular seminal passageways. He speaks of the condition (*passio*) that exists in some men from birth (*a nativitate*). Indeed, it is on this point alone that he goes so far as to contradict an authority directly. He mentions that Avicenna describes and then rejects an anatomical explanation—based on a branching of the nerve to the penis—of the disease Avicenna calls "*halubuathi.*" But, Peter insists somewhat inaccurately, the theory Avicenna rejects is just what Aristotle seems to be asserting in the text of the Problem. His voice seems to rise as he invokes Aristotle's most authoritative title, "The Philosopher," and speaks in the first person singular for the first and only time in this Problem:

"Avicenna, who seems opposed to the opinion of the Philosopher, adduces no reason, nor do I see what would prevent such a disorder and monstrosity from happening by birth, since immediately afterwards the same Avicenna writes about hermaphrodites, which appear more monstrous within nature."[29] His position is forceful and unambiguous: it is possible for men to be born this way, for them to be this way by nature and within nature.

At the same time, this natural occurrence is clearly irregular — a particular nature discordant with the general norms of nature or, as Peter calls it at several points, a "monstrous nature."[30] Although it certainly bore a negative connotation in this context, the term "monstrosity" conveyed the sense of an occurrence of and in nature.[31] The discipline of medicine did not limit the purpose of sexual pleasure and release of seed to reproductive purposes, nor was the philosophical work on which he was commenting much concerned with final causes. Thus Peter could sidestep the problem of divine and natural teleology and compare men susceptible to anal stimulation to hermaphrodites — a widely recognized natural category with specific physical causes but no identifiable natural purpose.[32]

In addition to justifying his opposition to Avicenna and emphasizing natural causes, the comparison to hermaphrodites plays a role in the rhetoric of normalization. Following the text of the *Problemata,* Peter also compares men disposed in this way to men unable to emit semen, to boys before the age of intercourse, to corpulent men (whose dry complexions affect their semen), to men with fevers, and to young women.[33] Like the attribution of "monstrosity," these comparisons are not flattering, but they are within the range of the familiar and the acceptable; they elicit no hint of moral blame; and they provide occasions for additional citations of authorities — Aristotle, Galen, and Avicenna.[34] Peter further normalizes his subject when he reproduces familiar explanations of the physiological and psychological origins of appetite in general and the standard account of sexual desire in particular — borrowed from the heterosexual context.[35]

However natural and normal Peter was able to make men "thus disposed,"[36] as he sometimes called them, declining direct naming, he clearly felt it was necessary to address the question of possible remedies. Following his initial description of the anatomy of blocked passageways, he rejected with adamancy the idea of a surgical correction.[37] Later, Peter endorses a different approach and, in doing so, explains what it is that needs to be cured: not the condition or disposition per se but rather the consequences of inadequate emission of semen. This redefinition of the problem reflects the medical view that sexual release was one way in which the healthy body managed superfluities. Such men are susceptible to insatiability and madness, like young women (another unflattering comparison) who desire to be rubbed to expel seminal moisture, but in whom rubbing causes an accumulation of seminal moisture, which, inadequately expelled because of their constitutions, in turn produces a greater desire to be rubbed. Although he mentions Avicenna's prescription for *halubuathi*—sadness, hunger, vigils, imprisonment, beating—Peter suggests that the buildup of spermatic fluid can be dispersed by specific foods and medicines.[38] Likewise at this point Peter, who has taken pains to establish the natural basis of men of this disposition, quotes directly and then passes over Avicenna's well-known assertion that "the origin of this sickness is meditative and not natural."[39] He returns to acknowledge this position later, in the context of those in whom the condition is not innate.[40]

## Natural/Unnatural by Habit

As Peter turns to those whose inclination occurs not at birth but "on account of a perverse, filthy habit," he would seem to have abandoned the project of naturalization, for he calls them "sodomites" and then "those who are damned by the polluted sodomitical vice," aiming his condemnations at the actors as well as at the act and the habit.[41] In one sense, the invective breaks the silence: the evasiveness of "these men" and the opacity of *halubuathi* have been replaced by a specific and familiar term. Yet the biblical and canonical resonance of the word "sodomite" introduces the ambiguities to which Jordan has called attention and, moreover, would seem to lift it out of reach of natural philosophy or medicine. In spite of and perhaps under cover of these moralistic phrases, Peter pursues his explanatory agenda: first, he establishes in physiological and psychological terms how these habits arise and become ingrained; second, he untunes the tonality of blame with the help of Aristotelian ethics.

Even if their passages and pores are not ill formed, individuals may have the experience of and develop the desire for "these abominable things."[42] This happens in boys, especially those before the age at which they begin to emit semen. Peter has already established the comparison between men with blocked seminal passageways and adolescents—both male and female—who are able to experience sexual stimulation but unable to emit seed in the normal manner of adults. Boys around puberty are frequently subjected (*supponi*) and rubbed around the anus. The experience gives them pleasure, the memory of which gives rise to desire, repetition, and habit.[43] This can also happen to young boys who are subjected to "this kind of dirty lust," because at this age "their nature is soft and tender," so the process occurs quickly with them.[44] According to Peter, Avicenna calls this result "*halubuathi*"[45] and mentions that, for this reason, many peoples outlaw intercourse with boys.[46]

Reserving the religious term "sodomites" for those who acquire these appetites by habit and the medical term *halubuathi* for the condition thus acquired has two effects. It leaves those to whom they belong at birth without a name, and it concentrates moral attention on the habitual group, evoking Avicenna's notion that the disorder is "meditative, not natural," and thereby posing all the more acutely the problem of rendering the condition "natural" in any sense of the word. But once again Peter uses the scholastic practices of attaching reassuring arguments from other disciplines and of citing authorities. The quotations also allow him to use the word "nature" repeatedly. According to Peter's questionable reading, Aristotle supports the general position that "frequent and long habit becomes just like their very nature, [which] is in children from birth."[47] Hippocrates speaks of the custom of mothers' elongating their babies' heads with their hands until "by habit the change is made into nature."[48] Cicero, recounting the origins of the art of persuasion, says "habit, from long duration, acquires the force of nature."[49]

In conjunction with the principle that habit acquires the force of nature, which Peter has constructed from well-manipulated fragments of authority, his reading of Aristotle's *Nicomachean Ethics* permits him to advance the most radical extension of his naturalistic approach. Conceding that, no matter how many times one throws a stone in the air, its nature remains heavy, he distinguishes between animate and inanimate beings and between "nature" as inclination and "nature" as necessary motion,[50] in order to secure his position: "Aristotle says in the seventh book of the *Ethics* that [these men] are 'outside the boundaries of vice [*malicie*].' "[51] Many in Peter's audience would have been familiar with the passage to which he is referring—Aquinas had proposed a reading of it quite different from Peter's.[52] Aristotle argues that the terms "incontinence" and "vice" cannot properly be applied to those who act because of their nature or a disease or a habit, just as no one would blame women for being passive in intercourse. Among his examples of such cases, which he compares to brutishness [*bestialitas*], Aristotle specifically includes men who engage in sexual acts with boys by nature or by habituation since childhood.[53]

## The Sounds of Silence

Circumscribed as it is by references to "abominable acts" and "perversions of the soul," Peter's causal account of natures acquired at birth or by habit by no means constitutes a vindication of sexual acts between men or of the men who engage in them. Neither the Aristotelian associations with animals and women nor the use of the word "sodomite" is overcome by the force of the physical and psychological explanations or by the weight of unimpeachable authorities and bland digressions. Furthermore, his erratic tone and language, combining condemnatory phrases with the neutral scholastic diction, gives the commentary on this Problem a persistent instability. Longing for allies in the past, we might be tempted to see Peter's discussion as a defense of proscribed sex acts and the men who practice them, but the text does not sustain such a reading.

At the same time, in spite of these ambiguities, Peter's treatment takes the naturalization and normalization of at least one dimension of homosexual desire farther than any other medical or philosophical text from the Latin West that has come to light. Indeed, because of these same ambiguities, Peter is able to incorporate not just anatomy and physiology but also psychology and ethics within the discourse of science and medicine—in particular, by the accretion of meanings of "nature."

A master of scholastic natural philosophy, Peter has derived standing and legitimacy from the Aristotelian text and, at the same time, has departed skillfully from it. Nowhere are the assertion of a naturalistic framework, the artful deployment of reliable authority, and the advantages of evasive language more evident than in the last sentences of Peter's commentary on Problem 26. He reintroduces Avicenna's term *halubuathi*, apparently to refer to the condition of those whose nature exists only as a result of habit, but he then recalls Aristotle's position that this "perversion" is not a vice, no matter whether acquired by birth or by habit. Having thus both restated and dismantled his own distinction between the two classes of men, Peter closes with references to Ptolemy's astrological writings, emphasizing in the end that these natural irregularities are the results of the natural and regular motions of the heavens.[54] Peter here manifests his tendency toward astral determinism, a position assiduously avoided by his more cautious contemporaries precisely because it might appear to remove free will and thus moral responsibility.[55] In doing so, he sounds a firm note to resolve the shifting tonality with which he treats anal sexual stimulation and the men inclined to it: this condition is a natural occurrence. It is likewise toward the end of this Problem that he articulates bluntly what behavior is at issue and, in doing so, indicates to the reader that, although this commentary may be an academic exercise tied to an ancient text, it is also a subject relevant to Peter's contemporaries:

> Some exercise the wicked act of sodomy by rubbing the penis with the hand; others by rubbing between the thighs of boys, which is what most do these days; and others by making friction around the anus and putting the penis in it in the same way as it is placed in a woman's sexual part, and it seems Aristotle is speaking rather about these.[56]

The analysis of a single Latin work cannot provide general conclusions about the silences of medieval science. Further research, such as systematic investigations of commentaries on the *Problemata* and other classical texts, may yield more clues.[57] Nevertheless, the richness of Peter of Abano's discussion and his prominent, if controversial, position as a natural philosopher and medical theorist make his opinions important, if not necessarily representative. More than thirty manuscripts of his *Problemata* commentary have come down to us in at least three versions, one of which indicates that it was used for teaching at the University of Paris after Peter's departure.[58]

The work in question sheds light, albeit partial and indirect, on the ideological dimensions of the medieval silence. Peter's language leaves no doubt that the subject was highly charged, for, in spite of the cool tone of the ancient text and his own inclination to clinical bluntness, the vocabulary of moral turpitude intrudes. Whether this linguistic confusion is a calculated cover on Peter's part or a sign of his own uncertainty, it suggests the pitfalls that medical authors, natural philosophers, and other medieval writers faced if they wished to enter into a nonpolemical discussion of men engaged in sex with men. Peter's predicament is analogous to but independent of Aquinas's trouble with behavior that might be either a secondary fault or the most essential betrayal of nature and thus of its Creator.[59]

Unlike Avicenna and such commentators as Jacques Despars, Peter does not exclude what all agree is a sexual irregularity from the domain of natural knowledge. The difficulties he faces, however, in establishing his right to speak as a naturalist underscore the weight in favor of silence. Never particularly respectful of disciplinary divisions, Peter pits Aristotle against Avicenna and excises what was clearly, for his contemporaries, a moral issue from the jurisdiction of ethics (by venturing into an interpretation of the *Ethics*). Then, ever seeking to extend the boundaries of natural philosophy, he uses all his tools, from anatomy to astrology, to fortify his explanation and takes the risks entailed in ignoring the claims of the individual will. Not many at the opening of the fourteenth century would have had the desire or the intellectual equipment to engage in this conversation. There were many reasons not to speak, and Peter's run-ins with the Inquisition, apparently in connection with his tendency to overstate the powers of nature, hint at the presence of political dangers, in addition to the disciplinary divisions and standards of decorum.

The reticence of medieval authors may be partly to blame for the inadequacy of language with which Peter seems to struggle, but his difficulties also raise the question of whether there was any medieval referent for which language was required. Certainly Peter's discussion suggests no serious analogue to the modern term "homosexuality"—an abstract construct to describe a state of being or identity that transcends particular acts and desires. Both Peter's intellectual style and the nature of the text on which he was commenting emphasized material and efficient causes at the expense of formal and final causes, so abstract essences found little place in this work.

Nor does Peter elaborate any broader physiological or psychological implications of the differences he establishes. He quotes Avicenna's phrase "their sickness,"[60] but, except for associating the habit of anal stimulation with sexual voracity, he does not suggest any other symptoms of the disease. He applies Aristotle's terms "bestiality"[61] and "monstrosity"[62] once each, but he does not extend the labels to other traits or acts of the men in question. Finally, having passed lightly over the active/passive distinction and having glossed "eunuchs and effeminates" to refer only to castrated men, he declines the opportunity afforded by humoral theory and other standard medical principals to elaborate the attribution of feminine qualities to men of this condition.

Peter's commentary thus offers no cultural or even broad physical concept of homosexuality within medieval natural philosophy or medicine, and, to this extent, it tends to confirm the view that homosexuality is a more modern construct and thus to explain the general silence of science and medicine. On the other hand, Peter clearly presents much more than particular sexual acts and desires. With respect to the construction of an identifiable category of men, he is not so much silent as inarticulate. He distinguishes two types—not the traditional active and passive, but rather the anatomical and psychological—but then he dismantles or at least blurs the distinction by reducing habit to nature. The status of "monstrous nature" hovers between individuality and generality; the application of the terms "sodomites" and "*halubuathi*" are partial and tentative. In spite of these uncertainties, the persistence of locutions like "such men" would suggest the subsistence of a general conception. By the very project of explanation in which he is engaged Peter constructs a category of men. Although this bipartite category is by no means congruent with the twentieth-century "homosexual," the medieval and the modern overlap with respect to significant areas of homoeroticism—however different the cultural readings of these acts and desires might be.

The construction of natural explanations may thus have permitted the creation, within the texts of science and medicine, of a more clearly delineated category related to the modern construct "homosexual" than could be created within other types of text. These disciplines, however, no matter how favorably endowed with ancient precedents, such as Part 4, Problem 26, of the *Problemata*, and no matter how well equipped to devise explanations based on natural processes, were part of a larger culture within which other social and ideological forces were at work, many of which are illustrated in the present volume. The silence of other physicians and natural philosophers, as well as Peter's own vacillations and evasions, is thus likely to have more than one cause. The political urgency of understanding our sexual past, the incompleteness of our research, the cultural tensions associated with men's relations with men in the Middle Ages, the diversity of medieval discourses, and the disjunction of medieval and modern categories all contribute to the medieval silences and modern controversies we confront.

# Notes

I am grateful to Monica Green and Pamela Scully for suggestions that have measurably strengthened this essay and to Kenyon College for research support.

1. The fullest account of both the silences and the texts is Danielle Jacquart and Claude Thomasset, *Sexuality and Medicine in the Middle Ages*, trans. Matthew Adamson (Princeton, N.J.: Princeton University Press, 1988), esp. 155–72.

2. Petrus de Abano, *Aristotelis stagirite philosophorum summi Problemata atque divi Petri Apponi Pativini eorundem expositiones* (Mantua: Paulus Johannis de Puzpach, 1475), referred to hereafter as Petrus, *Problemata*. Since this edition lacks foliation, I follow the signatures in the Pierpont Morgan Library copy (PML 33108; ChL 1265). Thus the text occurs on fol. h4ra-rb; the commentary on fols. h4rb-6ra. I have supplemented the text of this edition with readings from the Venice, 1482, and Venice, 1501, editions, referred to by date below. On Peter, see Eugenia Paschetto, *Pietro d'Abano medico e filosofo* (Florence: Nuovedizione Enrico Vallecchi, 1984); Sante Ferrari, "Per la biografia e per gli scritti di Pietro d'Abano," *Atti della Reale Accademia dei Lincei*, yr. 312, *Memorie della classe di scienze morali, storiche e filologiche*, ser. 5, 15 (1915):629–725; Lynn Thorndike, *History of Magic and Experimental Science during the First Thirteen Centuries of Our Era* (New York: Macmillan, 1923), 2:874–947; and Leo Norpoth, "Zur Bio-Bibliographie und Wissenschaftslehre des Pietro d'Abano, Mediziners, Philosophen und Astronomen in Padua," *Kyklos: Jahrbuch für Geschichte und Philosophie der Medizin* 3 (1930): 292–353. On the *Problemata* commentary, see Nancy G. Siraisi, "The 'Expositio Problematum Aristotelis' of Peter of Abano," *Isis* 61 (1970):321–39. I am grateful to Nancy Siraisi for having called this work to my attention.

3. See Joan Cadden, "Medieval Scientific and Medical Views of Sexuality: Questions of Propriety," *Medievalia et Humanistica* n.s. 14 (1986): 157–71.

4. Jacques Despars, *Expositiones in librum tertium Canonis Avicenne*, fen 20, tr. 1, ch. 6, cited in Jacquart and Thomasset, *Sexuality and Medicine*, 159.

5. Danielle Jacquart, "La réception du *Canon* d'Avicenne: Comparaison entre Montpellier et Paris aux XIIIe et XIVe siècles," in *Actes du 110e Congrès National des Sociétés Savantes (Montpellier, 1985)*, Section d'histoire des sciences et des techniques, vol. 2, *Histoire de l'école médicale de Montpellier* (Paris: Comité des Travaux Historiques et Scientifiques, 1985), 69–77.

6. Jacquart and Thomasset, *Sexuality and Medicine*, 157, identify the Arabic as *al-liwat*, which would seem to be transliterated in Peter's work by *halubuathi* (e.g., MS Cambridge, Peterhouse 79, fol. [32]ra), which was no doubt the origin (by confusion of minims) of *halubnathi*, etc. (e.g., MS Paris, Bibliothèque Nationale, lat. 6540, fol. 64vb). Such a reading may in turn explain the form *aluminati* in a printed version of Avicenna, *Liber canonis* (Venice: Paganinis, 1507; reprint Hildesheim: Georg Olms, 1964). The first edition of Peter of Abano's commentary uses *alguagi*, for which I am unable to offer an explanation. I have used *halubuathi*, the version apparently closest to the original. Translators from Arabic often resorted to transliterations when the Arabic meaning was unclear or no suitable Latin equivalent existed. In this case, some options were available, for example, the term *cinaedus*—imprecise and itself a transliteration from Greek but instantiated in classical Latin texts that circulated in the Middle Ages. Bartholomew of Messina used it in a Latin translation of a Greek philosophical text: Aristotle, *Physionomonica* [inc. Quoniam et animae sequuntur corpora...], Richard Foerster, ed., *Scriptores physionomonici graeci et latini*, 2 vols., Bibliotheca Scriptorum Graecorum et Romanorum Teubneriana (Leipzig: B. G. Teubner, 1893), 1:35, §21. Cf. Mark D. Jordan, *The Invention of Sodomy in Christian Theology* (Chicago: University of Chicago Press, 1997), 119.

7. Avicenna, *Liber canonis*, bk. 3, fen 20, tr. i, ch. 42, fol. 358ra: "Et stulti homines sunt qui volunt eos curare. Nam initium egritudinis eorum meditativum est non naturale."

8. See Mark D. Jordan, "Homosexuality, *Luxuria*, and Textual Abuse," chapter 2 in this volume, and *Invention of Sodomy*, 150.

9. Cf. Jacquart and Thomasset, *Sexuality and Medicine*, 160. For an example of the historical specificity of medical readings of female homoeroticism, see Katharine Park, "The Rediscovery of the Clitoris: French Medicine and the *Tribade*, 1570–1620," in *The Body in Parts: Fantasies of Corporality in Early Modern Europe*, ed. David Hillman and Carla Mazzio (New York: Routledge, 1997).

10. See Jordan, "Homosexuality, *Luxuria*, and Textual Abuse."

11. On the particulars and influence of Peter's sources, methods, and approach to scientific explanation, see Paschetto, *Pietro d'Abano*; Nancy G. Siraisi, "Pietro d'Abano and Taddeo Alderotti: Two Models of Medical Culture," *Medioevo* 11 (1985):139–62; John Herman Randall Jr., *The School of Padua and the Emergence of Modern Science*, Università di Padova and Columbia University, Saggi e Testi, 1 (Padua: Antenore, 1961); and Marie-Thérèse d'Alverny, "Pietro d'Abano et les 'naturalistes' à l'époque de Dante," in *Dante e la cultura veneta: Atti del convegno di studi organizzato dalla Fondazione "Giorgio Cini"... Venezia, Padova, Verona 30 marzo-5 aprile 1966*, ed. Vittorio Branca and Giorgio Padoan (Florence: Oleschki, 1966), 207–19.

12. Paschetto, *Pietro d'Abano*, ch. 9; Graziella Federici Vescovini, "Pietro d'Abano e le fonti astronomiche greco-arabo-latine (a proposito del *Lucidator dubitabilium astronomiae o astrologiae*," *Medioevo* 11 (1985): 65–96; Thorndike, *History of Magic and Experimental Science*, 2:890–901, and "The Latin Translations of the Astrological Texts of Abraham Avenezra," *Isis* 35 (1944): 293–302.

13. Late medieval and modern authors give various accounts of the substance of the accusations; see Paolo Marangon, "Per una revisione dell' interpretazione di Pietro d'Abano," in *Il peniero ereticale nella Marca Trevigiana e a Venezia* (Padua: Aldo Francisci, 1984), 66–104; Bruno Nardi, "Intorno alle dottrine di Pietro d'Abano," *Nuova Revista Storica* 4 (1920): 81–97, 464–81; ibid. 5 (1921): 300–313, reprinted in *Saggi sull'aristotelismo padovano dal secolo XIV al XVI*, Studi sulla Tradizione Aristotelica nel Veneto, 1 (Florence: G. C. Sansoni for Università degli Studi di Padova, Centro Aristotelico, 1958), 19–74; Thorndike, *History of Magic and Experimental Science*, 2:938–47, appendix 2, and "Relations of the Inquisition of Peter of Abano and Cecco d'Ascoli," *Speculum* 1 (1926): 338–43.

14. Aristotle, *Problems*, bk. 4, problems 30 and 18, Loeb Classical Library (Cambridge, Mass.: Harvard University Press, 1957–61), 1:132, 122.

15. Peter's Latin version of the *Problemata* commentary attributed to Alexander of Aphrodesias survives in at least two manuscripts: Vatican, reg. suev. 747, fols. 62r-104r, and Madrid, Escorial, La Real Biblioteca, f-I-11, fols. 31–42. Vatican lat. 2174, which I have not seen, contains a text that may be the Alexander commentary or simply Bartholomew of Messina's Latin translation of the Aristotelian text. See also *Alexandri Aphrodesei Problemata*, trans. Georgius Valla in *Problemata Aristotelis*... (Venice: Bonetus Locatellus, 1501), fols. 273ra-288ra.

16. Petrus, *Problemata*, fol. h4rb-va.

17. Petrus, *Problemata*, fol. h4rb: "Quare est quod gaudent sive delectantur illi cum quibus actus coytus pagitur ut mulieres aut proportionati eis."

18. Cf. Albertus Magnus, *Quaestiones super De animalibus*, ed. Ephrem Filthaut, in *Opera omnia*, ed. Bernhard Geyer, vol. 12 (Münster: Aschendorff, 1955), bk. 5, q. 3, pp. 153–55.

19. See Jordan, "Homosexuality, *Luxuria*, and Textual Abuse"; Joan Cadden, *Meanings of Sex Difference in the Middle Ages: Medicine, Science, and Culture* (Cambridge: Cambridge University Press, 1993), 145–50, 271–77. Cf. Elliott, "Pollution, Illusion, and Masculine Disarray."

20. Aristotle, *Problems* 4.26.879b5–9; Avicenna, *Canon*, bk. 3, tr. 2, fen 20, ch. 42, fol. 358ra.

21. Aristotle, *Problems* 4.26.879b26–30; Petrus, *Problemata*, fol. h5rb.

22. Elliott, "Pollution, Illusion, and Masculine Disarray," chapter 1 in this volume.

23. Petrus, *Problemata*, fol. h4va-b.

24. See, for example, Nikolaus M. Häring, "Alan of Lille, *De planctu naturae*," *Studi Medievali*, 3d ser., 19 (1978), ch. 1, meter 1, and John W. Baldwin, *The Language of Sex: Five Voices from Northern France around 1200*, Chicago Series on Sexuality, History, and Society (Chicago: University of Chicago Press, 1994), 46–47.

25. Petrus, *Problemata*, fol. h4va "...pori sive meatus non sunt naturaliter plasmati...."

26. Petrus, *Problemata*, fol. h5rb: "...in eos nulla humiditas evacuatur aut modica valde expellitur ex eis in locum quem expellitur in illis qui naturaliter et secundum naturam habent hos poros." See also fol. h4vb: "...hec humiditas non agreditur naturaliter...."

27. Petrus, *Problemata*, fol. h4vb: "...ita quod recte advenit contrarium eius quod oportet esse in choytu naturali...."

28. For example, James A. Brundage, *Law, Sex, and Christian Society in the Middle Ages* (Chicago: University of Chicago Press, 1987), 212–13, 398–99, 533–34; Jordan, "Homosexuality, *Luxuria*, and Textual Abuse."

29. Petrus, *Problemata*, fol. [74]va: "Avicenna non adducit rationem qui etiam contrarium videtur sententie Philosophi, neque video quid impediat a nativitate talem inordinationem et monstruositatem fieri, cum idem statim Avicenna faciat sermonem de hermaphroditis qui magis apparent apud naturam monstruosi." Avicenna's chapter on hermaphrodites follows immediately his chapter on *alguagi* or (*alumnati*): Avicenna, *Canon*, bk. 3, tr. 2, fen 20, chs. 42 and 43.

30. Petrus, *Problemata*, fols. h4vb and h5rb . The reading "menstruosa" occurs in the 1475 and 1484, but not in the 1501 edition. "Monstruosi" and "monstruositas" are reproduced consistently in the passage about Avicenna's error, fol. h5va.

31. Cf. Aristotle, *Generation of Animals* 4.4.770b11–17.

32. See Cadden, *Meanings of Sex Difference*, 198–202. Lorraine Daston and Katharine Park discuss the position of the hermaphrodite within the framework of the natural and show how what is a fairly untroubled category in the Middle Ages becomes a locus of anxiety: "The Hermaphrodite and the Orders of Nature: Sexual Ambiguity in Early Modern France," *GLQ* 1 (1995): 419–38.

33. Petrus, *Problemata*, fol. h5ra and va.

34. Petrus, *Problemata*, fol. h5ra.

35. Petrus, *Problemata*, fols. h4vb-5ra.

36. Petrus, *Problemata*, fol. h5rb: "sic sunt dispositi." Cf. ibid., "de huiusmodi dispositione."

37. As far as I can tell, no one had ever suggested a surgical approach. Peter may be thinking of Avicenna's comment that hermaphrodites may often be successfully treated surgically: *Canon*, bk. 3, fen 20, tr. i, ch. 43, fol. 358ra. Cf. Albertus Magnus, *De animalibus libri XXVI*, ed. Hermann Stadler, Beiträge zur Geschichte der Philosophie und Theologie des Mittelalters, 15 and 16 (Münster: Aschendorff, 1916 and 1920), bk. 18, tr. 2, ch. 3, §§ 68–69; vol. 2, pp. 1225–26, on surgery for congenital sexual "monstrosities."

38. Petrus, *Problemata*, fol. [74]rb-va.

39. Avicenna, *Canon*, bk. 3, fen 20, tr. i, ch. 42, fol. 358ra: "Nam initium egritudinis eorum meditativum est non naturale." The 1475 edition of Peter's *Problemata*, fol. [74]rb reads "...vitium egritudinis eorum medicamentum est non naturale...." as does that of 1482 (fol. 81ra); the 1501 edition reads "vitium" and "meditativum." The 1475 (mis)reading dates back to the fourteenth century. See MSS Cambridge, Peterhouse 79, fol. [31]vb, and Paris Bibliothèque Nationale lat. 6540, fol. 64va.

40. Petrus, *Problemata*, fol. h6ra.

41. Petrus, *Problemata*, fol. h5va: "Agit de illis quibus predicta propter pravam consuetudinem obscenam advenit, quales sunt sodomite....de illis qui scelerato vicio sodomitico sunt dampnati." See also fol. h5vb: "actum profanum"; "illud nephandum opus sodomiticum."

42. Petrus, *Problemata*, fol. h5vb: "hec...nefanda."

43. Petrus, *Problemata*, fol. h5vb.

44. Petrus, *Problemata*, fol. [75]ra: "...illi qui ante pubertatem supponuntur, dicens quod si huiusmodi turpis luxuria accidat tempore quo mollis et tenera est natura ipsorum qui supponuntur ut quando non possunt sperma emittere omnia predictorum istis cito adveniunt...."

45. Petrus, *Problemata*, fol. h6ra; Avicenna, *Canon*, bk. 3, fen 20, tr. 1, ch. 42, fol. 358ra.

46. Petrus, *Problemata*, fol. h5vb; Avicenna, *Canon*, bk. 3, fen 20, tr. 1, ch. 11, fol. 353ra.

47. Petrus, *Problemata*, fol. h5vb: "...nam frequens consuetudo et longa sit [1484: fit] sicut ipsa inesset natis a nativitate eorum natura," citing the end of *Posterior Analytics*, perhaps 2.19.100a4ff. Peter's sense is not evident in either *Analytica posteriora translatio anonyma* (p. 78) or *Analytica posteriora Gerardo Cremonensi interprete* (p. 96), ed. Lorenzo Minio-Paluello, 4/2 and 3 of *Aristoteles latinus*, Corpus Philosophorum Medii Aevi Academiarum Consociatarum Auspiciis et Consilio Editum, Union Académique Internationale (Bruges and Paris: Desclée de Brouwer, 1953, 1954), although it is closer to the former. Cf. "...habituata consuetudine fit transitus in naturam," citing *De memoria et reminiscentia*, pt. 1, ch. 28 (= pt. 2, 452a27–8) and "...acquiritur consuetudo que tandem multotiens convertitur in naturam," citing *Nicomachean Ethics* 2.[1], but which more closely approximates 7.10.1152a32 — see, for example, *Ethica nicomachea translatio Roberti Grosseteste Lincolniensis sive "Liber Ethicorum": A. Recensio pura*, ed. René Antoine Gauthier, *Aristoteles latinus* 26/1–3, fasc. 3, Corpus Philosophorum Medii Aevi Academiarum Consociatarum Auspiciis et Consilio Editum, Union Académique Internationale (Brussels: Desclée de Brouwer; Leiden: Brill, 1972), 7.14, p. 290.

48. Petrus, *Problemata*, fol. h5vb: "...Ypocras in libro *De aere et aqua* [14], inducendo quosdam quibus ex consuetudine matrum capita manibus post nativitatem elongando consuetudine mutatio facta est in naturam."

49. Petrus, *Problemata*, fol. h5vb: "...consuetudo propter vetustatem obtinet vim nature"; Cicero, *De inventione*, Loeb Classical Library, 1, 2, §3, p. 6.

50. Petrus, *Problemata*, fol. h5vb; cf. Aristotle, *Nichomachean Ethics* 2.1.1103a22–23.

51. Petrus, *Problemata*, fol. h5vb: "...quos Aristoteles 7 *Ethicorum* ait fore extra terminos malicie in quos extirpationem lex inclamat." Cf. Aristotle, *Nicomachean Ethics* 7.5.1148b35, and Gauthier, ed., *Ethica Nicomachea translatio Roberti Grosseteste*, 7, 7, fasc. 3, p. 281: "extra terminos est malicie."

52. See Jordan, "Homosexuality, *Luxuria*, and Textual Abuse."

53. Aristotle, *Nicomachean Ethics* 7.5.1148b24–35. The Greek is cryptic, and the Latin, even more so. Gauthier, ed. *Ethica Nicomachea translatio Roberti Grosseteste*, 7, 7, fasc. 3, p. 281: "Cum hiis autem venereorum masculis. Hiis quidem enim natura, hiis autem ex consuetudine accidunt, puta assuefactis ex pueris." Cf. Nicole Oresme, *Le Livre de Ethiques d'Aristote: Published from the Text of MS 2902, Bibliothèque Royale de Belgique*, ed. Albert Douglas Menut (New York: Stechert, 1940), bk. 7, ch. 9, p. 381: "et les autres en abus de delit charnel avecques enfans masles."

54. Petrus, *Problemata*, fol. h6ra. Peter refers to *Centiloquium*, 80 and *Quadripartitum*, 4, [5?]. Cf. Helen Rodnite Lemay, "Human Sexuality in Twelfth- through Fifteenth-Century Scientific Writings," in *Sexual Practices and the Medieval Church*, ed. Vern L. Bullough and James Brundage (Buffalo, N.Y.: Prometheus Books, 1982), 187–205.

55. Dante's disclaimer at *Purgatorio* 16:65–78 is typical of those committed to astrological principles and wishing to avoid the appearance of unorthodoxy.

56. Petrus, *Problemata*, fol. h5vb-6ra: "Notandum est quod illud nephandum opus sodomiticum quidam exercent manu fricando virgam. Alii puerorum inter cosas confricatione, quod et plurimi agunt hodie. Alii autem fricationem faciendo circa anum et virgam in ipsum imponendo sicut in vulvam imponitur et de talibus videntur esse sermo Aristotelis magis."

57. Jacquart and Thomasset's contribution to this investigation is based in part on a survey of some commentaries on Avicenna: *Sexuality and Medicine in the Middle Ages*, 155–72. I have undertaken a survey of *Problemata* commentaries.

58. For manuscripts, see Lynn Thorndike, "Manuscripts of the Writings of Peter of Abano," *Bulletin of the History of Medicine* 15 (1944): 201–19; "Peter of Abano and Another Commentary on the Problems of Aristotle," *Bulletin of the History of Medicine* 29 (1955): 517–23; Lynn Thorndike and Pearl Kibre, *Incipits of Mediaeval Scientific Writings in Latin*, rev. ed. (Cambridge: Mediaeval Academy of America, 1963); Charles Lohr, "Medieval Latin Aristotle Commentaries," *Traditio* 23 (1967): 313–413; 24 (1968): 149–245; 26 (1970): 135–216; 27 (1971): 251–351; 28 (1972): 281–396; 29 (1973): 91–197; 30 (1974): 119–44. One version contains alterations in the preface and minor changes in the text by Jean de Jandun, a controversial member of the arts faculty at Paris. See Zdzislav Kuksewicz, "Les *Problemata* de Pietro d'Abano et leur 'rédaction' par Jean de Jandun," *Medioevo* 11 (1985): 113–37.

59. Jordan, "Homosexuality, *Luxuria*, and Textual Abuse" and *Invention of Sodomy*, 147.

60. Petrus, *Problemata*, fol. h5rb: "vitium egritudinis eorum." See note 40.

61. Petrus, *Problemata*, fol. h6ra: "Causa vero istius actus nefandi dicit Aristoteles in 7 *Ethicorum* esse bestialitatem omninam [1482: omnimodam] et perversione anime..."

62. Petrus, *Problemata*, fol. h5rb: "...causam et modum huiusmodi menstruositatis [1501: monstruositate] et aliarum considerare voluerit 4 *De generatione animalium* diligenter inspiciat." Aristotle, *Generation of Animals* 4.4, treats "monstrosities" in general, including hermaphrodites, at 772b26–773a2.

✣

## CHAPTER 4

# Manuscript Illumination and the Art of Copulation

*Michael Camille*

Michel Foucault, in an early essay on Georges Bataille, described medieval sexuality in terms that might strike us as odd today, coming from someone who later made such strong claims for its "social construction": "never did sexuality enjoy a more immediately natural understanding and never did it enjoy a greater 'felicity of expression' than in the Christian world of fallen bodies and of sin."[1] My own essay starts from this rather atypical statement for two reasons. First, I also want to recognize in medieval culture, certainly compared with later periods, an openness to the visual representation of certain sexual acts—the "felicity of expression" that Foucault emphasized. However, this visibility is often combined with its very opposite, concealment, in a dynamic of partial disclosure that is crucial to medieval representation more generally. Second, I want to explore the category of the "natural" as it is presented in words and pictures. Sex and nature are closely linked today, in the age of sex therapy, couples counseling, eroticized mass media, and self-help publications like *The Joy of Sex*, first published in 1973, and more recently *More Joy of Sex, The Joy of Gay Sex, The Joy of Lesbian Sex,* and now *The New Joy of Sex: A Gourmet Guide to Lovemaking in the Nineties.* Foucault saw these contemporary signs of openness and praxis (how-to-do-it manuals, alongside *The Joy of Cooking* and *Auto Mechanic*) as actually masking fears and anxieties about our identities, which we increasingly construct in terms of what we do in bed. Outline drawings, rather than photographs, of lovers in various positions illustrate these publications, more recent editions containing firmer, pumped-up nineties bodies rather than seventies skinny ones.[2] As an art historian I am most interested in these pictorial historical transformations and how visual representations of the body serve to naturalize codes of corporeality and gender that cannot be expressed in words alone. Sexuality haunts the postmodern imaginary most thoroughly in the field of visual representation, through art, advertising, and film.[3] Yet how can any picture tell us what to do with our bodily members, and even more, how can a textbook and its illustrations provide us with our categories of desire?

These same questions also arise in the context of the very text on which I want to focus, a bodily "regime" that presents itself as "natural."

This thirteenth-century health treatise, the *Régime du corps*, contains an image of the sexual act that, we shall see, is just as laden with anxiety about performance as its modern counterparts, and one produced within a no less ruthlessly gendered sexual economy. However, its primary concern is not with the joy of sex, but with its outcome. The rest of this essay will then explore the multivalent iconography of the copulating male and female in thirteenth- and fourteenth-century manuscript illuminations produced both within and outside the orbit of the church's teachings. It treats gendered sexuality and what we would call heterosexual acts. Although it might be questionable to even use a modern concept like heterosexuality in discussing the Middle Ages, the images I shall be discussing present a clearly ideological positioning of male and female bodies in the act of intercourse. It is now well known that the Latin and vernacular medicotheological discourse of the Middle Ages fostered an imbalanced view of gender roles and relegated womens' bodies to a secondary and subservient position, literally underneath that of the male in the proper coital position. What is not so well understood is how images also worked to exactly the same ends. Presenting women's bodies as inherently inferior, as impermanent matter rather than eternal form, pictures also constructed women's bodies as "peinture" rather than "parole," image rather than text.

## Coitus and Creation in the *Régime du corps*

Aldobrandino of Siena's *Régime du corps* was the first hygenic and dietary treatise to be written in a vernacular language during the Middle Ages and is similar to the modern self-help sex guide to the extent that it uses the combination of text and image to inform lay readers of "truths" contained in a more prestigious "scientific" discourse to which they are denied access. Based on Avicenna's *Canon* and other Arabic medical texts that had recently been made available to the West in Latin translations, the *Régime* also incorporates material from Galen and Aristotle, especially in gynecological matters.[4] It promises to describe the art of "physike," which meant maintaining and monitoring the equilibrium of the body to carry man to his "mort naturel" at the age of seventy years. Circulating among an audience whose average life expectancy was not much more than thirty, it is not suprising that this work became so popular with noble lay readers in the next two centuries. At least sixty-eight manuscripts are listed as extant, many of them illustrated with miniatures or historiated initials heading each chapter. The title of the work, *Régime du corps*, or *Gouvernement de corps*, as it is sometimes called, evokes an interpenetration of the somatic and the social that is fundamental to understanding how this treatise sought to control and situate bodies, in the kind of process that Judith Butler describes as "identificatory practices governed by regulatory schemas."[5]

According to a dedicatory prologue found in a number of manuscripts, the work was written in 1256 by one "Aldobrandinus," physician to the Provençal court, at the request of Beatrice de Savoie, countess of Provence, who is described as "mother to the queens of France, England, Germany, and the countess of Anjou," specifically to "carry with her" when visiting her four well-married daughters.[6] It is divided into four books; the first, "parole de tout le cors," speaking of the whole body and things proper and improper to it, while the second describes its individual members following the standard medical model, which reads the body from top to bottom. The third book treats what medieval doctors called "the nonnaturals" and what we think of as diet. Finally the short last section is a treatise on physiognomy, which explains how the character and complexion of a person can be seen in their outward appearance. This ability to "read" bodies through their external signs and visible colors was crucial, not only to the practice of medieval physicians but for artists as well. Indeed, the illustration of medical discourse, both in the Latin and the vernacular treatises of this period, is a major site where the human body was positioned, constructed, and anatomized, long before its internal cavities were opened up in actual dissection.[7]

British Library MS Sloane 2435, which, like most of the earliest extant manuscripts, is in the Walloon dialect, was produced in northern France, perhaps Lille, circa 1285. It is one of the most lavishly illluminated and decorated of all copies of the work, suggesting that a wealthy patron was involved.[8] Although it contains no evidence of specific ownership, the opening rubric in gold is unique in describing the original patron of the work, not as the countess of Provence, but as a man: "Here begins the book to guard the health of the whole body and each of its members made by master Aldobrandino of Siena for Benoit of Florence." This first page is also important in providing a cosmic sacred frame in which to present this mundane vernacular discourse (Figure 4.1). The text is significantly bound with another popular French work on cosmology, the *Image du monde*, providing its owner with a microcosmic view of earthly bodies and then a macrocosmic view of heavenly bodies. Following the opening rubric, a large, four-part miniature represents God creating each of the four elements mentioned at the beginning of the text: earth, water, air, and fire. It was the relations of these elements within the human microcosm that, according to medieval doctors, determined complexional balance and therefore health. Beneath the creation scenes, still in the first column, is the human world of language—the "D" of the first letter of God's name ("Dex ki par la grant poissance le monde establi premierement fist le ciel et apries fist les quatre elemens"). Within this letter the author sits as creator of the text, which he writes out on a lectern before him. The masculine myth of origins, so crucial to the *Régime* and its illustrations, is underlined by the first sentences, describing how "God made man ("l'ome") in his own image as the noblest

Figure 4.1. Frontispiece to Aldobrandino of Siena, *Régime du corps:* creation scenes and author writing. British Library, London, Sloane MS 2435, fol. 1. By permission of the British Library.

creature that he had made on earth" ("a sa semblance, pour le plus noble creature k'il peust faire en terre"). There is no "femme" mentioned here. Not only is the story of Genesis being combined in this text with the new Aristotelian discourse of the female's biological inferiority, but its original royal female patron has also been replaced by a socially inferior but biologically superior "Benoit de florenche." Since he is unlikely to be the recipient of this particular manuscript, produced in northern France, it might suggest that this particular copy is being redirected toward a different, perhaps nonnoble audience. Despite the fact that the prologue goes on to refer to all those who see and hear ("verront et orront") this book, suggesting auditory, group reception, this manuscript strikes one as geared toward a wealthy individual who put special emphasis upon the seen aspects of the work, in its lavish gold and colored initials. At first glance one might mistake this book, both in its format and its decoration, for a Latin Psalter or part of a Bible. The scheme for the first page has indeed been adapted from contemporary Bible illustrations of the days of creation, appropriating for the vernacular discourse of the body the material manifestation of God's Word.

A golden-lettered rubric announces the subject of the seventh chapter: "li VII capitres dabiter avoec feme," or "to co-habit with a woman" (Figure 4.2). Also of burnished gold is the background, which is as brilliant as that glittering behind any crucifixion or annunciation in a contemporary Bible but here provides the foil for a fundamental rather than a transcendental act. Within the initial a man and a woman are revealed in the midst of intercourse by parted green curtains. These are not the theatrical curtains of display. Rather, they emphasize that we see something that goes on in private behind the usually closed curtains of canopied beds, which in this period were a major household item of the wealthy.[9] The flowing shape of these curtains, curling at the edges to form a kind of lip, is also metonymic. It represents the opening that cannot be represented, the part of the female body being penetrated. That the curtain joins with the woman's hair on the right side of the initial and does not touch the male figure at all reinforces this association between cloth and corporeality. The rent curtain was often used in poetic and visual terms to suggest vaginal penetration and can be paralleled in other thirteenth-century images.[10] If the woman's anatomy becomes part of the frame, what is depicted within is much less visible. The act literally takes place "under the covers." The artist has skillfully evoked the powerful muscular spasms of limbs in the rhythmic pulse of thick black pen lines that crisscross the bed to reveal mostly the massive curved thighs of the woman. Yet the body in question here, the body whose health is being maintained according to the accompanying text, is male. His long left arm pins the woman in place beneath him, serving simultaneously both to conceal and to reveal her, to cover her breasts and at the same time provide another metonymic means of representing what cannot be rep-

Figure 4.2. Initial to Book 7 of Aldobrandino of Siena, *Régime du corps:* "How to cohabit with a woman." British Library, London, Sloane MS 2435, fol. 9v. By permission of the British Library.

resented. The diagonal thrust of his tubular limb mimics the direction and design of his unseen member beneath the bedclothes.

This "C" initial opens the text with a powerful prescriptive statement aimed directly at the male reader: "Cascuns ki a sens et discretion doit metre sen entention et tout son pooir de savoir comment on doit habiter a feme, pour chou que c'est une principaux cose dou cors sainnement maintenir et dou cors metre a nient ki tempreement ne le fait et use" (He who has sense and discernment should devote his understanding and all of his efforts to learning how one should cohabit with a woman, for it is a principle means of maintaining one's health, and whoever does not do this moderately has a body that is good for nothing).[11] Aldobrandino goes on to detail the proper disposition of the male body, especially focusing on the "bonne eure"—the best time for engendering children.

What is going on in this image, then, has nothing to do with pleasure. But neither is it purely an act of procreation. It is about maintaining one's health, if one is a man.

In the tradition of medical literature to which this work belongs, stretching back to Galen and through various earlier treatises on coitus by Constantinus Africanus, the male is the body that matters.[12] The author of the *Régime* repeats the Aristotelian and Galenic view that all parts of the male body furnish material for the sperm and how "that part of the body of a man that he uses with a woman is nourished by a superfluity of humors from all the members." The man's body is described as being like a cooking pot in which fluids bubble and coagulate, and, following four necessary digestions, his veins carry the seminal matter ("le matere") from his brain down into the testes. The man's tight white nightcap, tied under his chin in the initial, is an important detail in this respect. It indicates the major problem for the male partner in sex—"loss of heat," which endangered his vulnerable body. Because heat was thought to rise upward, it was considered good sense to wear some form of protection on the higher of the two heads. It also emphasizes the intellectual insemination into his partner of his "gray matter," flowing directly from his brain through to his penis via two crucial veins, which are described in the text as running down the sides of his head and which, if cut, would result in sterility.[13]

The illuminator omits anything that might allude to pleasure here, so intent is he to make this an image of an act of intellectual inscription. The male figure stares blankly into space as if set on his task. His face does not touch hers, and the two bodies are represented as distinctly separate, significantly different from depictions of other copulating couples we shall look at, where the notion of two bodies coming together as one is suggested. His staring eyes seem almost vacant. He does not look up in the ecstasy of orgasm that the pseudo-Aristotelian *Problemata* described as a little death. His gaze is more serious and suitable to this crucial moment of conception. The whole emphasis in the text and this image is solely upon his performance. Men who indulge in too much sexual intercourse, who are drunk, or who are too young or too old, the text warns, will not easily "enfans engenrer."[14] The dangers alluded to here of too frequent intercourse, which was thought to deplete the body, weaken the brain, and even lead to premature death, was taken directly from one of Aldobrandino's major sources, Avicenna's *Canon*. But, the text goes on, "he who has a strong complexion and who is not too fat nor too thin and who has large veins, such a man will most easily engender children." Much of the chapter concerns choosing the right moment, when the male has reached a certain point in the digestive process and has eaten certain foods and has enjoyed a prescribed amount of rest. The chapters leading up to this seventh one are all concerned with maintaining a proper humoral balance. The fifth is about work and rest, and the sixth concerns bathing, a natural prelude to the sexual act. The initial illustrating the sixth chapter shows a man and a woman naked in separate bathtubs, the woman beckoning across to the man, their gazes meeting.[15] Only in this bathing image is there any reference to the role of sexual desire. Once in bed, the couple get down to business.

Aristotle and Galen after him gave the female partner no active role in conception, arguing that the female is less perfect than the male, is colder and wetter and produces an imperfect seed that in itself cannot generate an animal. Conception can only occur with the kindling of the male's innate heat and with insemination by his perfect seed, his "form." The male planted his seed, or his idea, inside the female. Indeed for Galen and Avicenna the thoughts of the father at this crucial moment could literally affect the form of the child produced. A certain king, having envisioned a monstrous black creature while having sexual relations with his queen, later fathered a deformed, dark child. So the stiff long neck and strong arm of the male in the initial can be paralleled in images of writers attentively working with their pens, as in the author portrait of Aldobrandino himself (Figure 4.1). The historians of medieval medicine Danielle Jacquart and Claude Thomasset might have been describing the Sloane manuscript's coitus image when they summed up the way medievals viewed the role of the female in conception, as "the perfect antithesis of the male, who acts on this unconscious mechanism in a responsible and conscious way."[16]

If the initial represents the perfect progenitor at the optimum moment for procreation, what of the woman underneath him? Like her partner, she wears her hair tight in a net. This indicates her married status and legitimates the act portrayed as taking place within the marriage bed. She definitely looks up to her partner/husband, and the illuminator has curved the line of her lower lip upward to suggest a smile. Thirteenth-century artists often utilized such expressions of joy, not only in the statues of smiling angels at Reims Cathedral, but in depicting lovers in secular manuscript illumination.[17] Does this expression here imply that she is experiencing a pleasure that is nowhere ascribed to her in the text? The *Régime du corps*, unlike some contemporary medical tracts, contains no mention of the opinion, held by some medical theorists, that female orgasm was necessary for conception to occur.[18] It is hard to say whether the smile on the lady's face here is an allusion to that medical belief or part of the misogynistic tradition that attributed desire, and its dangerous insatiability, more frequently to the female, in her urge to heat her cold, wet body. Both figures have tiny touches of red on their cheeks, representing their healthy status, but also in this case indicating the blood that is flowing through various veins at this crucial juncture. Facial expressions are interesting to consider in relation to the physiognomic discussions that occur in Book 4 of the *Régime*. Here "one can know the nature of each man from his appearance." He whose color mixes red and white, who has a lot of hair and a well-formed face, and who "delights in seeing and talking with women" is luxurious.[19] Although this elaborate discussion of complexions goes unillustrated in the Sloane manuscript, these codes played a fundamental role in the construction and interpretation of images of bodies as well as of actual ones. The very colors used to paint people in books and on panels was not so much an aesthetic choice on the part of the painter as a socially constructed code for both artist and audience. A woman's flesh had to be whiter and its tonality bluer and colder than the color used to delineate the male. The illuminator of our initial has not, however, distinguished flesh color in this way. It is the only visible marker that brings these two bodies together as "one flesh" in the biblical sense.

One reference in this chapter to what we today would term "the female partner" describes the best time to beget children as when "la feme est delivre un jour devant sa privee maladie," that is, one day before the onset of her period.[20] This "secret sickness" is an interesting reference to the shame and secrecy associated with the menstrual process. Aldobrandino, like many medical practioners, seems unwilling to discuss the woman's body in any detail. In describing the fact that it was from this excess "matere" of menstruation that the female body provides the material for the fetus, the author relates how retention of this is dangerous to women. This can be seen, he says, in widows and "women of religion and girls past the age of marrying, who often die suddenly." On the authority of one "Hali" (Ali Abbas), he recounts, they have "many sicknesses of which we are not going to speak." This conscious occlusion, a refusal to treat the medical "secrets of women," is typical of this text's preference for discussing the male body in the procreative act and ignoring that of the female.[21] Although the *Régime* was purportedly prepared for a female patron, it is written throughout with the male body as the paradigm, and even when discussing childbirth and wet-nursing in subsequent chapters, it does so from the male point of view. In this, however, it is only following what was already the common practice in its Arabic-Latin sources. Likewise the image's most powerful thrust is that of the male, who is represented as providing the seminal "idea," while the female provides only the matter for the fetus. As opposed to Thomas Lacquer's recent and controversial thesis that a "same-sex model" existed in premodern Europe, both text and image in the *Régime* emphasize and reinscribe the radical difference between male and female bodies in their specifically sexual roles.[22] The act of intercourse was structured in the *Régime du corps* so as to have none of the psychological and identity dimensions evident in any modern sex therapy manual. This is because the sexual body and its organs were not linked to an identity that was sustained and expressed through sex, but were thought of as tools in a finely calibrated "male" performance. Sexuality was not a matter of identity or of subjectivity during the Middle Ages; it was an art, like fencing or painting, which one could learn to do more or less well.

The role of the male in generation and the argument that only the man has seed were crucial in a society where legitimacy passed only through the father's line. Thirteenth-century diagrams of permitted and prohibited sexual relations between family members, called *Arbor consanguinitatis*, occur not only in legal compendia but also in works made for the nobility, crucially concerned, as a group, with maintaining their bloodlines.[23] These complex trees show a male crowned figure straddling a phallic vertical line of descent, through which, from father to son, the male blood of nobility descends. For the early patrons of the *Régime*, Beatrice of Provence and her four daughters, each married to a major thirteenth-century ruler, the role of incubator of royal blood was theirs from birth, although conception was very much a danger to their health as much as to that of their husbands, to judge from the high mortality rate during parturition. The *Régime du corps* regulated their bodies as ovens or incubators of this special blood. For less exalted owners of the treatise, the agnatic line of descent was also a concern. It affected the circulation of manuscripts like the Sloane volume, passed from generation to generation.

Whoever used the Sloane manuscript as their family health guide, whether it was a wealthy layman or a woman or both, the initial to chapter seven provided one clear and simple message among its many allusive signs. It is one that people continue to take for granted today, over seven hundred years later, with the effect that, at first, we do not even register it as a conscious choice on the part of the illuminator. Nevertheless it is a sign that we need to examine as constructed by rather than natural to medieval culture. It is fixed and fostered through representation and should not be seen as a reflection of some "medieval reality." The man is on top of the woman. This, the most basic visual cue to the sexual nature of the depicted event, can only be understood in its fuller ramifications when we compare it with other representations of copulation in Gothic manuscripts.

## "Let Me Count the Ways"

Although little studied and hardly ever published, images showing the act of copulation, like that in the *Régime du corps*, are not that uncommon in illuminated manuscripts of this period, and they occur in many genres of thirteenth-century manuscript illumination.[24] The pictorial convention, with its origins in classical art, of the male body on top of the female body in the act of performing sexual intercourse was already well established by this date and is found in a number of different discourses, not only in medical treatises but in Psalter and Bible illustrations, romances in the vernacular, and Latin texts of Aristotle's *Parva naturalia.* Indeed, a major source for Aldobrandino had been the scientific Latin literature of Aristotle, which became part of the university curriculum in the course of the thirteenth century. Here, in the very texts that defined the imbalanced gender positions of the two sexes, we often find initials, miniatures, and marginal images of men on top in the act of coitus. In a Vatican manuscript of Aristotle's *De generatione* produced around the same time as the *Régime,* the same scene occurs, with similar emphasis on the writhing bedclothes, although the bodies of both partners have later been obliterated by a prudish reader, such as often happens with sexually explicit scenes in medieval manuscripts (Figure 4.3). In an Oxford manuscript of Aristotle's *De animalibus* there is a kind of before and after sequence both in the initial and in the lower margin, where the couple are joined together on the left and on the right the woman is nursing her baby beside a fire (Figure 4.4). The fire that warms the newborn baby on the right signals not only the heat required for generation (the *Régime* also describes how it is better to have sex when "li cors est caus ke quant il est frois"), but also the Aristotelian conviction that the male as the fiery principle of the form gives life, unlike the cold, wet female, who provides only matter through her menstrual fluid. The two erect rabbits on either side are an obvious allusion to sexual arousal and its consequences, projecting any hint of pleasure onto the bodies of animals, making them metonymic of the human body's polymorphous perversity, just as they serve as punning signs for body parts in the fabliaux and other forms of vernacular literature.

Not only poets but also some doctors deemed that pleasure was crucial to conception. Constantinus Africanus, the eleventh-century writer whose ideas are appropriated by the author of the *Régime,* emphasized this: "The Creator, wishing the race of animals to remain firmly established and not perish, disposed that it would be renewed by coitus and by generation.... Therefore he shaped for the animals the natural members, which are apt and proper for this work, and provided them with such wonderful virtue and lovable pleasure that there is no animal that does not excessively delight in coitus. Because if animals hated coitus, the race of animals would certainly perish." Citing this passage in his own treatise on generation, *De animalibus,* Albert the Great went even further in discussing the importance of the senses and especially sight in arousing men and women to intercourse and argued that "human sexual relations are accompanied by a more exquisite level of pleasure than is found in other animals."[25] But it was hard for artists to represent this. A fascinating vernacular treatise on courtly manners based upon Seneca and Aristotle, now in Brussels, includes a chapter on the delights of love that actually emphasizes the position of Constantinus, that "malle avec femele" come together in the work of generation, and that God has made sex such an exquisite pleasure so that "they will have no disdain from

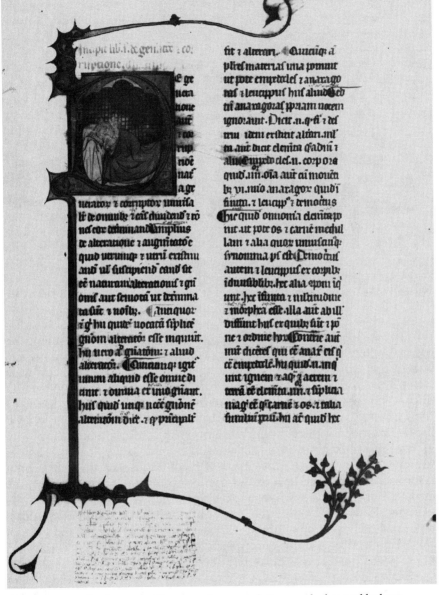

Figure 4.3. Initial to Aristotle, *De generatione:* copulating couple, later rubbed out. Biblioteca Apostolica Vaticana, Rome, Barb. lat. 165, fol. 234. By permission.

Figure 4.4. Detail of lower margin of Aristotle, *De animalibus:* copulating couple and woman with baby. Merton College, Oxford, MS 271, fol. 65v. By permission of the Warden and Fellows of Merton College.

the act."[26] The illuminator, however, had disdain for representing it. He painted a couple in the euphemistic, postcoital act of "sleeping together" within the same parted-curtain setting as in the *Régime* initial, a trick we still use today in television and film as a trope for having "done it" (Figure 4.5). A wariness about depicting the couple's bodies, let alone their pleasure, even though it is described explicitly in the text, is visible in a number of thirteenth- and fourteenth-century manuscripts.

The prescribed position of the man and woman in the *Régime* followed the one set down by the law itself. If medical discourse was all about finding the right time in terms of the humoral balance of the body, the discourse of church law was concerned with the right time in terms of the liturgical calendar. Copulation was not permitted on Sundays, Wednesdays, or Fridays, on any church feast day, or during Advent and Lent. It was also prohibited during pregnancy and after childbirth. Gratian further advised husbands to keep themselves chaste for up to eight days before accepting the Eucharist, for fear of contamination. In addition to these temporal restrictions, canon lawyers, writers of penitential handbooks, and theologians of the thirteenth century prescribed only one orientation of bodies as permissible, what has become known as the "missionary position."[27] The man had to be prone on top and the woman on her back facing him, the very position visualized in the initial of the *Régime.* It was also pictorially prescribed in thirteenth-century initials

Figure 4.5. *Li Ars d'amour:* the joining of "malle avec femele." Bibliothèque Royale, Brussels, MS 9543, fol. 53v. By permission.

and miniatures in Gratian's *Decretum,* especially in those laws dealing with marriage, adultery, and divorce. *Causa 33* deals with one of the few legitimate reasons for the dissolution of a marriage, impotence, and, in one late-thirteenth-century manuscript in Cambridge, shows the husband's futile attempts to perform his "conjugal debt" in this position (Figure 4.6). In reproducing this four-part picture in his study of medieval sexuality and law, James Brundage thought that the illuminator must have got the scenes out of order in placing the wife's complaint top left, followed by her unfortunate husband's attempt to the right, and then, in error, putting at the bottom left the priest performing the betrothal and

Figure 4.6. Gratian's *Decretum:* the dissolution of a marriage due to impotence. The Fitzwilliam Museum, Cambridge, MS 262, fol. 86v. By permission.

then to the right, the bishop annulling the marriage.[28] But in fact the two pairs of images serve to narrate the major points of the story more powerfully. The wife's explanation of her spouse's incapacity and its demonstration go together above, and the symbolic coming together of hands at the wedding below is contrasted with their separation. The joining of hands and their pulling apart in the last scene are metonymic of the more complete corporeal couplings that these ecclesiastical rites legitimated. Medieval narratives are often restructured for effect precisely to undermine our expectations of linear coherence, and this goes as much for sexual as for other stories. An even more explicit illustration to this *Causa*, in a manuscript in the Walters Art Gallery in Baltimore, does not depict the futile attempts to conceive. Instead the illuminator represented the wife's complaint of impotence being proved in public, when the husband's penis remains flaccid in front of the court, despite attempts to arouse it by a prostitute, specially called in for the job.[29] The medieval body was more in the public gaze. If that of the female was debased and specularized in its materiality, that of the male was rigorously vetted for any imperfection in its approximation to the divine archetype. My point here, returning to the *Régime* initial for a moment (Figure 4.2), would be that the male body is just as tyrannized in this scheme, despite its constructed primacy and authority. The anxiety in performance is registered here as much as anything.

In the Cambridge canon law image there is nothing in the second scene of coitus to tell the viewer that this was an unsatisfactory performance (Figure 4.6). The curly-haired youth on top of the woman also seems different from the old man at whom she points the disappointed finger in the first scene. Here, too, a smile is even more apparent on the woman's face, like the sweet smiling angels of late-thirteenth-century French Gothic art. But this couple are hardly angels, the nature of their act perhaps indicated by the fact that they do it, not in bed, but like animals, on the ground. They have their clothes hitched up in a more naturalistic way than usual, suggestive of hurried desire, the woman even retaining her shoes and gartered stockings. Perhaps the illuminator wanted to emphasize the church's teachings that passion has no place in procreation and often leads to sterility. For if this is her impotent husband, or if it is the woman's proverbial young lover, in both scenarios what is being represented here is sinful sex, sex not performed with procreation as its outcome. Gratian had been careful to state that sex had its place in marriage but only for the purposes of bearing children and not for pleasure. What he called "whorish embraces" were thought to be just as inappropriate for the marriage bed.

The scholastic philosophers, with their usual interest in classificatory schemes, debated the pros and cons of the various coital positions. Albert the Great listed four alternative or dangerous ones in addition to the traditional "natural" position; lateral, or side by side; seated; standing; and backward, or *a tergo*.[30] The first of these, side by side, is hard to isolate in miniatures since the spatial vocabulary of the thirteenth-century illuminator did not make much distinction between views from above or lateral views. Images of couples in bed where the faces of both are visible often occur in one particular genre, romance. In most romances characters are concerned with gratifying their desires and not with the possibility of conception. There are many miniatures showing sensuous representations of intercourse, especially in the extensive series of couples in bed that illustrate the Arthurian vulgate cycle.[31] These include the archadulterers Lancelot and Guinevere, whose intercourse follows the same basic pattern as that in the near-contemporary *Régime* initial, except that the two figures seem less regimented and more intertwined. Lancelot is often shown fondling the neck or breast of Guinevere, a gesture that the canonists would have abhorred but obviously one that had a different resonance for its courtly reader. However, even in romance the scene of intercourse was not only a site of pleasure. It often serves to mark the origins or conceptions of a new character, to carry its function of progeny-producing, which was as crucial as idealized love in these stories of family intrigues and generational secrets. A miniature from the *Merlin* in the same manuscript, for example, represents the conception of Mordret, who was engendered when neither Artus nor Lot's wife knew they were brother and sister.[32] This seemingly innocent image of pleasure was thus for readers of the period charged with the horrific scandal not only of adultery but also of incest (Figure 4.7). The action takes place within a little castle structure representing the room, with the door ajar at the left, indicating, as with the bed-curtains, a sense of secrecy to the action. But in contrast to the image in the medical treatise, the woman's breasts are visible and the heads of the two figures touch. Moreover, here it is the knight who smiles. Suggestive of foreplay and pleasure rather than the mechanics of conception, it is an image that was produced in the same northern French area as the Sloane manuscript of the *Régime*, but with quite different meanings and functions.

Albert the Great's second sexual position—seated—is alluded to in a number of initials to Aristotle's treatise on conception, *De generatione*, where the couple are often shown in the midst of an embrace on a bed. In one Parisian example the man is again shown as the active figure, his arms encircling the statuesque seated female figure in what might be taken as a "before" scene to the "after" of the *Régime* initial (Figure 4.8). The fact that figures are wearing clothes should not prevent us from interpreting such images in terms of genital sexuality. The third, the standing position, is seen in numerous images of the kiss in the thirteenth century, and, as I have shown elsewhere, often signified the act of penetration in the coming together of two mucuous membranes, even when both figures are fully clothed (Figure 4.9).[33]

It was the fourth position, described by Albert the Great as *a tergo* or backward, that was deemed most dangerous and that brought most condemnation. Still illegal for married couples in some states of America today, this was thought most sinful and unnatural since it made man into an animal. Yet the evidence of the penitentials on one hand and the fabliaux on the other suggests that anal sex was enjoyed by heterosexual couples.[34] Committing sodomy with one's wife, however, was deemed

Figure 4.7. *Vulgate Cycle:* the conception of Mordret from the prose *Merlin.* British Library, London, Add. MS 10292, fol. 113r. By permission.

as sinful as committing the act with a whore or a man. It was not so much the gender of the partner as what parts were put where that was labeled "against nature." The results of such unnatural sexual positions were thought to leave their mark on the infant, in diseases like leprosy, staining the child's body with the parents' sexual sin. Sodomy was considered even worse in planting seed where it will not grow. Only in the margins of manuscripts, in the extratextual realm of play where the deformed form is the norm, do we find anything close to these inverted positions.[35] Sexual relations between members of the same sex were never represented in thirteenth-century manuscript illumination, to the best of my knowledge, and certainly not using the couple in bed model. This would have been to normalize and place this most demonized form of sodomy within the procreative sanctions of the marriage bed. Although there are numerous instances of anal display in the margins of manuscripts, these can only hint at the fears and pleasures associated with anal penetration, using arrows and other instruments.[36]

Figure 4.8. Aristotle, *De generatione:* a couple embracing seated on a bed. Bibliothèque Nationale, Paris, MS lat. 12953, fol. 166. By permission.

Using the proper orifice but having the woman on top was also viewed with horror by theologians and by medical practioners, who thought that reversing the proper downward flow of semen could not only damage the fetus because the womb is "turned over," but may also cause harm to the man.[37] Reversing the natural order in this way, after all, caused God to bring the biblical flood (Romans 1:26–27), and its consequences were still thought dire for the bodies and souls of those seeking to gain pleasure from sexual experimentation. I have rarely seen this depicted in manuscripts, which suggests just how taboo this simple inversion of gender roles was. It is probably represented in an allusive way in depictions of the legend of Aristotle being ridden like a horse by Phyllis, frequently found in the margins of manuscripts.[38] One startlingly literal instance of the "woman on top" motif occurs unexpectedly in a late-thirteenth-century Psalter from Arras, the most widely used sacred text for laypeople during this period (Figure 4.10). David, author of the Psalms, is here shown in flagrante delicto, and not merely as guilty of the sin of looking upon Bathsheba from afar as she bathed, a voyeurism pictured in most other Psalters that focus upon his transgression. Moreover, wearing his crown even to bed, King David is shown in the lower, female position, his hand on his chin in a gesture of indolence. David is literally

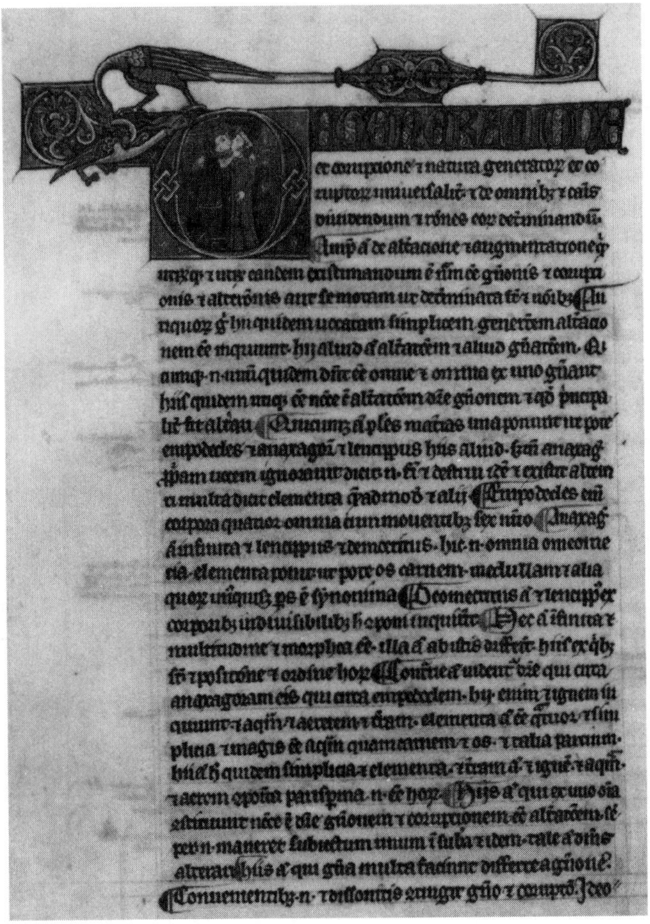

Figure 4.9. Aristotle, *De generatione:* a couple embracing standing up. Bibliothèque Nationale, Paris, MS lat. 6323, fol. 71v. By permission.

effeminized in this sexual position. The active partner in this scene is Bathsheba, who affectionately draws up the covers around her lover. There could be no surer way of condemning this adultery than through the representation of gestures that, although they might seem quite "natural" to us, allude to the "unnatural" genital reversal that is going on beneath the beautiful blue bedclothes, where fluids as well as bodies were thought to be going about it the wrong way. Whereas what were considered perverse sexual acts were commonly represented even in public sculpture in the twelfth century, the thirteenth and fourteenth centuries witnessed a more cautious attitude to the delineation of dangerously suggestive desires. Confessors were warned not to describe perverse sexual practices, for fear of stimulating the very desires they were meant to prohibit. The commonplace apology for religious images in the West was

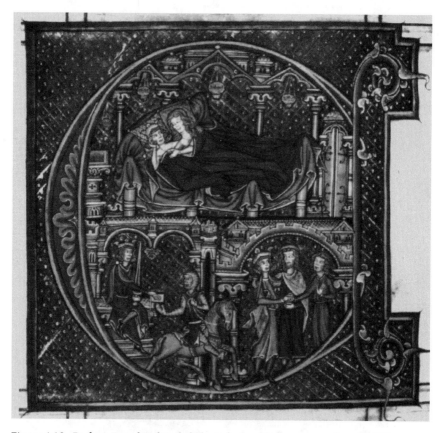

Figure 4.10. Psalter: David and Bathsheba in bed, with the woman "on top." The Pierpont Morgan Library, New York, M. 730, fol. 109v. By permission.

that they stimulated mimesis. People were likely to do what they saw, just as they took heed of what they heard in sermons. Images were thus even more powerful exemplars and invitations to action for medieval people than they are in our own image-saturated culture.

What all these thirteenth- and fourteenth-century depictions of copulation suggest in their variety of genres is an interest in the *representation* of the sexual act, both licit and illicit (with the exception of what we would call homosexual sex), on the part of medieval artists and their patrons, although part of that very process of representation involves omission, occlusion, or erasure. This is especially true in the tradition of popular medical discourse, of which the *Régime* is an early example. Another widely circulated text of the later fourteenth century that contains beautiful full-page pictures of coitus is the treatise on the "nonnaturals," or diet, known as the *Taquinum sanitatis*.[39] Here, too, while particular body parts might be covered, artists found visual ways of alluding to them in the image. This was to change in the opening years of the fifteenth century when a new, more prurient method of presenting the sexual act appears. This can be seen the illustration of the French translation of another great encyclopedic text, Bartholomeus Anglicus's *Livre de propriété des choses* (Figure 4.11). A miniature by one of the leading Parisian artists of the second decade of the century, known as the Boethius Master, sit-

Figure 4.11. Bartholomeus Anglicus, *Livre de propriété des choses:* copulating couple hidden by a curtain. Bibliothèque Nationale, Paris, MS 3122, fol. 179r. By permission.

uates the act of coitus behind closed curtains, cutting off the bodies of the couple. However, they are being observed by two voyeurs, a man and a woman inside the scene who can see what we, from outside, cannot. Illustrating Chapter 10, "How Material Things Are Made," the text quotes Aristotle on man's ability to "enform" base matter. Censorship here occurs at the same moment as the invention of an illusionistic and coherent pictorial space. It places the "work of art" and the conception of children under the veil of secrecy. Ironically, at the very moment the sex act is presented as private and happening behind closed doors, or in this case closed curtains, it becomes a spectacle of desire for others. In the new realms of the late medieval imaginary created by vernacular literacy and silent reading, a realm of privacy and pornography focused around the book meant that realms of individual pleasure could no longer be so easily controlled and policed through texts as it had been earlier.[40] If we think we have advanced beyond this ourselves, it is worth remembering that these acts, pictured without raising eyebrows in religious and devotional texts, are still occluded and censored in our media today. The prudish curtains of privacy that begin to appear in representations like this one around 1400 are tropes visible in every made-for-TV movie today.

## Copulating/Writing/Painting

The traditional association between the act of copulating and the act of writing, which was taught to every schoolboy in his first Latin lessons about conjugations and the gender of nouns, is something else that separates our epistemology from that of the Middle Ages.[41] It also explains the appearance of the copulating couple type that we have examined in a thirteenth-century university manuscript of a logical text, Aristotle's *Posterior Analytics* (Figure 4.12). For here Aristotle discusses the syllogism, in which from the combination of two terms, a third emerges. The fleshly merger of subject and predicate has here been rubbed out by a later, prudish reader, but at the time of its own conception, this scene was a pedagogical picture that used the rules of gendered sexuality to define language itself. In these final remarks I want to broaden my discussion from the close analysis of manuscript images like this one to address the more general underlying chain of metaphors that links not only writing but also the act of painting with the male role. More broadly, this conceptualization of the act of conception as an intellectual process only on the part of the male, or more literally in his pen (his writing penis), along with the ascription of a mere surface or material role to the woman (her blank parchment/flesh), was to open up a chasm between the male-gendered word and the female-gendered image, the full ramifications of which have yet to be explored.

In this essay I have been concerned with the representation of the genitally focused sex act, which hardly comprises the gamut of sexual-

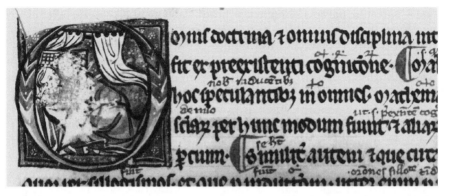

Figure 4.12. Aristotle, *Posterior Analytics:* copulating couple illustrating the concept of the syllogism (later rubbed out). Pembroke College, Cambridge, MS 193, fol. 215r. By permission.

ity as it might be seen in any culture in terms of roles and positions that can be taken up and performed. Images do *not* provide a mirror for sex, any more than they provide a mirror for Chaucer's world or anything else, for that matter. They are as permeated with ideology as any text. Their gendered hermeneutics, which associated writing with the phallus, was aided by the new natural science with its Aristotelian hylomorphism, which made even more of the form/substance dichotomy. This transformed the earlier tradition of patristic exegesis, in which writing itself was female and to be read by the masculine "spirit," into something much more focused on one-sided performance and the dualistic categories of activity and passivity. This matter/form dichotomy, which has been discussed of late by historians of science and medicine, had enormous repercussions on the appreciation of matter and form in the visual arts and is surely relevant to discussions of "text and image" that are so popular, if no longer in art history, then certainly in medieval literary studies. What is at stake is a theory of the relation between the verbal and the visual, which always prioritizes the act of writing over the more material manifestations of the image. The medieval theory of art was, as Umberto Eco has observed, "a theory of human technology seen as an extension of nature." The exemplary form of the art object was, in scholastic discussions of art, in the mind of the creator just as the form of the fetus was in the mind of the male as "an exemplary form in imitation of which something is made.... For we say the form of art in the artist is the exemplar or idea of the artistic product."[42]

The act of writing was viewed as a physical performance, inscribing signs in matter (associated etymologically with the term for both mother and materiality) in the same way as the male was thought to implant his idea within the woman's body in the act of coitus. It meant putting one's mark on fleshly parchment—a paradigm for the preservation of one's paternal name through the production of male heirs, what Carolyn Dinshaw has explored as a textual protection against "violations of the patriarchy."[43] For late-fourteenth-century poets like Jean le Fèvre, these metaphors associating writing with coitus and the production of poems with the making of offspring were commonplaces.[44] Just as the thirteenth- and fourteenth-century writer saw himself not as a subjective identity expressing itself in a book but more as the inheritor and progenitor of a tradition that he must pass on in the copy, sex and writing were not about the self at all but more about following rules, optimum performance, and calculated ends. But there were newer modes of writing, especially in the vernacular and in secular lyrics or allegories like the *Roman de la Rose,* in which the authorial pressure on the pen is also a pleasure in the penis, a literal *jouissance* in the act of pressing inky juices into the fleshly page. In Jean de Meung's poem Genius argues for the clerics to take up their pens and procreate:

> But those who do not use their pens, by means of which the mortal live for ever, on the beautiful and valuable tablets which Nature certainly didn't prepare for them in order that they should lie idle, on the contrary she lent them in order that all [men] should be writers upon them, so that all men and women might live; those who receive the two hammers and do not work straight at forging on the right anvil with them as they should; . . . those who despise such a mistress [as Nature] and read the text askew, and refuse to set about correctly understanding the right meaning, but rather pervert the text when they come to read it: may all these, along with the excommunication which damns them, since they are resolved to go that way, lose, before they die, the purse and the testicles which are the sign that they are male! . . . May the pens be taken from them, since they haven't wished to write on the precious tablets that were suited to them![45]

As Sarah Kay has suggested, this play of sexual difference runs through the *Roman de la Rose,* splitting body and soul, letter and spirit, reading and writing. It is a message that "implies a homology between the bodily and the spiritual: 'proper' sexuality and the joys of eternity are united in a 'proper' textuality."[46] Genius's words are full of irony at this point, urging the barons to invert their noble estate: "Plow for God's sake, my noble barons, plow and restore your lineage. . . . Tuck up your clothes in front, as if to take the air; or if you please be quite bare, but don't get too cold or too hot." This concern about temperature places Jean de Meung's allegory of coitus within the very medical tradition with which I began this chapter. It is men of religion, who according to the church's teachings are supposed to abstain from inscribing themselves upon the bodies of women, whom Jean castigates here as "disloyal creatures," not willing to "make a mark that shows." The tablets upon which they are meant to write are described as having "a very cruel future," since "they will become rusty if kept idle." This point, too, was based upon accepted medical notions of the woman's corruptible and insatiable appetite, as cited in the *Régime du corps,* which, if left unsatisfied, led to disease.[47]

The association between writing and copulation was made even more pointedly in one miniature illustrating this very passage in the *Roman de la Rose,* by an illuminator working in Paris in the 1390s, when it was still possible to present the act without the curtains pulled over it. This couple are even more cocooned within their bedclothes, but both seem more active than the pair in the *Régime* from over a century before, where only the male seemed to "make his mark" (Figure 4.13). Here, by contrast, the woman's hand is shown clearly manipulating the man's member beneath the covers and thereby drawing attention to the phallus that is the real subject of Genius's long diatribe. Their heads are placed on a pallet against a bedpost on the left, which has an angular wooden end and is surmounted by a curtain. This configuration is closely modeled on the furniture of scribes in the period. Indeed this artist represented such a bedhead/desk in imagining a scribe in a miniature decorating a Book of Hours, where Saint Mark faces the same left direction, making the site of textual inscription the same as the site of sexual inscription (Figure 4.14). The illuminator even shows his evangelist licking his pen/penis, ready to begin his impregnations of the flesh, pinned down on his desk/bed below him. This notion of masculine writing as origin was visible from the very first page of Aldobrandino's *Régime du corps,* where the author is associated with God the creator above (Figure 4.1). Words can penetrate images in the form of inscriptions, but images cannot penetrate them, although they can form the shapes, the womb of letters to contain the visible as a rupture within the text. The miniature or historiated initial is, in a very literal sense in the case of the *Régime* initial (Figure 4.2), an opening in the body of the page, vulnerable to the phallicized gaze, in an optics that is, like biology, most often gendered male. These metaphorical systems are, however, never neat, and they are often resisted. If the image as a material thing is often associated with the artifice and superficiality of the feminine, the image maker often reverses the association and seeks to present himself on the side of male conception. Louise Vasvari has shown how the Latin slang term *penicillus,* "little penis/paintbrush," with the same etymology as "pencil," is related to modern English sexual metaphors like "to score" and has emphasized the importance of the comic figure of the painter as penis in medieval Spanish texts.[48] It is *his* nascent independence from the craft tradition and his increasingly intellectual self-projection as the maker not just of matter, but of form, that the artist is forging in the thirteenth and fourteenth centuries.[49] What implications this might have had for female producers of texts or images in the period is an important aspect I cannot address here.

Figure 4.13. *Roman de la Rose*: Nature urges the clerks to coitus. The Pierpont Morgan Library, New York, M. 132, fol. 137r. By permission.

Art historians have tended to overlook the importance of these sexual metaphors, even though they were crucial in the formation of notions of artistic agency in the Middle Ages. The specularly gendered erotics of secular art in this period, especially tapestries and ivory carvings related to courtly love poetry, which again place woman on the pedestal in the realm of the image and man as lover on the side of language, we have hardly started to explore. Unlike literary historians, art historians have not yet begun to question the hegemonic models of gender hierarchy in medieval culture or to explore instances of their subversion, but tend to accept them as givens. This is especially the case with recent research on the function of devotional images, which has described cloistered womens' spirituality mainly in terms of gender reversal. In this scenario mystics can enter Christ's open, vulnerable body via his open wounds only by assuming the heterosexual position. However, we need to question whether the image of Christ with which women and men could interact, by being "on top," has always to be feminized.[50] Is the image that we have examined in this essay, that of the male body on top of the female body, so successfully constructed within the culture that, effaced and occluded as it often is, it nevertheless becomes the *only* model for human creativity?

Figure 4.14. *Book of Hours:* Saint Mark's foreplay, licking his pen. British Library, London, MS Add. 23145, fol. 19. By permission of the British Library.

I have only begun, in this essay, to map out the domination of this visual discourse of copulation, which, as we have seen from the very beginning in the *Régime du corps,* was associated not only with writing, but also with the making of visible marks, with the act of image making (the artist, unlike the writer, was always in danger of usurping God's role as maker of "all things"). This conjunction of the creative male contribution to coitus and the art of painting, the common image in medieval literature of the painter/paintbrush as phallus, needs to be examined in more detail and traced right through to the modern macho-ejaculations of the twentieth-century abstract expressionists.[51] Its medieval pedigree is most blatantly expressed in an exemplum that was popular throughout the Middle Ages and that elides the procreative and the painterly directly. Those who would seek to idealize the medieval artist's labor as an expression of an essential or "natural" talent or who view discussions of sexuality and gender as irrelevant to the study or appreciation of medieval art should take note. It concerns an artist, or painter (*pictor*), who was asked why, if he could produce such beautiful paintings, he had such ugly children. He replied that it was because he could make his pictures in the light of day, but was forced to make his children in the dark.[52]

## Notes

1. Michel Foucault, "A Preface to Transgression," *Language, Counter-Memory, Practice: Selected Essays and Interviews,* ed. D. F. Bouchard (Oxford: Oxford University Press, 1977), 29.

2. See the interesting comparison of the illustrations in *The New Joy of Sex* with those in the 1973 edition, in the *New Yorker,* October 7, 1991, 29–30, which compares the old male lover's member emerging from his hairy paunch to the new man's member which "fits like a dashboard accessory on his Greek body, and is rendered in six colors, as a long, vertical shimmering blur."

3. Jacqueline Rose, *Sexuality in the Field of Vision* (London: Routledge, 1986). While contemporary cultural studies takes much of its impetus from the intersection of sexuality and visuality, work within medieval studies still tends to isolate the visual from the verbal.

4. See the introduction to the edition by Louis Landouzy and Roger Pepin, *Le Régime du corps de mâitre Aldebrandin de Sienne* (Paris: Honoré Champion, 1911).

5. Judith Butler, *Bodies That Matter: On the Discursive Limits of Sex* (London: Routledge, 1993), 13.

6. For a list of manuscripts and their grouping, see Françoise Fery-Hue, "Le *Régime du corps* d'Aldebrindin de Sienne: Tradition Manuscrite et Diffusion," *Santé, Médicine et Assistance au Moyen Age,* Actes du 110e Congrès National des Sociétés savantes (Paris: C.T.H.S., 1987), 113–34. For citations of other illustrated examples, see the useful discussion of the *Régime* in Elizabeth Sears, *The Ages of Man* (Princeton, N.J.: Princeton University Press, 1986), 191; and for another northern French example in the Bibliothèque de l'Arsenal, see A. Stones, "Stylistic Associations, Evolution, and Collaboration: Charting the Bute Painter's Career," *J. Paul Getty Museum Journal* 23 (1995): 22, fig. 18. For the dedication to the Countess of Provence, see Landouzy and Pepin, *Le Régime du corps,* pp. lii–lix, who note that some manuscripts ascribe it to Frederick II and Richard de Fournival, but only one copy, Sloane 2435, mentions Benoit of Florence (lvi).

7. For the importance of medieval medical illustration in the history of the body, see Michael Camille, "The Image and the Self: Unwriting Late Medieval Bodies," in *Framing Medieval Bodies,* ed. Sarah Kay and Miri Rubin (Manchester: Manchester University Press 1994), 62–100; and for a good survey with numerous illustrations, see R. Herrlinger, *History of Medical Illustration from Antiquity to 1600* (New York: Editions Medica Rara, 1970). Pictorial analysis of the medical image of the body is needed, like the analysis excavating its textual metaphorics in Marie-Christine Pouchelle, *The Body and Surgery in the Middle Ages* (New Brunswick, N.J.: Rutgers University Press, 1990).

8. For British Library, Sloane 2435, see Fery-Hue, "Le *Régime du corps*," 116, who dates it "fin du XIIIe ou début du XIVe siècle." Peter Murray-Jones, *Medieval Miniatures* (London: British Museum 1984), 125–36, reproduces a number of initials from the manuscript, figs. 57, 61–63, and plate 11, but misleadingly states that its lavish illumination "best accords with a dedication to the countess of Provence." For color illustrations, see P. Murray-Jones and M. Pratellesi, "Il regime de corpo," *Kos* 2 (1985): 41–56.

9. For the bed as the site of birth and death and as the major economic expenditure in medieval households, see Michael Camille, *The Master of Death: The Lifeless Art of Pierre Remiet, Illuminator* (New Haven, Conn.: Yale University Press, 1996), 88; and for its literary and visual appearance in manuscripts, see Karin Lerchner, *Lectulus Floridus: Zur Bedeutung des Bettes in Literatur und Handschriftenillustration des Mittelalters* (Cologne: Böhlau Verlag, 1993).

10. A Louvre ivory mirror-back sets an erotic chess-game within a tent with similar parted curtains; see fig. 5 in C. Jean Campbell, "Courting, Harlotry and the Art of Gothic Ivory Carving," *Gesta* 34 (1995): 11–20.

11. Landouzy and Pepin, *Le Régime du corps*, 28.

12. This tradition is discussed in Joan Cadden, *Meanings of Sex Difference in the Middle Ages: Medicine, Science and Culture* (Cambridge: Cambridge University Press, 1993), 249–58. See also Paul Delany, "Constantinus Africanus' *De Coitu*: A Translation," *Chaucer Review* 4 (1969): 59, for the relation between diet and sex. See also the useful publication of a Catalan "codice medico-erotico" in Teresa Vicens, *Speculum al Joder: Tradado de recetas y consejos sobre el coito* (Barcelona: Hesperus, 1994).

13. For this Hippocratic notion, see Danielle Jacquart and Claude Thomasset, *Sexuality and Medicine in the Middle Ages* (Princeton: Princeton University Press, 1985), 34, and Helen Rodnite Lemay, "William of Saliceto on Human Sexuality," *Viator* 12 (1981): 165–81.

14. Landouzy and Pepin, *Régime du corps*, 29–30.

15. Reproduced in Murray-Jones, *Medieval Medical Miniatures*, plate 11.

16. Jacquart and Thomasset, *Sexuality and Medicine*, 144–45, discuss monstrous births in relation to theories of vision. The place of the gaze and vision in medieval courtly love is discussed in John W. Baldwin, *The Language of Sex: Five Voices from Northern France around 1200* (Chicago: University of Chicago Press, 1994), 118, 140, in which he describes what he terms "a privileged moment of gender symmetry in Western thought before the deluge of Aristotelianism" (p. 234). See also Gabriele Bartz, Alfred Karnein, and Claudio Lange, *Liebesfreuden im Mittelalter: Kulturgeschichte der Erotik und Sexualität in Bildern und Dokumenten* (Stuttgart: Belser Verlag, 1994).

17. Jan Svanberg, "The Gothic Smile," in *Kunstlerischer Austausch: Artistic Exchange: XXVIII Internationalen Kongresses für Kunstgeschichte*, II (Berlin: Akademie Verlag, 1993), 357–71.

18. On closing the eyes during orgasm, see Mary C. Wack, "Imagination, Medicine and Rhetoric in Andreas Capellanus' 'De Amore,'" in *Magister Regis: Studies in Honor of Robert Earl Kaske*, ed. Arthur Groos (New York: Fordham University Press, 1986), 106, and Robert M. Durling, "'Io son venuto': Seneca, Plato, and the Microcosm," *Dante Studies* 93 (1975): 110. For the association of orgasm and death, see Michel Maffesoli, *The Shadow of Dionysius: A Contribution to the Sociology of the Orgy* (Albany: State University of New York Press, 1993), 77. The problem of pleasure and the woman's seed in conception is discussed in Mary Frances Wack, "The Measure of Pleasure: Peter of Spain on Men, Women, and Lovesickness," *Viator* 17 (1986): 177, and Cadden, *Meanings of Sex Difference*, 93–97.

19. Landouzy and Pepin, *Le Régime du corps*, p. 201. For physiognomy, see J. Agrimi, "Fisiognomica e scholastica," in *Micrologus* 1 (1993): 235–79.

20. Landouzy and Pepin, *Le Régime du corps*, 29.

21. As a guide to the growing body of literature on this topic, see, in addition to Cadden's *Meanings of Sex Difference*, Monica H. Green, "Female Sexuality in the Medieval West," *Trends in History* 4 (1990): 127–58.

22. Thomas Laqueur, *Making Sex: Body and Gender from the Greeks to Freud* (Cambridge: Harvard University Press, 1990). See the review by Katherine Park and Robert A. Nye, "Destiny Is Anatomy," *New Republic* 53 (1991): 53–57. For discussion of how gender difference is exploited even in the illustrations in modern medical textbooks, see Rosalind A. Coleman and James Rolleston, "Anatomy Lessons: The Destiny of a Textbook, 1971–72," *South Atlantic Quarterly* 90 (1991): 153–73.

23. For a complete survey of these diagrams, see H. Schadt, *Die Dartstellungen der Arbores consanguinitatis und der Arbores affinitatis: Bildschemata in juristischen Handschriften* (Tübingen: Wasmuth, 1982).

24. For the copulating couple schema in art, see Raimond Van Marle, *Iconographie de l'art profane* (The Hague: Martinus Nijhoff, 1932), 482, and Sander L. Gilman, *Sexuality: An Illustrated History* (New York: Wiley, 1989), 67. For ancient prototypes, see C. Johns, *Sex or Symbol: Erotic Images of Greece and Rome* (London 1982), 61–72; and for a medieval amuletic badge showing the subject, see the fascinating discussion by Jan Baptist Bedeaux, "Laatmiddeleeuwse sexuele amuletten," in *Annus Quadrigia Mundi: Opstellen over Middeleeuwse Kunst* (Utrecht: De Walburg, 1989), 26. The subject's appearance in fourteenth-century model-books suggests its ubiquity: see Robert W. Scheller, *Exemplum: Model-Book Drawings and the Practice of Artistic Transmission in the Middle Ages* (Amsterdam: Amsterdam University Press, 1995), 263 n. 7.

25. See Albert the Great, *Man and the Beasts: De animalibus (Books 22–26)*, trans. J. J. Scanlan (Binghamton: Medieval and Renaissance Texts and Studies, 1987), 60. For an illustration of a fourteenth-century Parisian manuscript of Albert's treatise, which distinguishes the human from the animal sexual act as the only one involving shame, and thus covers up the lower bodies of the man and woman, see M. Camille, *Image on the Edge: The Margins of Medieval Art* (Cambridge, Mass.: Harvard University Press, 1992), fig. 23, p. 46. For an example in the fifteenth century, see Paris, Bibliothèque Nationale, MS fr. 9140, fol. 92, "des membres genitoires," which shows a similarly coy couple.

26. For this manuscript, see C. Gaspar and F. Lyna, *Les Principaux Manuscrits à peintures de la Bibliothèque royale de Belgique* (Paris: Imprimerie Nationale, 1937), 209–11. An identical series of miniatures illustrates the same text in Brussels, Bibliothèque Royale, MS 9543. The text has been published under the erroneous authorship of Jehan le Bel, by Jules Petit, *Li Ars d'Amour de vertu et de boneurté* (Brussels: Victor Devaux, 1867). See pp. 135–36 for the discussion of "amisté délitable" preceded by the miniature of the couple in bed.

27. For the medical arguments for this position, see Cadden, *Meanings of Sex Difference*, 245–47, and for legal opinions, see the fully documented article by James A. Brundage, " 'Let Me Count the Ways': Canonists and Theologians Contemplate Coital Positions," *Journal of Medieval History* 10 (1984): 81–93.

28. James A. Brundage, *Law, Sex and Christian Society in Medieval Europe* (Chicago: University of Chicago Press, 1988), plate 13.

29. Ibid., plate 14; see also the discussion by Jean-Claude Schmitt, "Le Miroir du canoniste: Les images et le texte dans un manuscrit médiévale," *Annales E.S.C.* 48 (1993): 1470–75, fig. 5.

30. Brundage, "Let Me Count the Ways," 86.

31. These are examined by Alison Stones, "Images of Temptation, Seduction and Discovery in the Prose Lancelot: A Preliminary Note," *Wiener Jahrbuch für Kunstgeschichte* 46–47 (1993–94): 887, Abb. 14–15. For the defacement of love scenes in romance manuscripts, see Lorie Walters, "The Image of Blanchefleur in Montpellier, BI, sect. Med. H. 249," in *Les Manuscrits de Chrétien de Troyes*, ed. K. Busby, A. Stones, and L. Walters (Amsterdam: Editions Rodoph), vol. 2, fig. 11, p. 447 n. 39.

32. H. O. Sommer, *The Vulgate Version of Arthurian Romances*, 7 vols. (Washington, D.C., 1909–13), 2:129.

33. See Michael Camille, "Gothic Signs and the Surplus: The Kiss on the Cathedral," *Contexts: Style and Values in Medieval Art and Literature: Yale French Studies* (1991),

151–71; see also Yannick Carré, *Le Baiser sur la bouche au Moyen Age: Rites, symboles, mentalités XIe-XVe siècles* (Paris: Le Leopard d'Or, 1993).

34. For contemporary applications of medieval sodomy laws, see Brundage, *Law, Sex and Christian Society*, 612–13, and Janet E. Haley, "Bowers vs. Hardwick in the Renaissance," in *Queering the Renaissance*, ed. Jonathan Goldberg (Durham, N.C.: Duke University Press, 1994), 15–40. See also Pierre Payer, *Sex in the Penitentials: The Development of a Sexual Code, 550–1150* (Toronto: University of Toronto Press, 1984), 29–30. As Jane Burns points out in "Knowing Women: Female Orifices in Old French Farce and Fabliaux," *Exemplaria* 4, no. 1 (1992): 87, "the confusion of *con* and *cul* is standard fare in Old French fabliaux," which have a tendency "to erase female genitalia by imposing the model of the male asshole."

35. For this artist and his works, see Michael Camille, *Image on the Edge: The Margins of Medieval Art* (Cambridge: Harvard University Press, 1992), 48–55, and "Play, Piety, and Perversity in Gothic Marginal Illumination," in *Sein Ganz Körper ist Gesicht*, ed. K. Kroll (Freiburg: Rombach, 1994), 171–93.

36. See Camille, *Image on the Edge*, figs. 50 and 55, for romances with marginal images of knights being shot in the ass by archers. There is as yet no full study of male or female homosexuality in medieval art, but see for now the plates in John Boswell, *Christianity, Social Tolerance, and Homosexuality* (Chicago: University of Chicago Press, 1980); Michael Camille, *The Gothic Idol: Ideology and Image-Making in Medieval Art* (Cambridge: Cambridge University Press, 1989), 90–91; John Paul Ricco, "Queering Boundaries: Semen and Visual Representations from the Middle Ages and in the Era of the AIDS Crisis," in *Gay and Lesbian Studies in Art History*, ed. Whitney Davis (New York: Haworth Press, 1994), 57–80.

37. Cadden, *Meanings of Sex Difference*, 245.

38. For this subject, see Lillian Randall, *Images in the Margins of Gothic Manuscripts* (Berkeley: University of California Press, 1966), figs. 554–57, and Susan L. Smith, *The Power of Women: A "Topos" in Medieval Art and Literature* (Philadelphia: University of Pennsylvania Press, 1995), 66–103.

39. Luisa Cogliato Arano, *The Medieval Health Handbook Taquinum Sanitatis* (New York: Braziller, 1972), plate 9, "Coitus."

40. This miniature was not included in George Duby's copiously illustrated *A History of Private Life*, vol. 1, *Revelations of the Medieval World* (Chicago: University of Chicago Press, 1989), but appeared in the second volume of Hans Peter Duerr's three-volume study *Der Mythos vom Zivilisationsprocess, Intimität* (Frankfurt: Suhrkamp Verlag), 83. Duerr wrongly identifies the scene as a doctor and a medical student watching coitus. Larry Benson makes a similar argument to mine about what he calls "the spread of courtly prudery" in the work of Bartholomaeus Anglicus; see L. Benson, "Chaucer and Courtly Speech," in *Genres, Themes, and Images in English Literature*, ed. P. Boitani and A. Torti (Tübingen: Gunter Narr Verlag, 1988), 20–21. The association between the origins of pornography and the rise of private or silent reading in the later Middle Ages was made by Paul Saenger, "Silent Reading: Its Impact on Late Medieval Script and Society," *Viator* 13 (1982): 367–414.

41. For sexuality and grammar, see E. R. Curtius, *European Literature and the Latin Middle Ages* (Princeton, N.J.: Princeton University Press, 1973), 414–16; Jan Ziolkowski, *Alan of Lille's Grammar of Sex: The Meaning of Grammar to a Twelfth-Century Intellectual* (Cambridge, Mass.: Harvard University Press, 1985); and Betsy Bowden "The Art of Courtly Copulation," *Medievalia et humanistica*, n.s. 9 (1979): 67–85. Another fascinating essay on the relations between grammar and deviant sexuality that has just come to my attention is Elizabeth Pittenger, "Explicit Ink," in *Premodern Sexualities*, ed. Carla Frecerro and Louise Fradenberg (London: Routledge, 1995).

42. Umberto Eco, *The Aesthetics of Thomas Aquinas* (Cambridge, Mass.: Harvard University Press, 1988), 167.

43. Carolyn Dinshaw, *Chaucer's Sexual Poetics* (Madison: University of Wisconsin Press, 1989), 18–21.

44. See Jacqueline Cercquiglini, *La Couleur de mélancolie: Les fréquentation des livres au XIVe siècle* (Paris, 1992), 80–100. For Richard de Bury, who writes a whole treatise on this notion of the book as offspring, see Michael Camille, "Book as Flesh and Fetish in Richard de Bury's *Philobiblon*," in *The Book and the Body*, ed. Katherine O'Brien O'Keefe (Notre Dame, Ind.: University of Notre Dame Press, 1997).

45. Guillaume de Lorris and Jean de Meung, *The Romance of the Rose*, trans. Charles Dahlberg (Hanover, N.H.: University Press of New England, 1983), 323–24. I have used the translation by Sarah Kay ("Sexual Knowledge: The Once and Future Texts of the *Romance of the Rose*," in *Textuality and Sexuality: Reading Theories and Practices*, ed. J. Still and M. Worton [Manchester: Manchester University Press, 1993], 75–76), which is closer to the original.

46. Kay, "Sexual Knowledge," 69–86.

47. *Roman de la Rose*, 324–25; and for the medical tradition on the detrimental effects of seed retention for women, which goes as far as to recommend masturbation, see Cadden, *Meanings of Sex Difference*, 275.

48. See Louise O. Vasvari, "Festive Phallic Discourse in the *Libro del Arciprestre*," *La Corónica: Spanish Medieval Language and Literature* 22 (1994): 104; and for the painter as a figure of phallic fun, see "Pitas Pajas: Popular Phonosymbolism," *Revista de Estudios Hispánicos* 26 (1992): 135–62.

49. I deal with the intersection of sexuality and subjectivity more fully in chap. 2 of *The Master of Death: The Lifeless Art of Pierre Remiet, Illuminator* (New Haven, Conn.: Yale University Press, 1996), 88–89.

50. See Karma Lochrie's argument in chapter 9 of this volume.

51. The male organ as a tool in modern art is discussed by Amelia Jones, "Dis/playing the Phallus: Male Artists Perform Their Masculinities," *Art History* 17 (1994): 546–83.

52. For the exemplum, based on Macrobius, see Thomas A. Wright, *Latin Stories* (London, 1842), p. 122, and Ernst Kris and Otto Kurz, *Legend, Myth, and Magic in the Image of the Artist* (New Haven, Conn.: Yale University Press, 1979), 115.

## CHAPTER 5

# Bodies That Don't Matter:
## Heterosexuality before Heterosexuality in Gottfried's *Tristan*

*James A. Schultz*

owadays most of us assume we will feel sexual desire either for men or for women and that we will be able to tell one from the other. This does not seem to be the case in Gottfried von Straßburg's *Tristan und Isold*. To be sure, women only desire men and men only desire women. Yet it's hard to see how they can keep themselves straight, since one can scarcely tell the men's bodies from the women's. When bodies are described as desirable, sex-specific features are not mentioned, and when men or women are described as beautiful, they are said to be beautiful in the same terms. And yet, somehow, the inhabitants of Gottfried's fictional world must be able to tell the men from the women, since they will always desire someone of the other sex. What sort of sexual economy ensures that women and men will always desire the other sex when the anatomy of desire scarcely distinguishes one sex from the other? How does heterosexuality work in a homomorphic world?

My answer to this question falls into three parts. The first is devoted to the bodies that are not differentiated by sex. The second considers the conventions of clothing that create gendered bodies. And the third traces the structures of desire in a world where, although much seems familiar, the relations of sex, gender, and desire are quite different from those to which we are accustomed.[1]

### Bodies: The Morphology of Desire

According to Judith Butler, culture produces bodies: "Historically revisable criteria of intelligibility...produce and vanquish bodies that matter."[2] Because the criteria change, "morphological possibilities" that are intelligible today would not necessarily have been intelligible in the past, and bodies that were intelligible in the past may not be so today. This is particularly true for the body as an object of desire. In 1928 Stephen Gordon, heroine of the *Well of Loneliness*, looked in a mirror and found her body, with its narrow hips and small breasts, "poor," "desolate," "monstrous"[3]—in other words, unintelligible; but things have changed, as Marjorie Garber notes, and the "monstrous body of 1928" is now "the ideal female body of the fitness generation."[4] What was desolate is now desirable. I want to describe the historically specific "morphological possibilities" represented by the desirable bodies in Gottfried's *Tristan.* In doing so I take seriously Caroline Walker Bynum's caution against assuming that medieval people eroticized the body in the same ways we do.[5] And I also take seriously what I understand to be the implications of Butler's argument: medieval "regulatory schemas" will have produced bodies different from ours, bodies in which morphological features that matter to us may not have been culturally intelligible and, in that sense, simply did not exist.

Although Gottfried is fascinated with the workings of desire, there are in fact only five bodies that he describes in any detail as the objects of desire: the body of Riwalin as he is jousting at Mark's springtime festival and is admired by the ladies of the court (699–719);[6] the body of Blanscheflur as Riwalin contemplates her beauty and falls more deeply in love (921–36); the body of Tristan as he enters Mark's court, just after he has displayed his skills as a hunter (3332–50); the body of Isold when she appears in splendor at her father's court, just before she departs for Cornwall (10885–11020); and the body of Isold again, this time as Mark looks at her through the window of the *Minnegrotte* (17557–607). These are the only passages in which a body is explicitly marked as desirable and is represented in enough detail that one gets some idea of its anatomical specificity. They are, in other words, the only passages in which one can investigate the relation of morphology and desire.

Of course, anatomy is not the only thing that sparks desire: the ladies of Mark's court are drawn to Riwalin not only for the shape of his arms and legs but also for the elegance with which he jousts, while Tristan and Isold, even though they have long been aware of each other's beauty, are only sexually attracted once they drink the fateful potion. And yet, although the body may not always be sufficient, it is nevertheless frequently accorded a crucial role in inciting desire. When Tristan appears at Mark's court, it is "his body" that makes him desirable, since it "was formed as Love required."[7] When Mark looks at Isold through the window of the *Minnegrotte,* it is "the beauty of her body" with which "Love enflamed the man."[8] Mark's reaction will not surprise those who share the assumption attributed to modern sex researchers that "the male body respond[s] to the presence of the female body, as if to a natural sign."[9] Medievals and moderns do agree that the body is important. But it is not the same body. For, as I hope to show, although Mark may be "enflamed" by the sight of Isold, it is not a female body to which he responds, nor is her body a natural sign.

Isold's body is not a female body for the simple reason that the desirable bodies in Gottfried's *Tristan* are not distinguished by sex. When the ladies of Mark's court admire Riwalin they note: "How perfect his body is! How evenly his magnificent legs move together!...How the spear becomes his hand!...How he carries his head and hair!...Fortunate is the woman who will have lasting joy from him!"[10] Although the last lines suggest that the women regard Riwalin as sexually desirable, the only parts of his body they mention are his legs, his hands, his head, and his hair, none of which is unique to males. In this Riwalin is like the knights in the French *Prose Lancelot*, the descriptions of whom, as Jane Burns shows in chapter 6 in this volume, "do not in any way tie [their] bodies to a gendered anatomy."

It is the same when Isold appears before the Irish court. As she enters, the narrator describes her as "tall, shapely, and slender....Her robe fell in folds around her feet....The beautiful maiden had inserted the thumb of her left hand [in a string of pearls holding her cloak together]....She had brought her right hand down to where the cloak should be closed, where she held it together elegantly with two of her fingers....On her head she wore a small crown of gold....Even the wisest man there, if he had not seen the gems [on the crown], would have insisted that there was no crown at all: so equal and so identical was her hair to the gold."[11] Although the description of Isold is considerably more elaborate than the praise of Riwalin, the elaboration is rhetorical rather than anatomical. In her case, as in his, the desirable body is represented by a limited number of parts that are visible to the public eye and that are common to men and women: head, hair, and the elements of the face; arms, legs, and feet. This is true not only for Riwalin and Isold but also for the other desirable bodies listed earlier.

Of course Gottfried might have mentioned parts of the body that distinguish one sex from the other: he could have given Riwalin a beard or referred to Isold's breasts, anatomical features that do manage to exist in other contexts. We learn, for instance, that when Rual arrives at Mark's court "the hair of his beard was so matted that he seemed to be a wild man"[12] and that when Isold wants to convince Mark of her devotion one night in bed she draws him "extremely close to her soft, smooth breasts."[13] But such anatomical signs of sex difference do not figure in the descriptions of bodies that are said to be beautiful.

There are historical reasons for this. While older men like Rual might have beards, the ideal of youthful male beauty in Middle High German (MHG) courtly texts requires young men to be beardless. Thus Wolfram von Eschenbach calls Parzival "the young man without a beard"[14] long after he has married, fathered children, and become lord of Pelrapeire; and Rudolf von Ems writes of knights who are just getting their very first beard hairs when they are nearly thirty.[15] Since thirteenth-century legal texts take the beginnings of a beard as a sign that a man is at least fourteen,[16] it seems unlikely that MHG writers really believed that men ordinarily remained beardless until they were thirty. Nevertheless, since courtly standards of beauty frowned on beards, these same writers insist that their heroes' faces are still smooth long after they have become adults.[17] Breasts are only slightly more common than beards. Before 1200 they do not figure in any descriptions of beautiful women in MHG texts.[18] In fact, Isold's embrace of Mark, mentioned earlier, and Jeschute's second encounter with the hero of *Parzival*[19] represent the first references by MHG writers to women's breasts in erotic contexts. Between 1200 and 1250 breasts figure in the description of the desirable woman's body in only two other MHG texts.[20] The vernacular writers are not alone in their reticence: according to Joan Cadden, when medieval medical and scientific authors discuss sex differentiation they do not often mention breasts.[21]

The evidence suggests then that Gottfried's omission of the most obvious anatomical signs of sex difference from his descriptions of beautiful bodies reflects more general medieval constructions of the body. According to these, beards are not part of the desirable male body and breasts play only a very occasional role in distinguishing the body as female, so that the standard of beauty for men and women is nearly the same. Thus, when Rennewart sits down next to his sister in Wolfram's *Willehalm*, the two are said to look the same—except that Rennewart's beard *has* begun to grow. This moves the narrator to comment: "I would be happier if [the hairs of his beard] were not there, for then one might have taken the man for the woman, their bodies were so similar."[22] The narrator *wants* to take the young hero for a woman; he thinks a beautiful man and a beautiful woman *should* look the same.

Just because, given the information that Gottfried provides about desirable bodies, it would be difficult to tell men's bodies from women's, that does not mean that all bodies are indistinguishable. When Rual appears at Mark's court, his clothes in tatters, his hair and his beard matted after years of searching for Tristan throughout Europe, Gottfried stops to assure us that, no matter how miserable his clothing, Rual was "in body and bearing, perfectly magnificent. His was a noble body."[23] After noting that Rual had a resonant voice and that he was in the prime of life, Gottfried concludes: "In the true dignity proper to a lord he was the equal of any emperor."[24] Although beautiful bodies do not reveal their sex, lordly bodies, even in hardship, reveal their class.

That, of course, is what Isold learns when she studies Tristan shortly before the famous scene in the bath. After inspecting his hands, face, arms, and legs, she declares: "It would be right and proper for him to have an empire at his service."[25] A bit later she recalls: "How well I have known all along since I have been observing him, and taking careful note of every detail of his body and his bearing and everything about him, that he was a lord by birth!"[26] Looking him over from head to toe—or rather from face to legs—Isold does not say: Great body, we've got to have sex; but: Great body, he's got to be a lord. Of course, she is right: Tristan is of royal blood.

Some have argued that Isold begins to fall in love with Tristan as she studies him in this scene,[27] a view for which I do not think the text gives much support. And yet, if it is true, if Isold really does begin to fall in love here, then the body she desires is one that is marked not as a *male* body but as a *noble* body. What Isold sees in Tristan is not sex but class.

Obviously these are not the bodies that Calvin Klein displayed so relentlessly a few years ago on billboards and buses throughout urban America—worked out, stripped down, lighted, and photographed so that every primary and secondary sexual characteristic leaps out at you and fills you with desire to buy new underwear.[28] Nor are they the bodies represented in a thirteenth-century manuscript of Aldobrandino of Siena's *Régime du corps*, which, as Michael Camille shows in chapter 4 of this volume, "emphasize and reinscribe the radical difference between male and female bodies." No, these are bodies that, as Gottfried represents them, simply do not have primary or secondary sexual characteristics. They are bodies that, although beautiful and desirable, do not distinguish morphologically between male and female. In this they are like the bodies of Lancelot and Guenevere, in which, according to Jane Burns, one cannot distinguish clearly between the man's mouth and hands and the woman's. And yet Gottfried's bodies can easily be distinguished by class: the body of Rual, travel-weary and filthy, and the body of Tristan, just recovered from nearly fatal wounds, are easily recognized as noble. Noble bodies reveal class more readily than desirable bodies reveal sex— even when the noble bodies look *least* courtly and the desirable bodies look *most* beautiful. Needless to say, in Gottfried's world sex does matter: desire for the other sex is the only possibility. And sex is always known. The point is not that one cannot tell women from men but rather that in the one domain where we think anatomical sex difference is of paramount importance, Gottfried clearly does not. When it comes to eliciting desire, Gottfried's female and male bodies are morphologically indistinguishable.

One should recall that Gottfried was writing before heterosexuality. I mean this not in the trivial sense that the term had not yet been invented, but in the more important sense that the cross-sexual relation between the desiring subject and the desirable object does not constitute either the identity of the subject or the morphology of the object in the profound way it is assumed to under a regime of compulsory heterosexuality. The modern Western organization of sexuality is unusual in that it takes sexual object choice as the primary criterion of sexual classification: if I desire men I am a homosexual, if I desire women I am a heterosexual, and it makes no difference whether I wear a necktie or a dress or who does what to whom in bed. Such a standard is not only unusual among human cultures but is, even in the West, very recent. The word "heterosexual"—along with its longtime companion "homosexual"— was not invented until 1868;[29] it only came to be widely used in its current meaning in the course of the twentieth century,[30] and even at the end of the twentieth century, as sex researchers discovered recently, it is "not well understood by many people."[31]

In earlier times sexual behavior was classified according to other criteria. In classical Athens people involved in sexual relations were divided into those who *did* sex (adult male citizens) and those to whom sex *was done* (women, boys, foreigners, and slaves).[32] In the thirteenth century Thomas Aquinas classified the species of lust according to their relation to reason (children must be raised by married parents) and to nature (the natural end of sex is procreation). Best are those "venereal acts" that respect reason and nature (the union of a married couple desiring children), worse are those that violate reason since they are outside marriage (fornication, seduction, adultery, rape), and worst of all are those that violate nature because conception is impossible (masturbation, sodomy, bestiality).[33] One could say that the ancient boy-lovers and the medieval sodomites were really homosexuals, and that most of the rest were heterosexuals. If one were to make this claim, however, one would blind oneself to the ways in which people in past times understood their sexual behavior. If we "perpetually look for precursors to our categories of sexuality in essentially different domains," writes Arnold Davidson, we will produce "anachronisms at best and unintelligibility at worst."[34]

For us the sex of the object is crucial since it is the primary criterion of sexual classification; it defines the sexual identity of the subject. Writing in a world before heterosexuality, Gottfried did not feel the pressure we feel to proclaim the sex of the object of desire. To be sure, the sex of the desired body does matter and it is always known. But it is not the obsession it is nowadays because less is at stake. Thus Isold can expect a response when she draws Mark to her breasts: she knows that directing her husband's attention to her specifically female body is likely to divert his mind from other matters. But at the same time Gottfried can ignore anatomical signs of sex difference when he describes desirable bodies: they are no more constitutive elements of the desirable body than is hair color, which he notes for Isold but ignores for Riwalin. One knows that this body is female, that one male, but this difference is not so important that it determines the morphology of the object of desire. Class, one of those "other regimes of regulatory production [that] contour the materiality of bodies,"[35] is written on the body more clearly than sex. Bodies differ in visible ways because they are noble or because they are beautiful (for which their nobility is a prerequisite). The nobility and the beauty of the desirable body are culturally visible in the morphology of the body itself. The sex of the desirable body is not.

## Clothing: Investing in Gender

While the sex of the desirable body is not culturally visible, the gender of the desirable body is. And of all the means by which gender is made visible in Gottfried's *Tristan*, the one that lies closest to the body is cloth-ing. The human body stands "in a relation of signification with clothing," according to Roland Barthes: "as pure sentience, the body cannot sig-nify; clothing guarantees the passage from sentience to meaning."[36] This is especially true when clothing signifies gender. When clothing signi-fies class, which it often does, it accomplishes something that, as has just been seen, bodies can also accomplish.[37] But when clothing signi-fies gender it does something that bodies cannot do, since Gottfried's desirable bodies do not distinguish themselves morphologically as men or women. Clothing, which relates differently to men's and to women's bodies, establishes thereby a difference between men and women: it guar-antees the passage to meaning. It creates the gendered body.

Although the basic elements of courtly clothing were the same for men and women in this period,[38] men's and women's clothes were not identical. Women's garments reached to the floor, while men's only ex-tended part of the way down the leg, and since the leg coverings fit very closely, the contours of men's legs were clearly visible. As a result shapely legs came to be regarded as the hallmark of masculine beauty.[39] When Tristan appears at Mark's court Gottfried tells us: "His feet and his legs, in which his beauty was most apparent, were praiseworthy indeed, as such things should be praised in a man."[40] Evidently, beautiful legs are an excellence that is peculiarly masculine. It is not surprising then that Riwalin's legs receive special praise from the ladies who watch him joust-ing and that Tristan's legs are noted again just after he is armed for the fight with Morold (709–10, 6705–6). Of course, legs in themselves are not peculiarly male. Thus one cannot say that men's clothes reveal a sexed body. Rather, men's clothes create a gendered body. Exposing the legs turns the body into a man's, since the body with visible legs can only be a man's. It is the clothes, not the legs, that make the body masculine.

Clothes reveal the body not only because they leave some parts ex-posed but because they fit other parts so closely. Like so much else that was prized in German courts of the twelfth and thirteenth centuries, the fashion for clothes that were cut to fit the torso had been imported from France.[41] When Isold appears in splendor before the Irish court, "she wore a robe and a cloak of purple samite, cut in the French style."[42] Close fitting clothes were also fashionable for men.[43] When Tristan is presented to Mark we learn that "his clothes were very courtly, having been cut to fit his body."[44]

But the close fit does not treat women and men in the same way. When Isold greets the Irish court, the contours of her robe are described as follows: "There, toward the place where the sides join the hips, her robe was fringed and narrowed and pulled close to her body by a sash, which lay precisely where a sash should. The robe was intimate with her and clung to her body; it was nowhere bulky and tried to keep close everywhere from top to bottom."[45] Gottfried's description of Isold's robe invites us to contemplate "the place where the sides join the hips" and to visualize the effect of a garment that was "pulled close to her body," that was "intimate with her," that "clung to her body," and that "tried to keep close everywhere." While Isold's robe clothes her body, it discloses her body at the same time. Of course, "sides" and "hips" are not peculiarly female: the body that is disclosed is not a sexed body. Rather the clothes create a gendered body: if you see through the clothes, then it must be a woman's body.[46]

The close fit of Tristan's garments has a different effect. In preparation for his grand appearance before the Irish court, Tristan dispatches Curvenal to bring him clothes "of the very best cut."[47] Once dressed, Tristan joins Isold, her mother, and Brangaene, and when the three women looked at him, "they thought: 'Truly, this man is a manly creature; his clothes and his figure create the man in him: they suit each other so well.'"[48] When Tristan enters the court a little while later the narrator repeats the women's thoughts in his own voice: Tristan's "body and his clothes harmonized marvelously with each other. Together the two of them formed a knightly man."[49] Gottfried seems to believe that "clothes make the man" in a very concrete way. The clothes cannot do it alone: they need a body with which they harmonize. But that body remains ungendered as long as it is unclothed. Ungendered body and suitable clothes *together* create the gendered man. The vocabulary of construction is Gottfried's, not mine. He is the one who claims that "the manly creature" is *created*, that the "knightly man" is *formed* only when he gets dressed.[50]

Clothes create gender in Gottfried's *Tristan* not because of their materials or their cut or their close fit, nor on account of the sexed body parts they reveal. Gender is created rather by the differential relation that clothes sustain with the body. If they clothe the body and disclose it at the same time, they create a woman. If they harmonize with the body and reveal the leg, they create a man. Through clothing, writes Barthes, "the body is taken 'in charge' by an intelligible system of signs, and sentience is dissolved in the signifier."[51] Gottfried's bodies, which are not differentiated by sex, are "dissolved" into their clothing. The clothing, which distinguishes women from men not so much by its form as by its formal relation to the body, creates difference: an intelligible system of signs. "Dissolved" in their clothing, bodies exist only as feminine or masculine.[52]

Predictably, when clothing creates gendered bodies it does not create them equal. Clothing collaborates with the man's body and confirms its nobility. It turns Tristan into the subject of heroic action, "a knightly man." Clothed, Tristan is admired, first by Isold, her mother, and Brangaene, then by the whole court, "many of whom said: 'Where has God ever created a figure better suited to the order of knighthood?'"[53] The woman's body, on the other hand, is exposed by its clothing and offered to public view. Isold is turned into the object of voyeuristic fantasy.

Clothed and thereby disclosed, Isold is desired: when she appears in court, "glances like feathered predators flew thick as snowflakes back and forth, hunting."[54] Through clothing Gottfried's bodies are indeed "taken in charge."[55] Undifferentiated morphologically by sex, they are, through their clothing, invested in a differential hierarchy of gender: Tristan to be admired as a knight, Isold to be desired as quarry.[56]

In making gender visible, clothes can represent many other "marks of gender"[57] that distinguish women and men. It is such signs—pronouns, names, behaviors, clothes—that enable the women and men in Gottfried's *Tristan* to keep themselves straight, even when their bodies seem to be very much the same. Among the marks of gender, however, clothing has a special status because of its proximity to the body. We assume that there is a sexed body underneath the gendered clothes, that the sexed body is prior and relatively stable, and that clothes are superficial and easily changed. For Gottfried, there is no sexed body underneath the gendered clothes. Clothes create gender difference for desirable bodies that do not differ morphologically by sex. Whatever distinction exists between women's and men's bodies results not from any anatomical *sex* differences, of which there are none, but from vestimentary *gender* differentiation. Bodies are understood to be female and male only because they are *already* known to be feminine and masculine.

It is hardly remarkable that, in a world before heterosexuality, gender should take precedence over sex. In nineteenth-century America no one imagined that two women who lived together were anything less than completely respectable—provided they both appeared suitably feminine.[58] Sexual relations, after all, could only take place between a man and a woman. Thus, if two females were sexually involved, one was assumed to have been "the man" (aggressive, sex-driven), the other "the woman" (passive, not interested in sex). Only the former, the "invert," was considered deviant. Not until sexual object choice was established as the crucial determinant of normalcy—not, that is, until the advent of heterosexuality—were both partners in a homosexual relationship considered perverts.[59] Even today, in many parts of the world, two men who have anal intercourse are not thought to belong to the same category: rather, the one who plays the "women's part" is considered deviant, while the one who acts the "man's part" is considered a "normal man."[60] As these examples show, where sexual object choice is not the determining factor in classifying sexual actors, gender often is. Since Gottfried was writing in a world before heterosexuality, one might expect that for him too gender is more important than sex.

## Desire: The Tyranny of the Object

If one shifts one's attention from the desired object to the desiring subject, here too gender differences matter a great deal. In Gottfried's *Tris-*

*tan* women's desire for men is something quite different from men's desire for women. And yet, shifting from Butler's "genealogical efforts" concerning the "materiality of the body"[61] to Foucault's "genealogy... of the desiring subject,"[62] one thing does remain constant: like the morphology of bodies and the gender of clothes, the structures of desire are produced by historically contingent "regulatory schemas." Foucault (re)defined his project as "a historical and critical study" of "the forms within which individuals...*are obliged* to recognize themselves as...subjects of desire."[63] Just as "the matter of bodies [is] a kind of materialization governed by regulatory norms,"[64] so desire can only be recognized when it observes certain obligatory forms. Regulatory norms on the one hand, obligatory forms on the other: desires, like bodies and clothes, are only intelligible when they conform to the regulatory schemas of the culture that produces them.

Since I am concerned with the relation between morphology and desire, I will limit myself to those passages where desire is clearly a response to a body described in some detail and explicitly marked as desirable. I return therefore to the five passages listed earlier.

When the women of Mark's court observe Riwalin jousting, their desire is distant but direct: " 'Look,' they said, 'the youth is a fortunate man: how wonderfully everything he does suits him! How perfect his body is! How his legs, worthy of an emperor, move in and out together! How firmly his shield remains glued to its spot at all times! How the spear becomes his hand! How all his clothes look good on him! How he carries his head and hair! How gracious are all his movements! How excellent he is! Fortunate is the woman who will have lasting joy from him!' "[65] The women remain distant, observing Riwalin from a certain remove but not talking to him. Yet they are direct, showing no hesitation about expressing their admiration, praising various parts of his body and his performance as a knight, and imagining the pleasure that he might bring to some woman. But it will be brought to some unnamed other woman, not to themselves. The ladies' direct but distant stance corresponds nicely to their brisk, declarative language: they list Riwalin's excellences as a series of exclamations, linked by parallel syntax and anaphora.[66]

When a man desires a woman, things are quite different—as is evident in the scene in which Mark observes Isold through the window of the *Minnegrotte*. The passage goes on for sixty lines, three times as many as the ladies get to watch Riwalin, and includes the following: "Her chin, her mouth, her complexion, and her body were so completely delightful, so lovely, and so charming that she pleased Mark: he was overcome with the desire to kiss her....His eyes presented everything to him: he looked very intimately at how her throat and her shoulder, her arms and her hands shone beautifully out of her garments."[67] Mark takes advantage of the fact that Isold is asleep to regard her "very intimately," following the rays of the sun as they play on her face, looking at her chin, mouth, complexion, body; then he returns again to look at her throat and shoulders, her arms and hands. He is so taken by what he sees that he wants to kiss her. Where the women watching Riwalin take note of his good points quickly, one at a time, and then move on, Mark lingers, returning his gaze to things he has already seen, and fantasizes about approaching the body he desires.

The lingering, repetitive, fantasizing gaze engenders a correspondingly expansive rhetoric, one whose figures are the simile, the extended metaphor, and the insinuation. Gottfried begins with similes: "Isold's complexion and her radiance glowed, sweet and lovely as a rose of several colors.... Her mouth flamed and burned just like a glowing coal."[68] A few lines later he combines the rays of the sun with the radiance of Isold into an extended metaphor: "Just then two beauties were playing a game with each other, light and light were shining together. The sun and the sun had staged a joyous festival there to the glory of Isold."[69] The metaphor of Isold as the sun is one of Gottfried's great conceits, inciting him to rhetorical bravura on a number of occasions, not only in connection with Isold but also in connection with her mother and Brangaene. Although radiance can be an attribute of male beauty—we know that Tristan's "complexion was radiant,"[70] for instance—the metaphorical elaboration of radiance is peculiar to women.

Gottfried takes time not only to develop the metaphor of Isold as sun but also to play a game of insinuation. At the beginning of the passage, he pretends to be unable to imagine what exertion might have caused Isold to look flushed as she sleeps next to Tristan—only to remember after ten lines that she had been out of doors that morning and that she must have acquired her color then (17561–75). Before he thinks of this explanation, of course, a different one has already occurred to us.

To judge from these two cases, women's desire is different from men's desire. Where the subject of desire is a woman, she is distant but direct. The language of desire is quick, favoring lists and anaphora. Where the subject of desire is a man he lingers, returns to what has already been seen, and attempts to draw near. The language is elaborate, metaphoric, and insinuating.

Remarkably, this difference does not seem to depend on the gender of the subject but on that of the object, as one can see from the behavior of the narrator. When the narrator sketches the portrait of Tristan as he first appears at Mark's court, he adopts the same spatial and rhetorical stance as the women who watch Riwalin joust. Like them he observes and describes from a distance—in this case from a position outside of the diegetic world. And like the women's praise, the narrator's is structured as a list of excellences held together by parallel syntax and anaphora: "His lips were red as a rose, his complexion radiant, his eyes clear...his arms and his hands well formed and white."

When the narrator sketches the portrait of a woman, however, he adopts the spatial and rhetorical stance of Mark at the window of the *Minnegrotte*. When Isold is led ceremonially through the Irish court by her mother before leaving for Cornwall, she is once again offered up to the male gaze under circumstances over which she has little control. Most of the passage is devoted to the description of her clothes—a description in which, like Mark at the *Minnegrotte*, the narrator lingers, moving his eye back and forth across Isold's body and trying to get close. That the narrator lingers is obvious: the passage goes on for 135 lines. As he lingers, his description of Isold's robe repeatedly draws us through the fabric to her body, as was noted in the discussion of her clothing. Gottfried's description is just like the robe: it is "intimate with her," clinging to her body and trying "to keep close everywhere from top to bottom."

The delight in rhetorical elaboration that Gottfried displays when the object of desire is a woman is evident not only in the description of Isold's clothes but also, once again, in the elaborate metaphor of Isold as the sun. The passage opens when the queen mother, the dawn, "led her sun by the hand . . . the radiant maiden Isold,"[71] and concludes by noting that "the joy-bringing sun spread her radiance over all, gladening the people in the hall."[72] Insinuation also plays a large role, not only in suggesting Isold's body beneath her robe but also in the description of her cloak. While the thumb of her left hand clasps a string of pearls holding the cloak together at the top, "she had moved her right hand farther down below, as you well know, to the place where the cloak should be closed, and she brought it together in an elegant manner with two of her fingers: from there it fell further on its own, falling in folds all the way to the bottom, so that you could see this and that—I mean the fur [lining] and the outer covering."[73] Like the passage about Isold's exertions at the *Minnegrotte*, this one also deliberately incites our fantasy—to imagine the place, farther down, that we know so well and to guess what might be revealed by Isold's cloak as it falls to the floor—only to draw a cloak of less titillating information over whatever it was that we had thought of. Here, however, the imagination is incited even further, bringing us even closer to the object of desire. The viewer is invited to shape Isold's body, to form, at least in the imagination, "this and that," the place "farther down," and the way her "robe fell in folds around her feet, just as much as any of you might wish."[74] The viewer is invited to construct the body—just as he might wish.

Desire takes two forms in Gottfried's *Tristan*. When men are desired, the subject is distant but direct; desire is articulated in anaphoric lists. When women are desired, the subject lingers, returns to what has already been seen, and attempts to draw near; the language is elaborate, metaphoric, and insinuating. The women who observe Riwalin desire according to the first paradigm; Mark at the *Minnegrotte* desires according to the second. One might reasonably assume that the choice of paradigm is determined by the gender of the subject: women desire one way, men another. However, the behavior of the narrator shows this not to be the case. When the narrator describes the desirable Tristan he adopts the stance of the women who admire Riwalin, but when he describes the desirable Isold he adopts the stance of Mark at the *Minnegrotte*. If the narrator can, as circumstances require, assume the subject position of Mark or the ladies at Mark's court, then the choice of one paradigm of desire or the other cannot depend on the identity of the subject. It is the gender of the object that determines the structure of desire, whether this is felt by a character or represented by the narrator.

That Gottfried treats desire for women at greater length, with more complex figures and more subtle devices than he treats desire for men, thereby making it a good deal more interesting, surely reflects and reinforces the hegemony of men and of men's desire for women within the culture in which he wrote. That women are held before our eyes, objects of insinuation and voyeuristic display, surely reproduces the position of women as the primary objects of desire in the sexual-political system of that world. That the narrator and the women at Mark's court accommodate themselves to the subordination and distancing that defines the desire for men is hardly surprising: "individuals are obliged" to desire according to the "forms" their culture makes available. By showing that the forms of desire are determined not by the gender of the subject but by the position of the object in the gender-power relations of the larger society, Gottfried demonstrates that the forms of desire are not authentic manifestations of an individual identity but rather cultural paradigms by which patriarchal power reproduces itself.

Again, Gottfried was writing before heterosexuality, which is to say, before our modern understanding of sexuality. We tend to believe "that sexuality comes from within, that it is a feature of the individual,"[75] and that it plays a crucial role in determining who we are: sexuality is "a constitutive principle of the self."[76] Part of the "self" that sexuality constitutes is our sexual identity, "a personal essence defined . . . in specifically sexual terms."[77] Gottfried believes none of this. Although he is committed to exploring the effects of passion on the individual, he does not locate the origin of desire within the individual but outside, in the sight of a beautiful body or in the effects of a love potion. And although Gottfried differentiates kinds of desire, he does not distinguish between heterosexual desire for the other sex and homosexual desire for the same sex, "other" and "same" being defined in relation to the sex of the *subject*, but between desire for the man and desire for the woman, "man" and "woman" describing the gender of the *object*. Of course, in Gottfried's world desire is always for the other sex: Mark cannot look through the window of the Minnegrotte and desire Tristan.[78] But the nature of desire does not define the nature of the desiring subject, the "sexual identity" of the subject, in the way that heterosexual and homosexual desire are thought to. Freed from having to define the individual sexual identity, Gottfried's desire for the man and desire for the woman directly and unambiguously reinforce women's and men's positions in the gender hierarchy.

Some will point to the "sex" of Tristan and Isold and insist that, in spite of everything, desire in Gottfried's *Tristan* is "heterosexual." But I believe this is a mistake, even if one takes only the most minimal definition of heterosexual, "attraction to the opposite sex."[79] There are no opposite sexes in *Tristan*. There are no attractions defined simply on the basis of sex. There is no realm of the sexual, independent of gender and class. Even less do these desires conform to the broader meanings we usually attach to "heterosexual": a sexual identity, defined by the opposite sex of the desired object, that is "a constitutive principle of the self." If we use the modern terms "heterosexuality" and "homosexuality" to describe sexual relations in medieval texts, we only make it more difficult to recognize that it is precisely certain familiar aspects of what we call (hetero)sexuality that are *absent* from texts like *Tristan*. In order to trace the relations of sex, gender, and desire in medieval contexts we need to clear a space as free as possible from modern assumptions about these relations. Terms like "heterosexual" and "homosexual" clutter up such a space with modern meanings and make it even more difficult than it would otherwise be to see the medieval relations clearly.[80]

## Before Heterosexuality

There are two striking differences between the sexual organization of Gottfried's world and that of our own. First, sex difference is not visible in the body of the object. Second, sexual desire is not determined by the identity of the subject. These two differences, mediated and thus shaped by culturally specific relations of gender, combine to produce structures of desire quite different from those we might expect. The beautiful human body, gendered by clothing and other markers as masculine, elicits a masculinist cultural desire for the man: distant and admiring. The beautiful human body, gendered by clothing and other markers as feminine, elicits a masculinist cultural desire for the woman: insinuating and possessive. A woman will not experience desire for a body morphologically male but for a beautiful body, made masculine by its clothing, that can therefore be admired from a distance. A man will not experience desire for a body morphologically female but for a beautiful body, made feminine by its clothing, that can therefore be looked at, approached, and possessed. The sex of the body matters not because, readily visible, it sparks desire in the opposite sex by a kind of biologically inevitable combustion but because, merely known, it determines which of two culturally determined kinds of desire will be experienced by someone of the other sex who has been attracted to a beautiful body. Where we assume that a visible difference in the sexed object will attract a desire preformed by the sexual identity of the subject, Gottfried represents a world in which a visible difference in the gendered object elicits a desire preformed by the gender relations of the larger society.

On cannot say that bodies don't matter in Gottfried's *Tristan*, only that they don't matter in the ways we expect them to. In a world "before heterosexuality" the hegemonic desire for the other sex does not exercise its tyranny in the same way it does today—perhaps because there is no competition in sight, perhaps because the identity of the individual is not at stake. The desired body, not required to certify its legitimacy as a heterosexual object, need not proclaim its sex so loudly. Differential desire, not required to certify the heterosexual normalcy of the subject, need not be rooted within the body of that subject. Not pressed into service defending heterosexuality, Gottfried's bodies can be mobilized to uphold other interests—noble precedence or masculine prerogative. It's not that bodies don't matter in Gottfried's *Tristan*. It's that they don't matter heterosexually.

## Notes

1. In writing this essay I have benefited greatly from the comments of Peggy Mc-Cracken, whose thorough critique of an early draft helped me figure out what I really meant and forced me to explain myself more clearly, and of Carolyn Dinshaw, whose detailed critique of a later draft challenged me to rethink and reformulate various parts of the argument. I am very grateful for their generous help.

2. Judith Butler, *Bodies That Matter: On the Discursive Limits of "Sex"* (New York: Routledge, 1993), 14.

3. Radclyffe Hall, *The Well of Loneliness* (Garden City, N.Y.: Sun Dial, n.d.), 211.

4. Marjorie Garber, *Vested Interests: Cross-Dressing and Cultural Anxiety* (New York: Routledge, 1992), 136.

5. Caroline Walker Bynum, "The Body of Christ in the Later Middle Ages: A Reply to Leo Steinberg," in Caroline Walker Bynum, *Fragmentation and Redemption: Essays on Gender and the Human Body in Medieval Religion* (New York: Zone, 1991), 79–117, here 85. See also Karin Lützen, "*La mise en discours* and Silences in Research on the History of Sexuality," in *Conceiving Sexuality: Approaches to Sex Research in a Postmodern World*, ed. Richard G. Parker and John H. Gagnon (New York: Routledge, 1995), 19–31, here 27.

6. Parenthetical references in the text and in the notes refer to Gottfried von Straßburg, *Tristan und Isold*, ed. Friedrich Ranke, 15th ed. (Zurich: Weidmann, 1978), by line number.

7. "dar zuo was ime der lip getan, als ez diu Minne gebot" (3332–33).

8. "Minne envlammete den man mit der schœne ir libes" (17594–95).

9. John H. Gagnon and Richard G. Parker, "Conceiving Sexuality," in *Conceiving Sexuality*, ed. Parker and Gagnon, 3–15, here 12.

10. "wie gar sin lip ze wunsche stat! wie gant im so geliche in ein diu siniu keiserlichen bein!...wie zimet der schaft in siner hant!...wie stat sin houbet und sin har!...o wol si sæligez wip, der vröude an ime beliben sol!" (708–19).

11. "lanc, uf gewollen unde smal....[der roc] nam den valt unde den val under den vüezen....da hæte diu schœne in geslagen ir dumen von ir linken hant. die rehten hæte si gewant...da man den mantel sliezen sol, und sloz in höfschliche in ein mit ir vingere

zwein.... Si truoc uf ir houbete einen cirkel von golde.... dan was kein alse wise man, hæter der steine niht gesehen, daz er iemer hæte verjehen, daz da kein cirkel wære: so gelich und alse einbære was ir har dem golde" (10894–985).

12. "sin har [was]... an barte verwalken also harte, als ob er wilde wære" (4004–7).

13. "zir senften linden brusten twanc sin vil harte nahen" (14160–61).

14. "der junge âne bart" (Wolfram von Eschenbach, *Parzival*, in *Wolfram von Eschenbach*, ed. Karl Lachmann, 6th ed. [Berlin: de Gruyter, 1926], line 307,7).

15. Rudolf von Ems, *Der guote Gêrhart*, ed. John A. Asher, 2d ed., Altdeutsche Textbibliothek, 56 (Tübingen: Niemeyer, 1971), lines 1540–45.

16. *Der Schwabenspiegel oder schwäbisches Land- und Lehen-Rechtbuch*, ed. F[riedrich] L. A. von Lassberg (Tübingen: Fues, 1840; reprint, Aalen: Scientia, 1961), Landrecht §27.

17. For a more extended discussion of beards, see James A. Schultz, *The Knowledge of Childhood in the German Middle Ages, 1100–1350* (Philadelphia: University of Pennsylvania Press, 1995), 120–21, and the literature cited there.

18. According to the evidence collected in Anna Köhn, *Das weibliche Schönheitsideal in der ritterlichen Dichtung*, Form und Geist, 14 (Leipzig: Eichblatt, 1930), 28–34, 92–93.

19. Wolfram, *Parzival*, lines 258,24–259,4.

20. Konrad Fleck, *Flore und Blanscheflur*, ed. Emil Sommer, Bibliothek der gesammten deutschen National-Literatur, 12 (Quedlinburg: Basse, 1846), lines 6395–401, 6904–5; Heinrich von dem Türlin, *Diu Crône*, ed. Gottlob Heinrich Friedrich Scholl, Bibliothek des Litterarischen Vereins in Stuttgart, 27 (Stuttgart: Litterarischer Verein, 1852; reprint, Amsterdam: Rodopi, 1966), lines 8213–17. Wolfram mentions the development of Sigune's breasts as a sign that she is maturing: Wolfram von Eschenbach, *Titurel*, in *Wolfram von Eschenbach*, ed. Karl Lachmann, lines 39,2–3.

21. Joan Cadden, *Meanings of Sex Difference in the Middle Ages: Medicine, Science, and Culture* (Cambridge: Cambridge University Press, 1993), 180.

22. "mir wær noh liep, wærn die her dan: man ersæhe den man wol für daz wîp: sô gelîche was ir bêder lîp" (Wolfram von Eschenbach, *Willehalm*, in *Wolfram von Eschenbach*, ed. Karl Lachmann, lines 274,24–26).

23. "an libe und an gebare vollekomen unde rich. er was des libes edelich" (4032–34).

24. "er was an rehter herschaft aller keiser genoz" (4044–45).

25. "im solte billich unde wol ein riche dienen" (10020–21).

26. "wie wol ich wiste al dise vart, sit ich in merkende wart, sit ich an ime lip unde gabar und sin dinc allez also gar besunder in min herze las, daz er gebürte ein herre was!" (10127–32).

27. Hugo Bekker, *Gottfried von Strassburg's* Tristan: *Journey through the Realm of Eros* (Columbia, S.C.: Camden House, 1987), 147; Bodo Mergell, *Tristan und Isolde: Ursprung und Entwicklung der Tristansage des Mittelalters* (Mainz: Kirchheim, 1949), 165; Gottfried Weber, *Gottfrieds von Strassburg Tristan und die Krise des hochmittelalterlichen Weltbildes um 1200* (Stuttgart: Metzler, 1953), 1:52, 58–59.

28. For gender and modern men's underwear, see Daniel Harris, "The Current Crisis in Men's Lingerie: Notes on the Belated Commercialization of a Noncommercial Product," *Salmagundi* 199 (Fall 1993): 130–39. For gender and medieval underwear, see E. Jane Burns, "Ladies Don't Wear *Braies*: Underwear and Outerwear in the French *Prose Lancelot*," in *The Lancelot-Grail Cycle: Texts and Transformations*, ed. William W. Kibler (Austin: University of Texas Press, 1994), 152–74.

29. Jonathan Ned Katz, *The Invention of Heterosexuality* (New York: Dutton, 1995), 52.

30. Ibid., 83–112.

31. Robert T. Michael, John H. Gagnon, Edward O. Laumann, and Gina Kolata, *Sex in America: A Definitive Survey* (Boston: Little, Brown, 1994), 31.

32. David M. Halperin, *One Hundred Years of Homosexuality: And Other Essays on Greek Love* (New York: Routledge, 1990), 29–30.

33. Thomas Aquinas, *Summa theologica*, trans. Fathers of the English Dominican Province, 3 vols. (New York: Benzinger, 1974), 2d part of the 2d part, question 154, articles 1, 12.

34. Arnold Davidson, "Sex and the Emergence of Sexuality," *Critical Inquiry* 14 (1987): 16–48, here 37.

35. Butler, *Bodies That Matter*, 17.

36. Roland Barthes, *The Fashion System*, trans. Matthew Ward and Richard Howard (New York: Hill and Wang, 1983), 258.

37. "Clothing was the fundamental medium to distinguish the status and privilege of aristocratic society from all other groups" (John W. Baldwin, *The Language of Sex: Five Voices from Northern France around 1200* [Chicago: University of Chicago Press, 1994], 100). See also Elke Brüggen, *Kleidung und Mode in der höfischen Epik des 12. und 13. Jahrhunderts* (Heidelberg: Winter, 1989), 113; Gabriele Raudszus, *Die Zeichensprache der Kleidung: Untersuchungen zur Symbolik des Gewandes in der deutschen Epik des Mittelalters*, ORDO, Studien zur Literatur und Gesellschaft des Mittelalters und der frühen Neuzeit, 1 (Hildesheim: Olms, 1985), 156.

38. Brüggen, *Kleidung*, 102.

39. Ibid., 104, 114.

40. "sine vüeze und siniu bein, dar an sin schoene almeistic schein, diu stuonden so ze prise wol, als manz an manne prisen sol" (3341–44).

41. Brüggen, *Kleidung*, 42, 72.

42. "si truoc von brunem samit an roc unde mantel, in dem snite von Franze" (10900–902).

43. Brüggen, *Kleidung*, 100 n. 299.

44. "sin gewant...was mit grozer höfscheit nach sinem libe gesniten" (3345–47). See also 2542. For a discussion of the fit of Tristan's clothes, see Raudszus, *Zeichensprache*, 149.

45. "der roc [was]...da engegene, da die siten sinkent uf ir liten, gefranzet unde genget, nahe an ir lip getwenget mit einem borten, der lac wol, da der borte ligen sol. der roc der was ir heinlich, er tet sich nahen zuo der lich: ern truoc an keiner stat hin dan, er suohte allenthalben an al von obene hin ze tal" (10902–13).

46. Brüggen considers this passage in some detail, although only as a matter of fashion and courtly behavior, which is consistent with her claim that writers before 1250 were concerned only with the description of the color, shape, and material of clothing and not with the revelation of the feminine body beneath (*Kleidung*, 41–44, 76). It seems to me that she underestimates the effect of insinuation, which will be treated in more detail below.

47. "diu von dem allerbesten snite" (10762).

48. "si gedahten...'zeware, dirre man der ist ein menlich creature; sin wat und sin figiure si schepfent wol an ime den man: si zement so wol ein ander an'" (10853–59).

49. "sin geschepfede und sin wat die gehullen wunnecliche in ein: si bildeten under in zwein einen ritterlichen man" (11098–11101).

50. While Tristan's body harmonizes with his civilian clothing, he is always *superior* to his armor, no matter how spectacular it is. At his knightly investiture Tristan is armed in the same way *externally* as those who will be knighted with him, but *inside* he is said to be much better (4975–5011). The armor that Tristan wears into the battle with Morold is splendid, but the workman who created what is inside the armor had done an even better job (6622–58). See also 6570–77. As a courtier, Tristan's noble body and his fashionable clothing correspond with one another and together turn him into a man. As a knight, Tristan exceeds the splendid armor that he is wearing.

51. Barthes, *The Fashion System*, 260.

52. Jochens notes that in Old Norse texts, as in MHG, one's clothes are "important markers of gender" (9), but that these clothes draw attention to "the most apparent sexual distinctions between men's and women's bodies" (penis, breasts) (21), which is not the case in *Tristan* (Jenny Jochens, "Before the Male Gaze: The Absence of the Female Body in Old Norse," in *Sex in the Middle Ages: A Book of Essays*, ed. Joyce E. Salisbury [New York: Garland, 1991], 3–29).

53. "ir genuoge sprachen daz: 'wa geschuof ie got figiure baz ze ritterlichem rehte?'"

(11203–5).

54. "gevedere schachblicke die vlugen da snedicke schachende dar unde dan" (10957–59).

55. For the role of clothing in securing masculine authority, see Dyan Elliott, "Dress as Mediator between Inner and Outer Self: The Pious Matron of the High and Later Middle Ages," *Mediaeval Studies* 53 (1991): 279–308.

56. This distinction parallels the one Jane Burns discovers in Old French texts between the armor by which a knight is "gendered masculine" and the exposed skin that defines femininity. Burns finds that this "highly polarized" system is actually much "more fluid" than it seems: when knights take off their armor to don the same courtly garments worn by women, perhaps even revealing exposed flesh, they thereby "shift into the hybrid status of lady/knight" (see chapter 6 in this volume). Burns calls this a "'feminization,'" an "erasing [of] sexual distinctions between armor and skin." This, it seems to me, would be true only if skin and courtly dress were *not*-masculine in the same way that armor is *not*-feminine. Since gender is constructed not only by prescription but also by proscription—it is "indissociable from relations of discipline, regulation, punishment" (Butler, *Bodies That Matter*, 232)—one must consider what is prohibited as carefully as what is recommended. But the unisex courtly chemise is not off limits for men. Burns herself notes that when knights don this garment they suffer "no loss of status," nor can I see anything in the texts to indicate that they are considered less masculine for being desirable. Where is the feminization? The economy of attribution and prohibition in the courtly romances suggests to me that vestimentary masculinity is defined not by armor itself but by the ability to move freely between armor, courtly dress, and exposed skin (knighthood, courtliness, desirability), while femininity is restricted to the last two, courtly dress and skin. Such a definition expresses the asymmetry of gender but is able to accommodate the fact that no one in the texts considers Lancelot and Tristan any less masculine when they exchange their battle gear for civilian dress. In the case of *Tristan*, at least, this may be because courtly clothes for men and women, although they differ little in form, nevertheless differ in function, providing men with something rather like armor while offering women something more like exposure. Nor are Lancelot or Tristan considered any less masculine when they reveal their bare skin. This may be because, as I have argued, the desirable body itself (including its skin) is neither masculine nor feminine.

57. Monique Wittig, "The Mark of Gender," in Monique Wittig, *The Straight Mind and Other Essays* (Boston: Beacon, 1992), 76–89.

58. Carroll Smith-Rosenberg, "The Female World of Love and Ritual: Relations between Women in Nineteenth-Century America," *Signs* 1 (1975): 1–29.

59. George Chauncey, "From Sexual Inversion to Homosexuality: Medicine and the Changing Conceptualization of Female Deviance," *Salmagundi* 58–59 (Fall 1982–Winter 1983): 114–46.

60. This is the case in much of Latin America. See Tomás Almaguer, "Chicano Men: A Cartography of Homosexual Identity and Behavior," *differences* 3, no. 2 (1991): 75–100, here 76–86.

61. Butler, *Bodies That Matter*, 17.

62. Michel Foucault, *The Use of Pleasure*, vol. 2 of *The History of Sexuality*, trans. Robert Hurley (New York: Pantheon, 1985), 5.

63. Ibid., 4–5, emphasis added.

64. Butler, *Bodies That Matter*, 16.

65. "'seht' sprachen si 'der jungelinc der ist ein sæliger man: wie sælecliche stet im an allez daz, daz er begat! wie gar sin lip ze wunsche stat! wie gant im so geliche in ein diu siniu keiserlichen bein! wie rehte sin schilt zaller zit an siner stat gelimet lit! wie zimet der schaft in siner hant! wie wol stat allez sin gewant! wie stat sin houbet und sin har! wie süeze ist aller sin gebar! wie sælecliche stat sin lip! o wol si sæligez wip, der vröude an ime beliben sol!'" (704–19).

66. Poag argues that the repetition of words related to *sælde* "implies that there is an

underlying connection between sexuality and felicity (at least for these female representatives of Tintagel)" (James F. Poag, "The Onset of Love: The Problem of the Religious Dimension in Gottfried von Straßburg's *Tristan*," in *Semper idem et novus: Festschrift for Frank Banta*, ed. Francis G. Gentry, Göppinger Arbeiten zur Gemanistik, 481 [Göppingen: Kümmerle, 1988], 285–305, here 290).

67. "ir kinne, ir munt, ir varwe, ir lich daz was so rehte wunneclich, so lieplich und so muotsam, daz ir Marken gezam: in gelangete unde geluste, daz er si gerne kuste.... sin ouge stuont im allez dar: er nam vil innecliche war, wie schone ir uz der wæte schein ir kele unde ir brustbein, ir arme unde ir hende" (17587–603). While at first glance it might seem that Mark, in looking at Isold's *brustbein*, is looking at a peculiarly female body part (Hatto translates the word as "breast"), it becomes apparant at line 18205 that Tristan also has one.

68. "ir varwe unde ir schin [luhte] als suoze und alse lose als ein gemischet rose.... ir munt der viurete und bran reht alse ein glüejender kol" (17564–69).

69. "zwo schœne hæten an der stunt ein spil gemachet under in zwein: da schein lieht unde lieht in ein. Diu sunne und diu sunne die hæten eine wunne und eine hohzit dar geleit Isote zeiner sælekeit" (17580–86).

70. "sin varwe lieht" (3335).

71. "vuorte ir sunnen an ir hant... die liehten maget Isote" (10887–89).

72. "diu wunnebernde sunne si breite ir schin über al, si erröute liute unde sal" (11006–8).

73. "die rehten hæte si gewant hin nider baz, ir wizzet wol, da man den mantel sliezen sol, und sloz in höfschliche in ein mit ir vingere zwein: vürbaz da viel er selbe wider und nam den valt al zende nider, daz man diz unde daz da sach, ich meine vederen unde dach" (10940–48).

74. "er nam den valt unde den val under den vüezen alse vil, als iuwer iegelicher wil" (10914–16). Brüggen treats this passage at length, but sees nothing in it besides clothing and courtly bearing (*Kleidung*, 41–44). Although Raudszus has less to say, she at least recognizes that this is a "sehr suggestive Beschreibung" (*Zeichensprache der Kleidung*, 155). Baldwin sees that Gottfried speaks "coyly" — although everything else he says about the passage is wrong (*The Language of Sex*, 104). According to Baldwin, "Iseut" holds the mantle together "suggestively" by placing her hand in the string of pearls "lest the opening reveal 'this and that.'" The heroine's name is not Iseut but Isold; the mantle is not held together by her hand but by the string of pearls; there is nothing suggestive about the way she places her hand there; it is *another* hand that holds the mantle closed; it is not closed *lest* something be revealed but falls in a way *so that* "this and that" is revealed. When Baldwin talks about other passages in Gottfried he is no more accurate: Tristan is not "wounded and unconscious" when Isold examines him, and he is not "in the bath" (102).

75. Michael et al. *Sex in America*, 16.

76. Halperin, *One Hundred Years*, 24.

77. Ibid., 25.

78. Krohn's reading of *Tristan*, according to which Mark's homosexual desire for Tristan is meant to defame him, has been rightly criticized by Jaeger: Rüdiger Krohn, "Erotik und Tabu in Gottfrieds 'Tristan': König Marke," in *Stauferzeit: Geschichte, Literatur, Kunst*, ed. Rüdiger Krohn, Bernd Thum, and Peter Wapnewski, Karlsruher Kulturwissenschaftliche Arbeiten, 1 (Stuttgart: Klett-Cotta, 1979), 362–76; C. Stephen Jaeger, "Mark and Tristan: The Love of Medieval Kings and Their Courts," in *in hôhem prîse: A Festschrift in Honor of Ernst S. Dick*, ed. Winder McConnell, Göppinger Arbeiten zur Germanistik, 480 (Göppingen: Kümmerle, 1989), 183–97.

79. William Morris, ed., *The American Heritage Dictionary of the English Language* (Boston: Houghton Mifflin, 1976), S.V. "heterosexual."

80. Thus it is not surprising that medievalists who use these terms, even those who write thoughtfully about the issues involved, end up discovering that the Middle Ages are more or less like the present. Simon Gaunt, who argues for the use of "homosexuality,"

discovers that "homophobia" in *Lanval* plays the same role "that Eve Kosofsky Sedgwick attributes to it in modern culture" ("Straight Minds/'Queer' Wishes in Old French Hagiography: *La Vie de Sainte Euphrosine*," *GLQ: A Journal of Lesbian and Gay Studies* 1 [1995]: 439–57, here 441–42). Carolyn Dinshaw, who argues for the use of "heterosexuality," finds that *Sir Gawain and the Green Knight* "theorizes heterosexuality in a way that accords with the theoretical articulations of Foucault and, particularly, Butler" ("A Kiss Is Just a Kiss: Heterosexuality and Its Consolations in *Sir Gawain and the Green Knight*," *diacritics* 24, nos. 2–3 [1994]: 205–26, here 214). For Dinshaw heterosexuality is a very capacious term, embracing not only marriage, procreation, gender, and the body but also all the binaries in the prologue to the *Canterbury Tales* — April and March, summer and winter, earth and sky, knowing and unknowing, public and private, and a good deal more ("Chaucer's Queer Touches/A Queer Touches Chaucer," *Exemplaria* 7 [1995]: 75–92, here 80–83). Defined in such generous terms, it is hard to see how heterosexuality could be anything *but* "invisible, cosmic and inevitable" (82). To be sure, Dinshaw insists that modern terms "need historical particularizing" ("A Kiss," 206). But while her analysis is rich in particulars from the texts under discussion, the historical particulars of "heterosexuality" are effaced. When *Cleanness* is found to allow sex for pleasure rather than for procreation, Dinshaw concludes: "Heterosexuality is thus subtly reconfigured here; at the same time, crucial structuring principles stay traditional" (217–18). What is arguably one of the most profound realignments in the construction of European sexuality (procreation to pleasure) is dismissed as a subtle reconfiguration, while the timeless principles of heterosexuality are reaffirmed. What I find missing is the middle ground, the space between the idiosyncrasies of a particular text and the inevitability of male-female relations. It is the space in which one might describe a distinctive historical structure of male-female relations in the context of which the details of a particular text will have been meaningful. If the history of sexuality is to be something more than the collection of idiosyncrasies or the affirmation of universal truths, then we must find a way of generalizing the former somewhere short of the latter.

CHAPTER 6

❖

# Refashioning Courtly Love:
## Lancelot as Ladies' Man or Lady/Man?

### E. Jane Burns

To introduce the topic of sexuality and clothing in Old French romance, I would like to offer an anecdote from the ceremony of papal investiture as it had evolved by the end of the fifteenth century. During the inaugural public procession, known as the *possesso*, the newly elected pope paraded from the Vatican to the Lateran palace, where his maleness was allegedly challenged in a series of demeaning ceremonies. As Richard Ingersoll has compellingly described these events, the pope, "while being invested with the insignia of his temporal authority—the keys to the Papal States, the *ferula*, or shepherd's crook, of the bishop of Rome, and a purse containing twelve precious stones, musk and seven seals (referring to the *Book of the Apocalypse*)—...sat on the *sedes stercoraria*," a "throne of shit," named after a line in Psalm 112 that is recited during the ceremony: "A pauper has been raised out of the dust and dung to sit with princes and reign in glory."[1] After first having made an awkward detour en route to the Lateran in order to avoid the spot where his infamous female predecessor, Pope Joan, was alleged to have given birth and thereby revealed the scandalous deception that marked her own investiture in the ninth century, the pontiff in the fifteenth century was purportedly "seated on an ancient birthing throne with a hole in the seat and...his genitals were ceremoniously examined as a guarantee that Pope Joan's dishonourable deceit would not be repeated." Ingersoll concludes, "The humiliating implications were that the celibate berobed spiritual leader could be mistaken for a member of the other, powerless gender."[2]

The *possesso*, named probably because of its association with the Pope's "taking possession" of the Church as bishop of Rome, enacts a triumphal display of social hierarchy that presumes gender identity to be biological, natural, and given. Whereas social status is understood in this paradigm as changeable and negotiable within gender-specific limits—the male pauper can become vested with the insignia and authority of a reigning prince—gender identity remains a strictly either/or proposition, attested by what is taken to be an unproblematic anatomical difference in genitalia. To the extent that the power vested in the pope's regalia is considered to be sex-linked—papal authority can only be conferred upon a man—the pontiff's vestments are not the crucial indicator of his ascension from the dirt of poverty to the regal throne of royalty. In fact the odd ritual of the *possesso* is designed precisely to guard against the embarrassing hoax of Pope Joan in which the papal robes actually obscured the presumed difference of a naturally sexed body.

## The Courtly Dress Code: How Clothes Make the Woman a Man—or Do They?

A very different paradigm for determining sexual difference and social status governs the courtly culture of twelfth- and thirteenth-century France, exemplified in particular by the complex imbrication of feudal homage and courtly love service. The ideological complexity of courtly homage was brought into relief most clearly a number of years ago in a scholarly dispute over how to decipher the sex of two figures appearing on the seal of a southern French nobleman, Simon de Mondragon.[3] The somewhat maverick historian of courtly love, John Benton, charged that the celebrated historian of feudal society, Marc Bloch, had crucially misidentified the two figures that the seal represents. Where Marc Bloch saw a scene of love service—an armored knight kneeling in supplication to his revered courtly lady—Benton saw an image of feudal homage and investiture: a knight kneeling in reverence before his feudal lord. The key to Bloch's putative misidentification, according to Benton, lay in the clothing—literally the dress—worn by the standing figure on the seal. In the absence of facial hair, armor, or any other distinguishing features of masculinity, Bloch assumed, we are told, that the figure wearing a long robe was a woman. He thus dubbed the image "the lover's homage."[4]

Benton reminds us, however, that civilian dress for aristocratic men in the twelfth and thirteenth centuries was in fact the kind of gown pictured on the seal, a unisex garment that could have been worn by either men or women.[5] The identity of the kneeling knight remains uncontested by both historians, who seem to presume that as long as a courtly figure is dressed in armor, whether in a visual image or in a literary text, one can readily recognize and identify him as a proper knight. But as soon as this male figure is "disarmed" (*desarme*, in Old French) and divested of that key marker of masculinity, his gender comes into question: he looks in fact more like an aristocratic woman.

In this instance, a determination of sexual difference could not be made on the basis of biology or anatomy for a number of reasons. Unlike the witnesses to papal investiture in the late Middle Ages, we cannot lift the hem of the standing figure on Simon de Mondragon's seal and peer beneath. Neither can we peel the clothing off fictional characters in courtly romance to see whether their outer garments match the imagined body they conceal. More important, even if we could establish what some might term the "natural sex" of romance characters, such verification would provide no sure clues to the system of gendered identity in the courtly world. The ideologies of gender and social status promulgated in French courtly texts of the twelfth and thirteenth centuries pointedly discourage any such line of inquiry on the part of medieval and modern audiences alike.[6]

Rather, the complex mechanisms of service and subservience that characterize French courtly society, as depicted in medieval literary texts, offer a richly fluid system of social interaction between women and men. The very position of the courtly lady, like that of her literary precursor in the Provençal *domna* of southern French lyric poetry, makes of her a third or hybrid gender, as Sarah Kay has cogently explained.[7] This lady is a woman who remains sexually female while possessing the social status of an aristocratic man: "From the poetry of Guilhem de Peitieu onwards, imagery derived from feudalism makes the *domna* the lover's lord and credits her with masculine powers such as making war, appearing in court and granting territories."[8] The *domna* of the southern tradition, so often emblematized by a masculine form of address (*midons*, my lord), is by definition a woman clothed in the social robes of a man. But unlike the *possesso*'s characterization of Pope Joan's concealed sex, Provençal lyric represents the feudal *domna* as having a constructed gender that derives more specifically from the social status imputed to it. So, too, the courtly lady of northern French romance is of "mixed" gender and status. Nominally vested with the authority of a feudal lord, as she receives putative homage from the knight in her service, this fictive woman occupies a cultural position balanced precariously between that of lady and lord: she must be a woman to receive the amorous advances of her heterosexual suitor, but she plays the seemingly empowered lord to his supposedly subservient vassal.[9] At the very core of courtly culture, then, cross-gendered performances are the norm, since social status, not anatomical sex, actively conditions gender identity.[10]

Whereas both Benton and Bloch seem compelled to choose one of two fixed gender norms, male or female, in identifying the figures on Simon de Mondragon's seal (thus following a logic similar to the fifteenth-century onlookers who wished to certify that the pope was male, not female), the very ambiguity of the visual icon they interpret resists such a reliance on a fixed, natural, or biological body. Indeed, in the courtly scenario, it seems that clothing supersedes anatomy as the prime indicator of gender identity. The body constructed by that clothing functions as a political and cultural object, resembling the "social body" described by Elizabeth Grosz: a body that undermines rather than underwrites the belief that sexual difference is fixed and primary.[11] The "social body" is the "political, social, and cultural object par excellence, not a product of a raw, passive nature that is civilized, overlaid, polished by culture. The body is a cultural interweaving *and* a production of nature."[12] Rather than having the status of some matter or ground on which cultural constructions are built, the courtly body can be understood in this light as a set of clothes that make, mark, delimit, and define the body presumed to lie beneath. In fact there is no body in any foundational sense prior to the garments placed upon it. As Judith Butler has explained for bodies more generally, "the mimetic or representational status of language, which claims that signs follow bodies as their necessary mirrors, is not mimetic at all. On the contrary, it is productive, constitutive, one might even argue *performative,* in as much as this signifying act delimits and contours the body that it then claims to find prior to any and all signification."[13]

Taking the courtly body as a clothed, cultural product, we can begin to see how the image on Simon de Mondragon's seal indicates many more possible gender identities than the two signaled by Bloch and Benton. In addition to reading this representation of courtly exchange as a knight kneeling to his lord or a knight kneeling to a lady who is playing the lord in the game of love service, Old French literature provides a number of other options that one might use to assess the seal's image. Foremost among them is the description of the love service between two companions at arms, Lancelot and Galehaut, in the thirteenth-century *Prose Lancelot.* When Galehaut takes Lancelot as his lord in love, saying that he is given over "body and soul" (8:483) to this man whom he loves more than any other man can (8:81), we find him playing the helpless and lovesick *fin amant* to Lancelot's more unforgiving and distant "ladylove."[14] In terms of the iconography on Simon de Mondragon's seal, this relationship would yield a knight doing service to another knight who is also, culturally speaking, a lady miming the role of a lord.[15] And what about the figure kneeling in armor? This sartorial marker of medieval maleness effectively occludes any clear determination of anatomical difference. As literary texts from the *Tournoiement as dames* to the *Roman de Fauvel* suggest,[16] the very fact that armor so thoroughly hides the body assumed to be protected beneath it makes this specifically "male" medieval costume the perfect mode of cross-dressing for women wishing to switch genders in the social sphere.

The social hierarchy at work in both pictorial and literary representations of courtly culture in twelfth- and thirteenth-century France, then, can be said to draw its gender boundaries socially such that "the dominant notions of gender depend not upon the supposedly manifest difference of the genitals but upon the precarious differentiation of the 'same,'" as Peter Stallybrass has argued for certain texts of the English Renaissance.[17] Looking to medical discourses of medieval and Renaissance Europe, he finds that "the body" in these later texts "is itself shaped and imagined through discursive categories which problematize inside and outside, male and female. . . . Gender was manifestly a production in which boundaries were produced and transformed rather than biologically given."[18] But what are the implications of this kind of gender fluidity for the normative sexuality promulgated in Old French romance and especially for the presumed heterosexuality of courtly love? How can heterosexual lovers come together in the adulterous liaisons that we have understood to be fundamental to courtly coupling if their bodies are not clearly sexed as male and female? What are the paradigms governing sexuality in Old French romance, and how do they interact with the gender fluidity that informs courtly love service?[19]

In many ways, courtly narratives play out a crucial tension, current in a number of medieval discourses, between heteronormative sex-based identities and a range of less rigidly conceived gender identities. Joan Cadden's recent study offers abundant evidence that medieval scientific texts, which expressed a profound and compelling discomfort with "displaced" gender identities and attempted to impose a two-term system of gender difference, also acknowledged the existence of middle terms such as hermaphrodites, eunuchs, women dressing as men, and homosexuals. In so doing, these early medical texts outlined a system based on degrees of sexual difference that posed a significant challenge to any strict either/or categorization of the sexes.[20] Roberta Krueger has shown how a number of didactic treatises and courtesy manuals that appear in northern France in the thirteenth century also attest to an uncertainty about the fixity of sex roles, even as their moralizing authors attempt concertedly to enforce traditional categories of gender.[21] Susan Crane has argued that "despite the dominance of a hierarchized conception of gender difference [in medieval romance narratives from the English and French traditions], romance also represents gender contrarily as unstable, open to question, and in danger of collapse."[22]

I have argued elsewhere that the quintessential courtly couple, Lancelot and Guenevere, function in the *Prose Lancelot* as loci of displacement, substitution, and slippage between the categories of male and female, thereby calling into question the presumed natural alignment of sex and gender in courtly romance.[23] I would like to broaden that investigation here, surveying evidence from the *Prose Lancelot* and its literary predecessor, *Le Chevalier de la charrete,* to examine more specifically how the varied gender identities of this courtly pair are vested in the clothing they wear.[24] Indeed, for Lancelot and Guenevere the boundaries of the properly socialized body are drawn less through clearly sexed body parts than through garments that outline more ambiguous body shapes. This essay asks, then, how clothes make the "man" (whether he is a knight, a lord, or a lady) and the "woman" (whatever her ascribed social and sexual status) in court culture. It explores how clothing constructs a range of gender and social identities for the courtly couple, not in terms of immutable sex differences but as spacings on a continuum[25] that can produce, at different moments, "different densities of sexed being."[26] I want to demonstrate, in brief, that even though the ideology of courtly love seeks to regulate sexual practice through compulsory heterosexuality by dressing bodies in gender-specific clothing, that same clothing often produces gender identities that fall beyond the sex-based binary terms of "male" and "female."

## The Church's Dress Code:
## How to Keep Men From Becoming Women

From the twelfth century on, churchmen in France sought to regulate dress as a means of constructing and enforcing rigid boundaries of gender identity for knights, courtiers, and clerics.[27] Saint Bernard, well known for having railed against the luxurious extravagances of Abbot Suger's artifacts at Saint Denis, also launched a pointed attack on the sartorial excesses of what he termed "old" or secular knights in comparison with the celestial knighthood he sought to promote. In 1130, his *In Praise of the New Knighthood* critiques the chivalric tendency "to devote such expense in labor and fighting for no purpose except death and sin" by attacking the costly and unnecessary accoutrements of war:

"You deck your horses with silk, and plume your armor with all manner of rags. You paint your saddles and shields with emblems. You adorn your bits and spurs with gold and silver and precious stones. And in all this glory you gallop in shameful frenzy and mindless stupidity to your own death!"[28] And further, "Why... do you blind yourselves with effeminate locks of hair, and trip yourselves up in long and flowing tunics with cumbersome sleeves in which you bury your tender, delicate hands?"[29] The problem with these excesses, as Bernard makes clear, is not only wasteful expense but the blurring of gender categories that they suggest: "Are these the trappings of a warrior, or are they not rather the *trinkets of a woman*?" (my emphasis here and following).[30]

Around 1140, the Norman monk Oderic Vitalis blamed the general degeneration of aristocratic manners among the Norman upper classes on the influence of womanish effeminacy:

Our wanton youth is sunk in effeminacy, and courtiers, fawning, seek the favours of women with every kind of lewdness. They add excrescences like serpents' tails to the tips of their toes where the body ends, and gaze with admiration on these scorpion-like shapes. They sweep the dusty ground with the unnecessary trains of their robes and mantles; their long, wide sleeves cover their hands whatever they do; impeded by these frivolities they are almost incapable of walking quickly or doing any kind of useful work. They shave the front part of their head, like thieves, and let their hair grow very long at the back, *like harlots.*[31]

He compares these contemporary degenerates to their predecessors at the court of William Rufus, "effeminates" who "parted their hair from the crown of the head to the forehead, grew long and luxurious locks *like women*, and loved to deck themselves in long, over-tight shirts and tunics."[32] Even these "tight shirts" appear to depart somehow from the contours of the "naturally" sexed male body to construct an anatomy seen as foreign and other, that is: female. Earlier, Saint Anselm's biographer, Eadmer (d. 1124), complains that from roughly 1096, "almost all young men at court wore long hair *in the manner of girls*; they combed it thoroughly each day and then walked around lasciviously, taking small steps."[33] Anselm himself is said to have preached against the effeminancy of long hair on Ash Wednesday around 1096 and succeeded in cutting short the hair of men in the congregation who repented this excess.[34] Whereas these efforts were made in the name of stemming moral decay, it is significant that they equate moral degeneracy specifically with a collapse of gender boundaries that must be reinstated to preserve the social order.

When the prior of Vigeois (1184) denounces the excesses of checkered and speckled robes and full, floor-length mantles, he critiques them in particular for having been contaminated by a feature belonging to the opposite sex, "long trains *like those worn by women*."[35] Clerics, too, came under attack and were charged, among other vices, with taking even greater care in their appearance than women: "You will see them in public with hair *as curly as women's*, clean shaven, their skin softened by cosmetics, their head uncovered and shoulders bare, with arms waving, wearing gloves, lightly shod, their robe split to the hipline, and to ensure that no part of their outfit falls out of balance, you will see them constantly checking their mirror."[36]

The danger posed by such transgressions of moral boundaries goes much further than the question of self-indulgence or excessive spending. The equally threatening danger, voiced indirectly in the ecclesiastical pleas for curbing luxury garments among knights, noblemen, and clerics alike, is the collapse of what is presumed to be the God-given sexual difference between women and men. William of Malmesbury makes the case overtly when describing "one of these long-haired men who, *forgetting their natural sex*, like to transform themselves by taking on the appearance of a woman."[37] Knights who wear "trinkets," young men with long hair and trailing gowns, and clerics with soft skin and bare shoulders risk looking, in an echo of the ambiguous figure on Simon de Mondragon's seal, more like women than men. And yet, that ambiguously defined charge of "effeminacy," so often leveled by medieval churchmen against those who, through cross-dressing, were seen to deny their biological sex, finds no ready equivalent in the depiction of romance heroes. However blatantly Arthurian knights may cross the gender line into the socially defined domain of femininity, their behavior is not measured against an anatomical standard. In the earliest tales of courtly coupling, "natural sex" seems not to be at issue.

117

## Armor and Skin: The Status Quo of Sexual Difference

If courtly ideology, as it appears in tales featuring Lancelot and Guenevere, typically constructs the elite social body in two discrete and easily recognizable categories—male and female—it locates that sexual difference for men, in particular, in distinctive dress and clothing. Indeed, the properly socialized body in Arthurian romance results from encasing the male anatomy so fully in armor that no skin shows. Knights are by definition "totes armez," as is Méléagant, whose arrival in the opening scene of the *Chevalier de la charrete* establishes the standard of chivalric dress that persists throughout this romance and continues in the thirteenth-century *Prose Lancelot*: "A tant es voz un chevalier / qui vint a cort molt acesmez, / *de totes ses armes armez* / Li chevaliers a tel conroi / s'an vint jusque devant le roi" (Then a knight arrived at court well attired, in full armor, and thus equipped he approached the king).[38] The first time we see Lancelot in the *Charrete*, although unhorsed and disoriented, he is nonetheless a "chevalier," "*tot armé*, li hiaume lacié / l'escu au col, l'espee ceinte" (fully armed, helmet laced up, shield around his neck and sword belted on, lines 317–18). In a later battle with Lancelot, Méléagant remains "toz armez" (line 3538), his body parts fully contained within an armored surface: "Molt estoit genz et bien aperz / Melïaganz, et bien tailliez, / de braz, de janbes, / et de piez, / et li hiaumes et li escuz / qui li estoit au col panduz / trop bien et bel li avenoient" (Méléagant was noble and fit with well-formed arms, legs, and feet. His helmet and the shield hanging from his neck suited him perfectly, lines 3540–44).[39] The knightly body in this scenario is deemed comely and attractive to the extent that it is controlled and constrained (*tailliez*); limbs and head, trunk, hands, and feet remain invisible to the eye, which reads only the armored casement surrounding the flesh.[40]

Conversely, visible flesh not only invites wounding but marks a knight's formal defeat. Thus does Lancelot end his battle with the *orgueilleux* in the *Charrete* by removing the opponent's helmet to expose his head: "si li fet le hiaume voler / del chief, et cheoir la vantaille; / tant le painne, et tant le travaille / que a merci venir l'estuet" (He flung the helmet off his [opponent's] head, causing the visor to close, and tormented him and made him suffer until he was forced to surrender, lines 2740–43). The final battle of the *Charrete* shows Lancelot defeating Méléagant by first exposing his head to view: "Lanceloz vient, si li deslace / le hiaume, et la teste li tranche" (Lancelot approaches, unlaces his [Méléagant's] helmet and decapitates him, lines 7086–87). Typically, knights in the *Prose Lancelot* are considered "desarmé" and dangerously close to death once their helmet is gone: "et cil a poor qui a la teste *desarmee* " (The knight, whose head was uncovered, feared for his life, 1:143).[41] Unprotected flesh connotes chivalric shame, as Lancelot explains on one occasion: "Ce seroit trop grant honte, si je m'en aloie *desarmés* " (It would be an intolerable shame for me to go without armor, 2:306). Indeed when we encounter this knight relieved of his armor and most of his weapons, we confront a man "stripped bare," we are told ("pur le cors," 2:306), although he remains fully clothed. Thus the courtly knight's masculinity and social status derive from the fact that his specific body parts are encased and literally unseen. He is gendered masculine precisely to the extent that his anatomical sex is concealed and unverified. He is a knight and a man, curiously, to the degree that he has no clearly sexed body.

Consequently, the courtly knight can switch genders with relative ease. The most vivid example of this phenomenon is provided by Gauvain's assertion in the *Prose Lancelot* that he would give anything to secure Lancelot's liberation from prison and forever have such a valiant man with him/for himself:[42] "Je voldroie orendroit estre la plus bele damoisele del mont saine et haitie, par covent qu'il m'amast sor toute rien toute sa vie et la moie" (I would like to be the most beautiful damsel in the world, in perfect health, provided that he love me more than anyone else for the duration of his life and mine, 8:94). Gauvain here imagines himself in the role of the beautiful *damoisele,* a female object of desire loved and adored by Lancelot, that is, in the role typically allotted to Lancelot's official ladylove, Guenevere. I consider Gauvain's suggestive comment in this scene to be a key example of unmarked transvestism in the *Prose Lancelot,* as I have argued elsewhere.[43] Gauvain's imagined and rhetorical cross-dressing also functions as a gender performance in Judith Butler's definition of the term; it constitutes an expression of gendered subjectivity that does not presume or depend upon a natural alignment of anatomical sex, gender identity, and gender performance.[44] Here, no necessary link joins masculinity with maleness or femininity with femaleness. Rather Gauvain qualifies as a knight and a man at the very moment he casts himself in the role of Lancelot's ladylove principally because of the armor he wears.

The courtly lady, by contrast, gains social status "as a woman" to the extent that her flesh is exposed to view.[45] A passage from the *Prose Lancelot* juxtaposes male and female modes of dress as follows: "si voient venir .II. routes de chevaliers *tous armés,* si i a .X. chevalier en chascune route, et ... chevauche une dame moult cointement aschesmee de palefroi et d'autre ator; et fu vestue d'un samit vermeil cote et mantel a peine d'ermine; si fu *toute desliie* et ele estoit de merveilleuse biauté" (They saw two columns of fully armed knights approach, ten knights in each column and ... a lady on horseback, equipped very attractively with a palfrey and other accoutrements, dressed in a red silk gown and a cloak lined in ermine. She [her head] was completely uncovered and of wondrous beauty, 7:385). The lady's costume is characteristically open (headdress undone: *deslie*) so that her beautiful face can be seen.[46] Even though the standard portrait of the courtly "dame" often describes her as clothed in *cotte* and *mantel,* it also typically delineates her plump breasts, alert nipples, and curving thighs as if she were standing naked before us. Much is made, typically, of the white skin that covers the elite lady's face and neck, chest and hands.[47] It is not that this lady is unclothed per se, but that skin itself constitutes the aristocratic woman's typical garment.

Guenevere, as a temporary prisoner of King Bademagu in Gorre, is defined, in the *Charrete*, in terms of flesh alone when Bademagu assures Lancelot of her safekeeping by stating that no one has touched her *char*: "La reine a boene prison / que nus de *char* a li n'adoise / neis mon filz cui molt an poise" (The queen fared well in prison; no one touched her [literally, her flesh], not even my son, for whom it was difficult, lines 3362–64). An extreme version of this characterization of femininity as skin and flesh is found in the courtly temptress of the *Charrete*, who, as the starkest contrast to the "chevalier toz armez," appears to us instead to be "tote descoverte" (line 1067). Later described as "descoverte jusqu'au nonbril" (uncovered down to the navel, line 1082), this nearly ravished woman reveals disturbingly how the courtly association of female attractiveness and visible skin might rest in fact on a principle of women's vulnerability to attack,[48] even when they are fully clothed.

This is, indeed, what the *coutume de Logres* confirms: that the company of armed and armored knights, bound to one another through ceremonies of homage and dubbing, are authorized by the customs of Arthur's realm to trade unarmored women and ravish them if they please, "Mes, se ele conduit eüst / uns autres, se tant li pleüst / qu'a celui bataille an feïst / et par armes la conqueïst, / sa volenté an poïst faire / sanz honte et sanz blasme retraire" (If she was in the care/company of one [knight] and another wanted to fight with him and win her in combat, he could do with her as he pleased, incurring no blame or shame, lines 1311–16).[49] The terms of this relationship are clarified in an especially striking passage where the disobedient son refuses to give up his claim on an unnamed *pucele* and explains that to relinquish the woman he escorts would be tantamount literally to losing his armor: "Einz iert de mon escu la guige / ronpue et totes les enarmes, / *ne an mon cors ne an mes armes* / n'avrai je puis nule fiance, / ne an m'espee, n'en ma lance, / quant je li lesserai m'amie" (The strap of my shield and its handles would be broken; I would no longer have any confidence in my body, arms or armor, not in my sword or my lance, if I gave my ladylove to him, lines 1720–25). The courtly knight's armor cannot function properly unless he has a lady in tow (lines 1716–19). For him to be armored effectively, she must be uncovered and physically vulnerable, in need of chivalric protection. If knights in the Arthurian world are "made" literally when a lord confers upon them the armor that creates their social body, ladies, who experience no such ritual investiture, are defined by the absence of any equivalent garment.[50] Instead of armor, it is the lady's skin that confers social status upon her; and her status is that of an objectified body to be traded by armed knights.[51]

Roughly midway through the *Prose Lancelot,* Lancelot's female guide subtly oversteps this allotted role and draws a strong rebuke from "the most perfect knight." Having begun the journey through the forest as the lovely and deferential Arthurian lady who "takes pains to serve and praise" (1:317) the knight in her company, this damsel suddenly switches rhetorical modes and begins to solicit Lancelot's amorous attention as a lover: "De totes les choses le semont de quoi ele le cuide eschaufer, si se deslie sovent por mostrer son vis et son chief qui de tres grant bialté estoit et chante lais bretons et autres notes plaisans et envoisies, et ele avoit la vois et haute et clere et la langue bien parlant et breton et françois et mains autres langages" (Everything she said to him was designed to heat him up; she repeatedly unlaced her headgear to reveal her very beautiful head and face as she sang Breton songs and other pleasing and seductive tunes. She had a high, clear voice as her tongue pronounced words in Breton, French and many other languages, 1:317). This alluring maiden who has taken pains to unveil her skin, is nonetheless not reduced to skin alone, for she has moved tentatively into the subject position, actively constructing a possible love scenario between herself and the hapless Lancelot: "Et quant ele voit un bel lieu plaisant, si li mostre et dist: 'Veez, sire chevaliers, dont ne seroit il bien honis qui tel lieu passeroit avec bele dame ne avec bele damoisele sans fere plus?'" (Showing him a lovely place by the roadside, she said, "Look sir knight, don't you think that anyone who passed by such a place, while traveling in the company of a beautiful lady or maiden, and didn't act further, would be dishonored?" 1:317–18). Although couched in properly courtly syntax, this damsel's request appears thoroughly unladylike. It provides a cogent example of bodytalk, as I have defined that phenomenon, in which fictive females can be seen to resist, through the speech attributed to them, the very stereotypes of femininity that their gendered anatomy is designed to convey.[52] Lancelot immediately brands such resistant speech as unacceptable within a courtly code that does not allow ladies to speak this way: "Je n'avoie pas apris que pucele parlast en tel maniere" (I never knew a maiden could speak in such a way, 1:318). Curiously, no equivalent censure follows Gauvain's crossover speech, which casts him in the role of Lancelot's ladylove, or Galehaut's unproblematic depiction of Lancelot as his lord in love (8:81, 483). Yet the damsel accompanying Lancelot in the forest cannot as readily step into the cross-gendered role of the desiring subject. Her movement off the pedestal of courtliness into a more sexually aggressive, combative, and knightly pose meets with considerable resistance.

Later in the scene, the young woman guide undresses and slips into bed next to the timorous and incredulous Lancelot who repeats his earlier rebuke, this time more specifically in terms of physical aggression: "Kar onques mes n'oï parler de dame ne de damoisele qui volsist prendre chevalier par force" (I've never heard of a lady of damsel who tried to take a knight by force, 1:323). "Ladies" don't make sexual advances; "ladies" don't attack with force. That is to say, in effect, that ladies don't wear armor; they can't cross-dress as knights. Unmarked transvestism practiced by females is actively policed by a courtly code that sees men as relatively bodiless while consigning women to the realm of skin. Whereas knights can play at being armored men or robed women in the Arthurian world, ladies themselves cannot as easily cross the gender lines dictated by courtly culture. Ladies should wear only one outfit, it seems, a loose and flowing gown, which, diametrically opposed to the knight's armor, is tied typically to her exposed and gendered flesh. The lady escorting Lancelot through the forest has injudiciously stepped over the hypothetical line dividing armor from skin. In cross-dressing metaphorically as a knight she has made gender trouble in the courtly world.[53] And yet this is precisely the dilemma posed by the quintessential courtly lady, Guenevere, who so often eschews proper courtly conduct,[54] and by the hybridized Provençal *domna* before her.

## Unisex Dress: Where Genders Cross and Knights Become Ladylike

We can see from the preceding examples that whereas the courtly code attempts to impose strict gender identities by insisting that "knights are knights" and "ladies are ladies," because knights wear armor and ladies do not, such a highly polarized regulation of sexual difference falters from its very inception. The fact that ladies can, although with difficulty, break through the limiting restrictions of their beautiful skin and that knights can, much more readily, shift into the hybrid status of lady/knight attests to a more fluid relationship between armor and skin than the traditional strictures of courtly coupling would suggest.

Indeed within the courtly world, the terms of masculinity and femininity can shift and recombine in surprising constellations that are figured along a continuum from armored, invulnerable subject to naked, vulnerable object. In one scene alone we watch the perfect knight Lancelot travel across the full spectrum of socially defined modes of dress and their assigned gender identification: he passes from the standard masculine armor to the unisex court garb of *mantel* and *chemise,* until falling finally into the category of lowest, most embodied, status when he takes on the quintessential marker of femininity as the courtly code defines it: white flesh. When Lancelot arrives at the temptress's castle in the *Chevalier de la charrete* and exchanges the military shield, which hangs typically around the knight's neck (*l'escu au col*), for a courtly mantle that the lady places around his shoulders—"Quant cele li ot *au col mis /* le mantel..." (When she placed the cloak around his neck and shoulders, lines 1019–20, 1000, 1012–13)—he becomes as vulnerable to attack as the temptress herself. His thin mantle offers no protection against armed assailants: "et li quarz qui l'a assailli / fiert si que le mantel li tranche, / et la chemise et la char blanche" (And the fourth one to attack him struck so as to slice through his cloak and *chemise* and through his white flesh, lines 1144–46). The subsequent seduction scene reveals Lancelot to be even more fully denuded (*desnuer*, line 1205) in a way that recalls the temptress's own state of being "tote descoverte" earlier in the tale.[55] However, in that fleeting moment when we are allowed to glimpse what lies beneath this knight's clothing, we see not the body of a man, but the vulnerable, uncovered body of the aristocratic woman, "la char blanche," and his concomitantly lowered social status.

More commonly, however, knights cross-dress overtly, moving with ease and no loss of status into the socially prescribed realm of "ladies." Key to this process is the fact that knights change clothes regularly in romance narrative. Their numerous arrivals and departures are marked by elaborate rituals of hospitality,[56] which include the shedding of armor and the donning of elegant garments worn at court, that is, the kind of unisex aristocratic dress worn by the standing figure on Simon de Mondragon's seal. In the *Prose Lancelot*, Hector is greeted by a *pucele* who removes his armor and offers instead a garment identitical to her own indoor dress, clearly distinct from the battle armor that only men can wear. The *pucele* "le fait desarmer desus une moult bele queute pointe; et ele misme le desarme ... Si li aporte la puchele .I. court mantel, si li met au col" (had his armor removed on a beautiful coverlet; she removed it herself ... and brought him a short cloak which she placed around his neck and shoulders, 8:303). In disarming/undressing the knight, she removes the insignia of his chivalric maleness and clothes him as she clothes herself, erasing sexual distinctions between armor and skin. This visual "feminization" of the knight who steps off the battlefield to enter the world of courtly extravagance is made especially clear in the encounter between the duke of Clarence and his female cousin. After a valet removed the duke's shield and armor, "est issue une damoisele d'une chambre qui porte sur son col un mantel d'escarlete et li dux le voit molt bien venir.... Lors li met la damoisele le mantel al col et maintenant rest entree en la chambre dont ele estoit issue" (The duke saw a damsel, wearing a silk cloak around her neck and shoulders, emerge from a room. The damsel placed the cloak around *his* neck and shoulders and reentered the room from which she had come, 1:181). In this instance the mantle passed from lady to knight does not only resemble a woman's garment; the mantle he dons belongs in fact to her. The description of the knight Bors arriving at Bademagu's court "vestuz d'uune [*sic*] robe d'un samit vermoil foree d'ermine dont il avoit cote et mantel" (dressed in a red silk gown lined in ermine with a tunic and cloak lined in ermine, 4:374) offers a close reflection of the queen, Guenevere, "vestue d'unne [*sic*] robe de porpre qui toute estoit batue a or, si en avoit cote et mantel forré d'ermine" (dressed in a rich, dark-colored gown, completely worked in gold, with a tunic and cloak lined in ermine, 4:385).[57]

What lies beneath the knight's armor in courtly romance, then, is not sexual difference but the sexual ambiguity of a social body that can move quite readily between genders and between social stations. Even in combat, the body parts of fighting knights remain remarkably gender neutral. Descriptions of "les bras, les espaules, li cors, li dos" (arms, shoulders, body, back, 1:337), "la char, li os" (flesh, bones, 2:127), "la teste" (the head, 1:344) do not in any way tie these bodies to a gendered anatomy. The armor that constructs the properly socialized body in the courtly world seems rather to connote both masculinity and its fundamental mutability. Knights can dress as men (in armor) or cross-dress as women (in robes) without risking effeminacy or diminished social status.

Even the putatively male suit of armor itself proves less gender specific than it originally appears. When the Dame du Lac first arrives at King Arthur's castle to request that the young Lancelot be dubbed a knight, she insists on supplying his apparel: "Or vous requier je dont que vous chest mien vallet qui chi est me faites chevalier de teus *armes* et de teil harnois com il a" (I ask that you make this young man, here before you, into a knight, with the arms and armor that he now has, 7:267). One of her horses carries "*la robe* au vallet dont il devoit estre chevaliers et une autre ruebe a porter" (the robe he should wear to become a knight and another to carry with him, 7:265), in addition to a shield, helmet, and sword. When Arthur replies that he can only create a knight out of his own robes and his own arms, not hers — "Mais en che que vos me requerés avroie je honte, se jel faisoie, car je n'ai pas a coustume que je fache nului chevalier se de mes *robes* non et de mes *armes*" (It would be dishonorable for me to do as you request; I have only made knights using my own robes, arms, and armor, 7:267) — the Lady of the Lake responds, "Et bien sachiés que chis vallés ne puet estre chevaliers ne ne doit d'autres *armes* ne d'autres *robes* que de cheles qui chi sont" (Be assured that this youth cannot become a knight using any arms, armor, or robes other than these, 7:268). At stake in this scene are many issues: Who will make Lancelot a knight? A man (the king) or a woman (his surrogate mother, the Lady of the Lake)? And what clothing will be used to make the young Lancelot into a knight? But clearly the knightly self that is fashioned from this clothing will not derive from arms and armor alone. The unisex robes are as much a part of Lancelot's putatively male outfit as they are for knights wearing armor elsewhere in Arthurian romance. Lancelot, when fighting with Griffon, is said to have "tote sa robe . . . ensanglentee" (his robe completely bloodied, 2:305), and Galehaut on another occasion explains to Lancelot that he set out with a band of knights "armé desos lor robes" (wearing armor under their robes, 1:36).

In addition, the helmet that fully covers the knight's head often veers surprisingly close to an evocation of the aristocratic lady's typically white skin. The *orgueilleux* who suffers defeat at Lancelot's hand in the *Charrete* is said to have "la vantaille et la coiffe blanche" (a white visor and head covering, line 2908), just as Lancelot and Méléagant, later locked in battle, sport "les hiaumes et les haubers blans" (white helmets and halberks, line 3613). As these metallic items of chivalric dress take on the color attributed characteristically to the aristocratic lady's skin, the courtly dichotomies that construct male and female bodies, as well as those that fashion knights and ladies as distinct and clearly separate categories, begin to erode. It is in this world of blurring sexual differences that even the most masculine of knights such as Gauvain can occupy, at times, an indeterminate social space between dichotomous extremes of purely female or wholly male. Whereas courtly love attempts to convince us that sexual difference is biologically conditioned, the very phenomenon of courtliness also reveals tellingly that sexual difference in King Arthur's world, constructed as it is by courtly costume, does not involve a fixed choice between only two options, male and female. This does not mean that body parts are absent or insignificant in court culture. Indeed, they play a key role in the homage ceremony. Yet in the move from feudal homage to courtly love service, body parts tend to lose their gendered specificity.[58]

## Homage Refashioned in Courtly Clothes

The ceremony of feudal homage focuses on two body parts in particular: the mouth and hands. A feudal vassal typically vows to become the "man" (*homme*) of his lord, and more specifically to be "un homme de bouche et de mains" (a man of the mouth and hands).[59] This ritual differs from courtly love service in that homage joins the hands of two men, while courtliness unites the hands of a woman with those of a man. But can we really tell the difference? Lancelot, the perfect knight, the anomalous quester, the conundrum of courtliness personified, is said to be "bien tailliés" (well formed) with a "pis espés, col gros" (thick chest, fat neck); but he also bears the more typically feminine features of a noble lady: "bochie petite" (small mouth) and "mains longues et plaines et soés a baillier" (long, smooth hands, soft to the touch, 1:128–29). Elsewhere Lancelot is said to have the perfectly proportioned neck of a noble lady: "De son col ne fait il mie a demander, car s'il fust en une tres bele dame, si fust il assés couvenables" (No need to ask about his neck. If it had belonged to a beautiful woman, it would have suited her perfectly, 7:73). This knight has, moreover, long, straight arms that end not in a man's hands but in those of a lady: "les mains furent de dame tout droitement" (7:73).

What does it mean to say that Lancelot has the mouth, neck, and hands of a lady, while also asserting that he has the hips and stance, the chest and shoulders of the perfect knight? What kind of hybridized sexual and social status is suggested here? Certainly these allusions to a lady's face and hands provide a striking contrast to the more rugged description of Lancelot recuperating from combat at the lady of Malehaut's castle. Lying "naked on a bed," Lancelot is said to have a swollen face, battered and bruised by the chain mail of his hauberk. More specifically, his neck is flayed and his wrists hugely swollen and covered with blood: "le vis enflé et batu et camoissiés de mailles, le col et le nes escorchié... les puins gors et enflés et plains de sanc" (8:33). Indeed, the typical knight's neck and hands take such a beating during combat because they are crucial to his successful self-defense: the hands wield the sword and lance while the neck, as we have seen, bears the weight of the shield, hung from a leather strap (8:107). Elsewhere, Lancelot's capable and heroic hands lift the tombstone at the Doloreuse Garde (7:332). If the fighting knight's hands and neck are typically concealed beneath protective armor and thus invisible (7:286), they emerge during the ceremony of dubbing. In Lancelot's case we are told twice that at the moment when Lancelot became a knight he was fully armed "except for his head and hands" (tous armés fors de mon chief et de mes mains, 8:111 and 7:285–86). Yet Lancelot becomes a knight in a highly anomalous manner.

The scene of his dubbing by Queen Guenevere constitutes the most significant rewriting of the homage ceremony, in which the vassal becomes his lord's "homme de bouche et de mains." Indeed Lancelot explains to Yvain that he does not want to be a knight "de la main le roi" (by the king's hand, 7:286).[60] Rather, with his hands and neck bare he will become, it seems, "a knight of the queen's hand." And, in fact, in response to the young Lancelot kneeling before her, Guenevere first "takes him by the hand" and asks him to rise (7:285) and then "pulls him up by the hand" (7:286). The gesture reassures Lancelot: "il est moult a aise, quant il sent a sa main touchier la soie toute nue" (He was pleased to feel the touch of the queen's naked hand against his own, 7:286). As these naked hands touch, not only is the homage ceremony eroticized, but the traditional bonding between men—the ceremony that makes one man another man's man—shifts significantly. Guenevere extends her courtly and delicate hand to touch... is it the hand of a knight or is it, as we have seen before, the "hand of a lady" (7:73)?

In this instance the ideology of courtly love that tries concertedly to control the social body by constructing it according to a binary logic of masculine and feminine also shows how such rigid categorization, figured in terms of armor and skin, proves woefully inadequate. Lancelot has none of the social vulnerability that characterizes the physically beautiful and delicate *damoiseles* whose bare hands are traded among armed knights in the Arthurian forest.[61] Nor does he exhibit the vulnerable *char blanche* of his predecessor in Chrétien's tale.[62] The prose hero's masculinity is not feminized in a way that would reduce his social or sexual status. Rather, his hybrid existence as the atypical but quintessential courtly knight further challenges the categories of masculinity and femininity already called into question by Gauvain's rhetorical cross-dressing and Lancelot's own layered performance as Galehaut's lady/lord in love. Indeed, the very phenomenon of courtly love, which, in the examples we have seen, tends to blur distinctions between lord and ladylove, between a man's hands and a woman's or the mouth of a knight and that of a lady, undercuts the importance of being able to identify the sex of who is kneeling before whom in courtly encounters.

## Sexuality as Spacings on a Gendered Sartorial Continuum

The examples we have seen from the twelfth- and thirteenth-century tales of the archetypical courtly lover, Lancelot, reveal, in specifically medieval terms, how the constituent elements of gender cannot be made to signify monolithically, how in medieval French culture maleness and femaleness, masculinity and femininity are not impermeable or mutually exclusive categories. Even within the heteronormative model of Arthurian romance, which tries relentlessly to construct men as knights and women as ladies, we find ample evidence that gender might better be understood as "queer" in Eve Sedgwick's definition of the term, that is, that the constituent elements of sexuality move within "an open mesh of possibilities, gaps, overlaps, dissonances and resonances, lapses and excesses of meaning."[63] This does not mean that the categories of male and female have disappeared altogether,[64] any more than Peter Stallybrass's contention that gender depends upon a precarious "differentiation of the same" might suggest that the ability to differentiate has thoroughly vanished.

Indeed, we have seen how the "mesh" of sexuality's component elements remains more open for men than for women in the Arthurian world, where the ideology of courtliness polices female sexuality with greater rigor. But those key moments in which courtly ladies do veer problematically across the gender divide, those moments not of literal but of metaphorical cross-dressing, outline a range of possible scenarios that courtliness tries to suppress: that ladies could be knights — that they could court men, make sexual advances, refuse the terms of the courtly contract, dress in armor, and do battle. If this kind of behavior is unbecoming to the properly socialized Arthurian lady and denigrated by the courtly code that deems it inadmissable for ladies to cross the gender line in such ways, courtly romance shows us nonetheless what might happen if ladies did "dress" as knights, just as knights can fashion themselves as ladies.

Yet the productive blurring of gender categories is not limited to romance narrative alone. Even medieval ecclesiastical discourses that attempt to set male apart from female, monolithically as armored knight and metaphorically as naked lady, cannot help but bring the two extremes together. Within the churchmen's strongest condemnations of gender mixing we hear the message articulated more overtly in romance texts: that knights and ladies can best be defined as spacings on a gendered sartorial continuum, as figures exhibiting many different densities of sexed being, depending to a significant degree on what they wear. A particularly striking example of the rhetorical difficulty of insisting that knights cannot be ladies appears in a sermon delivered in 1273 by the Dominican preacher Gilles d'Orleans, who rebukes Parisian women for being simultaneously too knightly and too seductive:

> En apercevant une de ces femmes, ne la prendrait-on pas pour un chevalier se rendant à la Table Ronde? Elle est si bien equipée, de la tête aux pieds, qu'elle respire tout entier le feu du démon. Regardez ses pieds: sa chaussure est si étroite, qu'elle en est ridicule. Regardez sa taille: c'est pis encore. Elle serre les entrailles avec une ceinture de soie, d'or, d'argent.

> [Upon seeing one of these women, wouldn't one take her for a knight of the Round Table? She is so well equipped, from head to toe, that she breathes the devil's fire. Look at her feet: her shoes so narrow, she looks ridiculous in them. Look at her waist; it's even worse. She has squeezed her innards with a silk belt of gold and silver.][65]

A woman as a knight of the Round Table? Because she is so well "equipped"? And her equipment consists, in this case, of a belt made of silk, gold, and silver and a knight's armor. How is it, this sermon asks specifically, that this "miserable" and lowly (female) creature dares to wear the "armor" of a knight: "D'ou vient qu'une misérable and fragile créature ose se revêtir d'une armure pareille?" But what precisely is that armor made of by this preacher's own definition? None other than courtly armor's gendered opposite: skin, more precisely the skin of a woman, revealed on her open chest by a plunging neckline. The preacher continues, "C'est à Paris surtout que régnent ces abus. C'est là qu'on voit des femmes courir par la ville toutes décolletées, toutes *espoitrinées*" (It's in Paris that these abuses are especially prevalent. There, one sees women running through the city completely uncovered, their chests bare).[66]

In attempting to protect knights from the contamination of ladies, this thirteenth-century preacher attests to the necessary permeability of both social and sexual status. His own speech constructs that most feared and evocative hybrid: the lady/knight, figured in this instance as a non-noble woman wearing a sash fit for a king *and* as a knight of the Round Table whose armor is fashioned from the delicate skin of a lady's chest. Is "she" a man or a woman? Is "he" a woman in disguise? S/he bears the cultural mark of both armored knight and skin-clad lady, with flesh as delicate as it is steely. This constructed flesh, quite unlike that of the pope enthroned during the ritual *possesso* in Rome two hundred years later, cannot be used to determine sexual difference. This skin is armor, too; it marks thereby that crucial zone of gender indeterminacy that lies at the heart of courtliness.

## Notes

I would like to thank Sarah Beckwith, Judith M. Bennett, James Schultz, Helen Solterer, Gabrielle Spiegel, and Theodore Evergates for their insightful comments on earlier versions of this essay.

1. Richard Ingersoll, " The *Possesso*, the Via Papale, and the Stigma of Pope Joan," in *Urban Rituals in Italy and the Netherlands*, ed. Heide de More and Anna Vos (Assen: Van Gorcum, 1993), 39.

2. Ibid.

3. John F. Benton, "Clio and Venus: A Historical View of Medieval Love," in *The Meaning of Courtly Love*, ed. F. X. Newman (Albany: State University of New York Press, 1968), 36. For a recent reprinting of the image, see Brigitte Bedos-Rezak, "The Social Implications of the Art of Chivalry: The Sigillographic Evidence (France: 1050–1250)," in *Form and Other in Medieval France: Studies in Social and Quantitative Sigillography* (Brookfield, Vt.: Ashgate, 1993), 199, fig. 12; Bedos-Rezak identifies the image as a scene of homage (21); and so, earlier, does Marc Bloch, *Feudal Society*, vol. 1, trans. L. A. Manyon (Chicago: University of Chicago Press, 1970), plate 4.

4. In her exhaustive analyses of medieval seals, Brigitte Bedos-Rezak mentions only two seals that depict a kneeling knight paying homage to a "lady"; "Medieval Women in French Sigillographic Sources," in *Medieval Women and the Sources of Medieval History*, ed. Joel T. Rosenthal (Athens: University of Georgia Press, 1990), 8.

5. For more on unisex dress in twelfth- and thirteenth-century France, see E. Jane Burns, "Ladies Don't Wear *Braies*: Underwear and Outwear in the French *Prose Lancelot*," in *The Lancelot-Grail Cycle: Texts and Transformations*, ed. William W. Kibler (Austin: University of Texas Press, 1994), 152–74.

6. I do not mean to imply that there is a difference in kind between the seemingly more "real" bodies involved in the ritual *possesso* and the fictive bodies figured in Arthurian romance. Both kinds of bodies are cultural products, each deriving from a different structuring ideology. The interpretation of the bodies involved in the *possesso*, as I have described it, results from a presumption that bodies can be naturally sexed; the ideology governing the creation of gender identity in Arthurian romance, by contrast, makes no such blanket or exclusive presumption.

7. Sarah Kay, *Subjectivity in Troubadour Poetry* (Cambridge: Cambridge University Press, 1990), 86.

8. Ibid., 91–92.

9. It is important to emphasize that the Provençal *domna* and courtly lady do not actually acquire the lord's power or authority but remain only fictively empowered. See E. Jane Burns and Roberta L. Krueger, introduction to "Courtly Ideology and Woman's Place in Medieval French Literature," *Romance Notes* 25, no. 3 (1985): 205–19; and E. Jane Burns, "The Man behind the Lady in Troubadour Lyric," *Romance Notes* 25, no. 3 (1985): 254–70.

10. The system remains, however, crucially distinct from the Old Norse culture described by Carol Clover, in which "maleness and femaleness were always negotiable" (378) and gender was not coextensive with biological sex but based on "winnable and losable attributes" (379). The Old Norse sagas retained a clear hierarchy of sex difference that "at the level of the body knows only the male and at the level of social behavior, only the effeminate, or emasculate, or impotent" (387). See Clover, "Regardless of Sex: Men, Women, and Power in Early Northern Europe," *Speculum* 68, no. 2 (1993): 363–87. Epithets such as "effeminate" or "impotent" do not typically accompany gender crossings in French courtly romance.

11. This does not mean that considerations of sexual difference are insignificant. On the contrary, I have argued in *Bodytalk: When Women Speak in Old French Literature* (Philadelphia: University of Pennsylvania Press, 1993), as here, that it is important for feminist readers of Old French literature to take the body into account but to understand that body as necessarily a product of historical, cultural, social, and linguistic processes. For more on the importance of "sexed bodies," see Elizabeth Grosz, *Volatile Bodies: Toward a Corporeal Feminism* (Indianapolis: Indiana University Press, 1994), 187–210.

12. Grosz, *Volatile Bodies*, 18.

13. Judith Butler, *Bodies That Matter: On the Discursive Limits of "Sex"* (New York: Routledge, 1993), 30. The psychoanalytic perspective on courtly love confirms the absence of any actual, prior, historical, or biological object of male desire. Lacan explains in the *Ethics of Psychoanalysis* (New York: Routledge, 1992) that the "feminine object is emptied of all real substance" (149), and in *Encore* he shows that the place of the "lady-thing" is originally empty, a void around which male desire is structured through indirection and postponement; *Le Seminaire Livre XX: Encore* (Paris: Editions du Seuil, 1975), 65. For an overview see Slavoj Žižek, *Metastases of Enjoyment* (London: Verso, 1994), 89–112.

14. "Et que ferai jou, qui tout ai mis en vous mon cuer et mon cors?" *Lancelot: Roman en prose du XIIIe siècle*, ed. Alexandre Micha (Geneva: Droz, 1982), 8:483, and "Et sachiés que vous porrés bien avoir compaignie de plus riche homme que je ne sui, mais vous ne l'avrés jamais a homme qui tant vous aint" (8:81). (Subsequent references are to this edition.) For additional textual references, see Reginald Hyatte, "Recoding Ideal Male Friendship as *fine amor* in the *Prose Lancelot*," *Neophilologus* 75 (1991): 505–18. Hyatte's article is insightful in mapping out the details of the role reversals involved here, although his conclusion—that Lancelot and Galehaut are simply friends rather than homosexual lovers—unfortunately minimizes the richness of the textual material he presents.

15. Kevin Brownlee has shown how even Chrétien de Troyes's twelfth-century *Lancelot* (*Le Chevalier de la charrete*) experiments with gender inversions as "Godefroi's Lancelot plays the role of Chrétien's Guenevere. At the same time, Godefroi casts Méléagant's sister in the role of Chrétien's Lancelot, i.e., the desiring subject, the active and successful quester"; Brownlee, "Transformations of the *Charrete*: Godefroi de Leigni Rewrites Chrétien de Troyes," *Stanford French Review* 14, nos. 1–2 (1990): 161–78.

16. See, for example, Helen Solterer, "Figures of Female Militancy in Medieval France," *Signs* (Spring 1991): 522–30, and Nancy Freeman Regalado, "Allegories of Power: The Tournament of Vices and Virtues in the *Roman de Fauvel* (BN MS Fr. 146)," *Gesta* 32, no. 2 (1993): 135–46.

17. Peter Stallybrass, "Boundary and Transgression: Body, Text, Language," *Stanford French Review* 14 (1990): 9.

18. Ibid., 19; and see Elizabeth Spelman, *Inessential Woman: Problems of Exclusion in Feminist Thought* (Boston: Beacon Press, 1988), who shows how, in his political works, Aristotle distinguishes among three categories: men, women, and slaves, thus producing gender as a class distinction that does not derive from biological sexual difference. See, esp., 37–56, and the essay by James Schultz, chapter 5 in this volume, that shows how gender is constructed by clothing and class in Gottfried's *Tristan*, such that "sex difference is not visible in the body of the object" and "sexual desire is not determined by the identity of the subject."

19. On courtly love generally, see Roger Boase, *The Origin and Meaning of Courtly Love* (Manchester: Manchester University Press, 1976); Jean Frappier, "Vues sur les conceptions courtoises dans les littératures d'oc et d'oil au XIIe siècle," *Cahiers de civilisation médiévale* 2 (1959): 15–56; Moshé Lazar, *Amour courtois et 'Fin'amors' dans la littérature du XIIe siècle* (Paris: Klincksieck, 1964), and subsequent bibliography in Roberta L. Krueger and E. Jane Burns, "A Selective Bibliography of Criticism: Women in Medieval French Literature," *Romance Notes* 25, no. 3 (1985): 375–90; Stephen Jaeger, *The Origins of Courtliness: Civilizing Trends and the Formation of Courtly Ideals, 939–1210* (Philadelphia: University of Pennsylvania Press, 1985); Maria Rosa Menocal, *The Arabic Role in Medieval Literary History* (Philadelphia: University of Pennsylvania Press, 1987); R. Howard Bloch, *Medieval Misogyny and the Invention of Western Romantic Love* (Chicago: University of Chicago Press, 1991); Laura Kendrick, *The Game of Love* (Berkeley: University of California Press, 1988); Peter Allen, *The Art of Love: Amatory Fiction from Ovid to the Romance of the Rose* (Philadelphia: University of Pennsylvania Press, 1992).

20. Joan Cadden, *Meanings of Sexual Difference in the Middle Ages: Medicine, Science, and Culture* (Cambridge: Cambridge University Press, 1993), 202–12.

21. Roberta Krueger, "Constructing Sexual Identities in the High Middle Ages: the Didactic Poetry of Robert de Blois," *Paragraph* 13 (1990): 105–31; and for the fourteenth century, see "Intergeneric Combination and the Anxiety of Gender in *Le Livre du Chevalier de la Tour Landry pour l'enseignement de ses filles*," *L'Esprit Créateur* 33, no. 4 (1993): 61–72.

22. Susan Crane, *Gender and Romance in Chaucer's* Canterbury Tales (Princeton: Princeton University Press, 1994), 13. Many recent studies that show how medieval French literature problematizes gender identity focus on the *Roman de Silence*: Peter Allen, "The Ambiguity of Silence," in *Sign, Sentence, Discourse: Language and Medieval Thought in Literature*, ed. Julian N. Wasserman and Lois Roney (Syracuse, N.Y.: Syracuse University Press, 1989): 98–112; Simon Gaunt, "The Significance of Silence," *Paragraph* 13 (1990): 202–16; Michele Perret, "Travesties et Transexuelles: Yde, Silence, Grislandole, Blanchandine," *Romance Notes* 25, no. 3 (1985): 328–40; and most recently Peggy McCracken, "The Boy Who Was a Girl: Reading Gender in the *Roman de Silence*," *Romanic Review* 85, no. 4 (1994): 515–34, who shows specifically how this complex romance "challenges the primacy of anatomy as the location of gender identity" (532).

23. See E. Jane Burns, "Which Queen? Guenivere's Transvestism in the French Prose *Lancelot*," in *Lancelot and Guenivere: A Casebook*, ed. Lori Walters (New York: Garland, 1996).

24. I choose these texts because ever since Gaston Paris coined the term "courtly love" in 1883, scholars have taken these early tales of Lancelot and Guenevere to be the founding narratives of courtly love in the northern French tradition; Gaston Paris, "Etudes sur les romans de la Table Ronde, Lancelot du Lac: II: *Le Conte de la charrette*," *Romania* 12 (1883): 459–534. Various permutations of courtliness are, of course, attested in a broader range of romance narratives.

25. I borrow this useful term from Leslie Rabine, "A Feminist Politics of Non-Identity," *Feminist Studies* 14, no. 1 (1988): 11–31.

26. Denise Riley, *Am I That Name? Feminism and the Category of "Women" in History* (Minneapolis: University of Minnesota Press, 1988), 6.

27. For examples from the German tradition, see Joachim Bumke, *Courtly Culture: Literature and Society in the High Middle Ages*, trans. Thomas Dunlap (Berkeley: University of California Press, 1991), 138–55.

28. Theodore Evergates, ed. and trans., *Feudal Society in Medieval France: Documents from the County of Champagne* (Philadelphia: University of Pennsylvania Press, 1993), 99; "Operitis equos sericis, et pendulos nescio quos panniculos loricis superinduitis; depingitis hastas, clypeos et sellas; frena et clacaria auro et argento gemmisque circumornatis, et cum tanta pompa pudendo furore et impudenti stupore ad mortem properatis" (*Tractatus et opuscula*, vol. 3 of *Sancti Bernardi Opera*, ed. Jean Leclercq and H. M.

Rochais [Rome: Editiones Cistercienses, 1963], 216]. See also the military code established in 1188 by Phillip Augustus and Henry II prohibiting crusaders from wearing costly fabrics: "Nobody shall wear colored cloth, gray cloth, squirrel fur, sable or purple cloth" (Nullus vario vel grisio vel sabellinis vel escarletis utatur); Bumke, *Courtly Culture*, 129.

29. Evergates, ed., *Feudal Society*, 99; "Vos...oculorum gravamen ritu femineo comam nutritis, longis ac profusis camisiis propria vobis vestigia obvolvitis, delicatas ac teneras manus amplis et circumfluentibus manicis sepelitis" (*Tractatus*, 216).

30. Evergates, ed., *Feudal Society*, 99; "Militaris sunt haec insignia, an muliebria potius ornamenta?" (*Tractatus*, 216). The subject of lavish knightly dress was still at issue in 1279 when Phillip the Bold instituted his sumptuary laws. As J. Quicherat notes, the bourgeoisie was prohibited from using luxury chariots, golden spurs, and harnesses; *Histoire du costume en France*, Paris: 1977, 204. Bernard's comment should also be set in the long tradition of cosmetic theology, exemplified by Tertullian's writing on women's apparel and discussed by Marcia Colish, "Cosmetic Theology: The Transformation of a Stoic Theme," *Assays* 1 (1981): 3–14, and Bloch, *Medieval Misogyny*, 39–47.

31. *The Ecclesiastical History of Oderic Vitalis*, ed. and trans. Marjorie Chinball (Oxford: Clarendon Press, 1973), 4: 188, 189: "Femineam mollitem petulans iuuentus amplectitur, feminisque uiri curiales in omni lasciuia summopere adulantur. Pedum articulis ubi finis est corporis colubrinarum similitudinem caudarum imponuntent, quas velutscorpiones prar oculis suis prospiciunt. Humum quoque puluerulentam interularum et palliorum superfluo sirmate uerrunt, longis latisque manicis ad omnia facienda manus operiunt, et his superfluitatibus onusti celeriter ambulare uel aliquid utiliter operari uix possunt. Sincipite scalciati sunt, ut fures, occipatio autem prolixas nutriunt comas ut meritrices."

32. Ibid.: "Nam capillos a uertice in frontem discriminabant, longos crines ueluti mulieres nutriebant, et summopere comebant, prolixisque nimiumque strictis camisiis indui tunicisque gaudebant."

33. Eadmer, *Historia novorum*, lib. I, *Patrologiae: Cursus completus...series latina*, ed. J.-P. Migne, vol. 159 (Paris, 1844–64), c. 576; cited in H. Platelle, "Le Problème du scandale: Les nouvelles modes masculines aux XIe et XIIe siècles," *Revue Belge de philologie et d'histoire* 53, no. 4 (1975): 1078. See Platelle for further discussion and additional examples.

34. Ibid., 1080.

35. Pierre Kraemer, *Le Luxe et les lois somptuaires au moyen âge* (Paris: Ernest Sagot, 1920), 36, quoting H. Baudrillart, *Histoire du luxe privé et public* (Paris: Hachette, 1880), 4:640.

36. Ibid., 37–38, quoted from Hélinaudin, *Histoire littéraire de la France*, vol. 17.

37. "Crinitis nostris, qui obliti quid nati sunt, libenter se in muliebris sexus habitum transformant"; William of Malmesbury, *Historia novellae* 1. 4, *PL* 179, c. 1396–97, cited in Platelle, "Le Problème," 1082. Behind these injunctions to maintain two clearly defined sexes lies Paul's remark in 1 Corinthians 11:14–15: "It is shameful for a man to have long hair, although it is glorious for a woman to do so, for hair was given to her as a kind of veil" (Platelle, "Le Problème," 1087).

38. Chrétiende Troyes, *Le Chevalier de la charrete*, ed. Mario Roques (Paris: Champion, 1970), lines 44–48. (Subsequent references are to this edition.) For examples in the *Prose Lancelot* of a knight completely covered, see Micha, *Lancelot*, 1:136, 291, 363; 2:52.

39. In the *Prose Lancelot*, the *escu* carries special weight as the exemplary marker of a knight's identity: "Por Dieu, dites nos la verité del meillor chevalier del monde, por quoi il ne li pendra jamés escu al col et se il est ou mors ou vis..." (1:351). Having the "escu al col" signals Lancelot as a living, breathing, functional knight. If he is accused of adultery, we are told, Lancelot would lose his status as a knight and the right to carry a shield and wear armor: "ains iroit tos jors mes en langes et nus piés, ne jamés n'avroit escu a col ne arme vestue" (1:352). Indeed, Lancelot's *escu* is venerated and fetishized as a substitute for his very being in 1:361. For a sampling of other instances in which the knight's identity is vested in the *escu*, see 1:361, 387. Other knights described as "bien taillies" include Hector (8:277), Gauvain (2:408), Segurade (8:177), and Lancelot (1:128).

40. It is this thorough covering that makes both literary and historical knights into what John of Salisbury called "les mains armées du roi" (the king's armed and armored hands); J. Flori, "La Chevalerie chez Jean de Salisbury," *Revue d'histoire ecclésiastique* 77, nos. 1–2 (1982): 35–77.

41. See also 1:344 and, further, how Galehaut, riding without a helmet, receives an unexpected blow to the face (1:359).

42. "Et vous, fait il [Galehos], mesire Gauvain, se Diex vous doinst le santé que vous desires, quel meschief feries vous por avoir tous jours mais .I. si preudome?" (And you, Sir Gauvain, Galehaut said, if God were to restore your health, what misdeed would you do to have such a valiant man with you forevermore?, 8:94).

43. Burns, "Which Queen?"

44. Judith Butler, *Gender Trouble: Feminism and the Subversion of Identity* (London: Routledge, 1990), 137.

45. Danielle Regnier-Bohler has shown how in Old French narrative generally men of varying social ranks must be covered to be fully socialized, whereas women are always already nude since their identity is fundamentally sexual rather than social; "Le Corps mis à nu: Perception et valeur symbolique de la nudité dans les récits du moyen âge," *Europe: Revue Littéraire Mensuelle*, October 1983, 51–62.

46. See also 2:376 and Guenevere "desvelopee" in 1:18.

47. See Burns, *Bodytalk*, 109–12, and Alice Colby, *The Portrait in Twelfth-Century French Literature* (Geneva: Droz, 1965).

48. It is often that very beauty, revealed in female skin exposed to view, that is said to provoke knights to seize women, as in the following passage from the *Prose Lancelot*, where a "bone pucele" is "si bele de cors" that "an tout le païs n'avoit si bele ne chevalier si puissant que volentiers ne la preist por sa biauté" (there was not a more beautiful maiden in all the country nor a powerful knight who would not readily seize her on account of her beauty, 4:134).

49. Roberta Krueger has explained how Guenevere's abduction constitutes a version of the *coutume de Logres*; "Desire, Meaning and the Female Reader: The Problem in Chrétien's Charrete," in *The Passing of Arthur: New Essays in Arthurian Tradition*, ed. Christopher Baswell and William Sharpe (New York: Garland, 1988), 31–51. For other examples of noblewomen being "handed off" as the prize in a tournament, see Jean-Louis Picherit, "Le Motif du tournoi dont le prix est la main d'une riche et noble héritière," *Romance Quarterly* 36, no. 2 (1989): 141–52, esp. 149.

50. My interest in investigating how knights and ladies are "made" in the Arthurian world was sparked by Marjorie Garber, "Spare Parts: On the Surgical Construction of Gender," *Vested Interests: Cross-Dressing and Cultural Anxiety* (New York: Routledge, 1992), 93–117.

51. I do not mean to suggest here that the courtly lady's skin is somehow more concrete, real, or material than the knight's armor. Rather, that while his gendered identity is created by and located in the suit of armor, hers is fabricated and read as skin.

52. Burns, *Bodytalk*, 4–7.

53. This damsel, it should be noted, is not the typical courtly lady, but a temptress whose actions were designed by a third party to test the knight's resistance, as Lancelot later learns (1:326). Yet this in no way diminishes the force of the scene in revealing what can happen when courtly ladies are not "ladies."

54. Burns, "Which Queen?"

55. Actually, Lancelot is here described as "denuded," although he retains his *chemise*, much as many female figures in Arthurian romance are said to be "nue en sa chemise." See Burns, "Ladies Don't Wear *Braies*," 163. A narrative progression similar to the one outlined in the scene with the temptress occurs in the *Charrete* on pp. 78–82, where Lancelot exchanges his armor for a mantle (lines 2534–37) and is helpless to defend himself against the charges of the *chevalier orgueilleux*, at least until he rearms (line 2661ff.) and exits the castle. The exchange of *escu* for mantle does not always prove problematic, as the scenes on pp. 63ff. and 90ff. attest.

56. See Matilda T. Bruckner, *Narrative Invention in Twelfth-Century French Romance* (Lexington, Ky.: French Forum, 1980).

57. See also the Dame du Lac dressed like Lancelot ("la dame si fu atornee moult richement, car ele fu vestue d'un blanc samit, cote et mantel a une pene d'ermine," 7:266) and Lancelot wearing a "robe d'un blanc samit, cote et mantel, et estoit li mantiax fourés d'ermines" (7:259); the ailing Gauvain wearing a *damoisele's* robes (1:212); and the recovering Lancelot borrowing a lady's gown (6:210). We must, of course, remember that the unisex robe and mantle also belong to the wardrobe of the courtly lord, such that the more an unarmored knight comes to look like a lady, the more he also resembles an empowered aristocratic man.

58. These examples of Lancelot's gender crossing provide a very different picture from the scenario of the "man in the dress" mentioned in Gregory of Tours that Nancy Partner interprets as exhibiting a "core gender identity of maleness"; "No Sex, No Gender," *Speculum* 68, no. 2 (1993): 442.

59. Marc Bloch, *Feudal Society*, 146.

60. See the dubbing ceremony, 8:106.

61. See, for example, how Arthur takes Guenevere "by the hand" in the opening scenes of the *Charrete* (lines 188–96) and hands her off to the armored Keu (*toz armez*), who will later fight the equally armed Méléagant for possession of the queen.

62. There is one key moment in the *Charrete* where Lancelot's status as the "perfect knight" derives precisely from his ability to cross gender boundaries without losing social status. He proves his mettle as the superhero of Arthurian romance by doing exactly what knights cannot do: remove portions of armor and perform heroic feats. In the episode of the sword bridge, for example, Lancelot uses bare hands and feet to traverse the deadly blade while wearing, it seems, no more than the otherwise degrading chemise: "Bien s'iert sor l'espee tenuz, / qui plus estoit tranchanz que fauz, / as mains nues et si deschauz" (He held tightly to the sword blade, sharper than a scythe, with his bare hands and feet, lines 3100–02); "Le sanc jus de ses plaies tert / a sa chemise tot antor" (The blood from his wounds stained his *chemise*, lines 3136–37). Are these the hands and dress of a lady? Far from the standard of masculine prowess signaled by the fully armored and contained body of the rival Méléagant (line 3541), Lancelot's body in this episode remains equally removed from the vulnerable body of the temptress "tote descoverte" or the compliant and possessed body of the *damoisele* in tow. Lancelot seems here to be both "naked" and adequately clothed at once, vulnerable yet empowered.

63. Eve Kosofsky Sedgwick, *Tendencies* (Durham, N.C.: Duke University Press, 1993), 8.

64. Sedgwick's project could hypothetically lead to such an end, however, as Elizabeth Weed has cogently argued: "The risk, then is that the cleavage of sexuality and gender in some queer criticism will—has already—rendered the difference of sexual difference *once again* unreadable; Weed, "The More Things Change," *differences* (Summer–Fall 1994): 268.

65. Lecoy de la Marche, *La Chaire française au moyen âge* (Paris: Librairie Renouard, 1886), 438.

66. Ibid.

CHAPTER 7

✤

# The Love of Thy Neighbor

## Louise O. Fradenburg

In *A Preface to Chaucer*, D. W. Robertson Jr. cites Saint Augustine's "classic Christian" definition of "the two loves," charity and concupiscence: charity is "the motion of the soul toward the enjoyment of God for His own sake, and the enjoyment of one's self and of one's neighbor for the sake of God"; cupidity "is a motion of the soul toward the enjoyment of one's self, one's neighbor, or any corporal thing for the sake of something other than God."[1] As is well known to students of medieval literature, Robertson's inference that "charity is the basic lesson of Christianity" becomes in turn the basis for his exegesis of medieval culture and literature.

The purpose of this essay is to take some steps toward a psychoanalytic and culturalist rereading of charity and its implications for the study of medieval literature and sexuality, in order to analyze, rather than replicate, the vicissitudes of medieval bodies and pleasures. In doing so this essay will explore several related figures of benevolence and self-abnegation: chivalric fantasies of rescue, the "gentil herte" and its capacity for "pity," woman as "helper" in the work of generation, and the queen as "intercessor" and epitome of charity. Ethical discourse will likewise be an important concern because of the way it proposes to repair the fault in man's being through acts of (self-)rescue — through what Michel Foucault refers to as "subjectivation," "in which one is called upon to take oneself as an object of knowledge and a field of action, so as to transform, correct, and purify oneself, and find salvation."[2]

The re-creation of the subject is central to premodern ethics and ideologies of love, as well as to the ethics of psychoanalysis. And creationist formulations of sexual difference have often been central to ethical deliberations on pleasure: for example, to the project of thinking (and ennobling) an identity whose access to pleasure and to the Good, and therefore to fullness of Being, is ensured by its informed capacity to choose right action, and thus to recreate and rescue itself.[3] I will therefore be focusing on Saint Thomas Aquinas's sexing of ethical generativity in the *Summa Theologica* and *Commentary on the Nicomachean Ethics*, and on the rescue fantasy of Chaucer's F-Prologue to *The Legend of Good Women*, which teaches us what "Etik seith."[4] I will also be dealing with two psychoanalytic texts: Freud's analysis of Daniel Paul Schreber's

135

*Denkwurdigkeiten eines Nervenkranken,* a study in the ethical and sexual outrage createdness can occasion in the hearts of obedient subjects; and Jacques Lacan's *The Ethics of Psychoanalysis,* which rethinks charity and thereby clarifies the ethical resonance of psychoanalytic understandings of the subject as founded on the image of the other.

## Aquinas

Aquinas's *Commentary on the Nicomachean Ethics* considers how ethical judgments can be made about women and about men with bad habits. The problem posed by men who "take pleasure in pulling out their hair, biting their nails, eating coal and earth, and having sexual intercourse with males" is that one can only speak of continence and incontinence without qualification when the person being judged has sufficient power of reason to exercise "universal judgment," a power impaired in men with bad habits because of their "psychological sickness."[5] According to Aquinas, [women,] because of the imperfect nature of their body, . . .

> do not govern their emotions in the majority of cases by reason but rather are governed by their emotions. Hence wise and brave women are rarely found, and so women cannot be called continent and incontinent without qualification.[6]

People who have bad habits or imperfect bodies are unable to rule and rescue themselves or others; they rarely attain full ethical subjectivity, conceptive power, or the sacrificial generativity of heroism ("wise and brave women are rarely found").

While Aquinas distinguishes men with good habits from women and imperfect men, these categories are not secure. Women are not the same as men, but they resemble some men (the kind with bad habits) closely; as ethical subjects their resemblance to perfect men is flawed ("qualified"), but unmistakable. This figure of flawed but evident similarity formulates an intimate or proximate other, a distanced but still recognizable (self-)image, an imaginary support for the perfect ethical subject.[7]

It is therefore not surprising that one of Aquinas's most significant deliberations on generativity and sexual difference concerns the ethical power of the flawed similar: that is, the question of how a female, a "misbegotten male," can possibly be a "helper" to man.[8] Woman is only helpful in the "work of generation," "since man can more efficiently be helped by another man in other works" (*ST,* 466). But generation is not to be scorned; as a form of "active power," generation is, in plants, the "noblest vital function," and among human beings the "active power of generation belongs to the male sex" (*ST,* 466). Woman's status as helper, then, resolves a problem about the Creator's own reasonableness, the question that Aquinas's theodicy seeks at this point to answer: "It would seem that the woman should not have been made in the first production of things" (*ST*, 466). Aquinas's argument, formally and substantively, seeks to secure the reasonableness of man and of man's Creator: man, helped by woman in the work of generation, helps himself better than she can, has a nobler power of life; moreover, "man is yet further ordered to a still nobler vital action, and that is intellectual operation" (*ST*, 466).

One further possible problem with the reasonableness of creation is that if "subjection and limitation were a result of sin," but woman is "naturally of less strength and dignity than man," then "woman should not have been made in the first production of things before sin" (466). But, besides "servile" subjection, "by virtue of which a superior makes use of a subject for his own benefit"—that is, the kind of subjection that is self-interested, which began after sin—there is another, charitable kind, "called economic or civil, whereby the superior makes use of his subjects for their own benefit and good; and this kind of subjection existed even before sin" (*ST*, 466). Moreover, the reason why woman is subject to man, which is also the reason why he helps her more than she helps him, is that "in man the discretion of reason predominates" (*ST*, 467). Fundamental, then, to Aquinas's mapping of gender and class onto conceptive power and charitable benevolence is the distinction between self and other—a distinction of intense interest not only to Augustine but also to Ockham and Bradwardine, and to the psychologists of enjoyment, the casuists of charity, the writers of mirrors for princes and princesses, and theorists of the "common good."[9]

Thus Aquinas's answer to the third reason why women should never have been made ("occasions of sin should be cut off") is that it would not have been "fitting for the common good to be destroyed in order that individual evil might be avoided; especially as God is so powerful that He can direct any evil to a good end"; moreover, "if God had deprived the world of all those things which proved an occasion of sin, the universe would have been imperfect" (*ST*, 466–67). The full perfection of the created universe, its reasonableness and its lack of any significant lack, is linked here to the "common good" and its precedence over "individual evil"; the common good acquires a creationist status, as product and sign of absolute conceptive power, of the ability to think universals that transcend change, loss, destructivity.

Although itself a bravura display of conceptive power, scholastic philosophy's structure of ceaseless question and answer opens up certain fissures in the seamless rationality of creation. The voice of the creature who discovers that it is mortally wounded, which means also and inevitably wounded in its perceptivity, that is, in the way in which reality is affirmed for it, has a way of raising itself, in inquiry if not in reproach. Aquinas's work indicates for us one mode of rescue available to such a creature: the profoundly ethical project of ennobling subjectivity by justifying its relation to its Creator. Ethics, that is, tracks a path that emerges in its psychoticized form as the "redeemer fantasy," wherein the help the subject can give, to himself or to others, desperately affirms the very principle of rescue—the phantasmatic notion that absolute help might be on the way, that one's faults might be stably and lastingly supplemented by a subject-other mutual aid society.

## Schreber

The inability of fantasies of rescue to recuperate fully the fault in being—for example, the empty or imponderable (non-)origin that an encounter with shame might expose—is evident in the case of Schreber, who writes late in his struggle with his "illness" that "I have now long been aware that the persons I see about me are not 'cursorily improvised men' but real people, and that I must behave towards them as a reasonable man is used to behave toward his fellows."[10] Freud's observations on "megalomania" clarify the role, in redeemer fantasies, of the fragility of the subject's relation to the other, of the destabilization of the subject's ability to believe in the reality of a supplement or object invested with the power to rescue the subject.

This deficit in reality, however, can be refound and phantasmatically repaired within the megalomaniacal subject only because the subject, in psychoanalysis, is always already modeled on the other. Megalomania reveals the ease with which the subject "becomes" the other in love or in mourning; it reveals also the difficulty of distinguishing categorically between injury to the subject's ideal image and injury to the image of the other. Thus if a subject's (self-) love is too lost, perhaps because it loves in a way that reasonable reality finds shameful (a man with bad habits), or because it has an imperfect body and can neither remain constant nor judge constants (a woman), the subject may decide " *'I do not love at all—I do not love anyone'* ... I love only myself." The resulting "megalomania" resembles the "overvaluation of the love object" that takes place in mourning; its purposive grandiosity, that is, is commensurate with the impossibility of the desire the subject cannot address.[11]

Schreber's *Denkwurdigkeiten eines Nervenkranken* demonstrates the shattering cost of theodicy when the creature in question has become unintelligible to himself. Schreber's metamorphosis is an almost parodic carnalization of ethical subjectivation. He dates his illness from a time when it occurred to him that "it really must be very nice to be a woman submitting to the act of copulation" (*DN* 36, *SE* 13). After this he begins to develop his rescue fantasy. God wants Schreber to become a woman; slowly and painfully (because God is not very good at miracles), Schreber's body is changed into the body of a woman, impregnated by divine rays in order to redeem the world. His transformation reveals the workings of sexual difference and proscribed desire in the wish to become a redeemer—in the wish for a certain power of alteration, figured so often not only by the transfigured body (whether crucified or beatified into a phantasmatic image of the power to endure), but also by the subject as object of its own ethical powers of self-re-creation.[12]

But the kind of redeemer Schreber wants to become is more like the "immaculate virgin" than the son of God. His rescue fantasy reheroizes a mortified subject who wishes to "become" a "woman" (Schreber associates women with voluptuousness and silliness) and who wishes at the same time to possess unassailable honor and wisdom.[13] This is an exacting process: bird-souls with girls' names inject "corpse-poison" into Schreber's body, he is mockingly called "Miss Schreber," his organs are shattered, he dies and decomposes. Schreber's ordeal redeems femaleness—or at least his desire with respect to it—by turning it into an *ascesis* that will demonstrate the indestructibility of the messianic self Schreber adopts as the object of his love and the touchstone of his certainty.[14]

And one aspect of this messianic self is its triumphant remasculation. Schreber writes:

> Every attempt at murdering my soul, or at emasculating me for purposes *contrary to the Order of Things* (that is, for the gratification of the sexual appetites of a human individual), or later at destroying my understanding... has come to nothing. From this... struggle between one weak man and God himself, I have emerged as the victor... because the Order of Things stands upon my side. (*DN* 61, *SE* 19)

Soul murder, the destruction of understanding, and emasculation are, for Schreber, parallel assaults; because he wants to become a woman despite the dangers of so doing, he decomposes emasculation into two kinds, one authorized by the Order of Things (having as its grand purpose world redemption), the other contrary to that Order ("for the gratification of the sexual appetites of a human individual").[15] Schreber gets the Order of Things on his side by hyperlibidinizing his own body-soul— he is the apple of God's eye, however dubious the distinction—and by risking the very reality of that body-soul, that is, its survival but also its prestige, its credibility, its ability to comprehend reality, in battle with the Other to end all others, namely, the divinized image without whose support his subjectivity cannot survive but whose existence *as* Other is equally threatening to Schreber's project of self-regeneration.

This God resembles the "bird-souls" to whom Schreber gives "girls' names" "because of their voluptuous bent": God demands a "constant state of enjoyment"; he is "childish" and completely ineducable.[16] He resembles Schreber in his shameful desires: "Deuce take it! What a thing to have to say—that God lets himself be f——d!" (*DN* 194, *SE* 27n2; Schreber is likewise mocked by rays of God: "So *this* sets up to have been a Senatsprasident, this person who lets himself be f——d!"). The specularity of this series of figures, along with the theme of coercion that links them (the bird-souls are forced to say things they don't mean, it is against Schreber's will that he says nasty things about God), indicates that the fault in the creature is mirrored in a faulty Creator. With Schreber the endlessness of the suffering associated with this decomposition of ideality pays homage to the irreparable nature of the wound thus dealt to the subject's capacity for certitude, and seeks to relieve that wound by demonstrating in the flesh—by substantiating—the subject's capacity to endure.

At the core of Schreber's rescue fantasy, then, is the question of a man's honor, and for Schreber this is an ethical question, that is, a question of educability. Schreber's reformulation of the symbolics of the rescuing and (self-)rescued subject is so testily carnal because Schreber is aware of a contradiction: sexual difference is part of the Order of Things (femaleness is shameful, and so on), but it is also negotiable, profane. Even God doesn't care about it when his *jouissance* is at stake, a fact that jolts Schreber to the core, since he has had to pay a very high price (in the way of shame) for his bad habits, his ineducability, his femaleness. In an attempt to restore sexual difference (and reasonableness) to the Order of Things while recognizing that at the same time sex is changeable, Schreber pays for what he learns and likes about the mortality and contingency of powers by mortifying his flesh, ransoming his own and his deity's fecklessness through a perdurable suffering.

Schreber's carnal theodicy thus simultaneously excoriates and redivinizes a creationist positing of man's identity in relation to the field from which he originates. Schreber's response to the discovery that sex can be changed is to materialize an art of self-transformation addressed, as Lacan would put it, to the ethical question of what it means when "man" fashions the signifer ex nihilo. In other words, Schreber's story addresses the ethical problems raised not only by man's production of the artifact, but also by man's (and God's) production, *through* ethics, as artifact, out of nothing: that is, man and his God emerge as such ex nihilo, out of that which they are not, as do their works—a fact that they are always trying to conceal, by passing the signifier off as that which it is not.

## Queens, Charity and Courtly Love

The later Middle Ages has been seen by some scholars as a particularly bad time for the notion of woman's capacity to exercise reason.[17] It has also been seen as a bad time for women rulers. Pauline Stafford argues that queenly power suffered from the diminishing importance of household politics; Paul Strohm writes that queens were "progressively excluded from affairs of state" and "compensated in sumptuous but highly inflated symbolic coin."[18] Increasingly the queen, like Alceste in the Prologue to *The Legend of Good Women,* is patron and intercessor, and little else; Diane Bornstein explains that the *Speculum dominarum,* the first "mirror for the princess," develops the political role of the queen almost entirely in terms of charity—"her reputation for mercy should make her visits a welcome solace to the poor, the oppressed, and the unfortunate"—and teaches the queen "virtuous love" "of God, relatives, neighbors, fellow Christians, husband, and children."[19]

But "affairs of state" and "symbolic coin" are difficult to separate; power is not purely a matter of public administration, nor is the love a queen might inspire in her subjects necessarily easy to manage politically. Bornstein argues that courtesy books written by men emphasize women's "sexual and familial roles" out of "an anxiety about women overreaching their domain."[20] The late medieval "mirror for the princess," with its inculcation of the "passive" virtues of "humility, obedience, modesty, piety, and chastity," is apotropaic; it tries to ethicize the queen's dangerous status as sublime object.[21] And one aspect of her sublimity is the indeterminacy of her gender.

The queen is a paradoxical figure because she links sovereignty to the feminine. She is, as Ian Maclean puts it, a "point of contradiction," a "dislocation" in the "structure of thought."[22] Because of this, her power is fascinating. And as late medieval representations of female patronage make evident, the problem of her pleasure likewise becomes exigent.[23] The ethicizing of queenship represents a compelling indeterminacy as dangerous but educable; the fantasy of the queen's benevolence specularly reassures the narcissism of those she can compel.[24] It is true that the figures of queenly petition and intercession lend sovereign authority to sexual difference and heterosexualize sovereignty, but despite such indications of a straightforward gendering of charity, the apotropaic figures of petition and intercession are perilously unstable, as their careful handling in royal ritual suggests.[25] To understand this fact, and its implications for Alceste in the *Legend,* we need to see the queen as part of a broad medieval ethicizing of the proximate other—the neighbor, consort, spouse, friend, brother—and we need in particular to explore the role of the lady in the ethics of courtly love.

If the goal of premodern ethics is a subject that can will itself into a nobler state of being, the embrace of passion by *fin' amors* might seem to pose a problem. But *fin' amors* (courtly love) crafts an aristocratic subject whose pathos is the ground of its *ascesis,* who wills its own passional suffering. *Fin' amors* develops a sexuality—an identitarian stylization of sex, or in this case of not-yet-sex—for which temporality, and therefore the mortal suffering bound up with signification, is constitutive of the specific prestige of its pleasures.[26] The *finamen* (courtly lover) possesses a special body capable of deferral and lack; it can endure, because it so chooses, and its endurance marks its special aliveness, its power of alteration over its own flesh. Thus the *finamen* can speak endlessly of its suffering flesh, of the "gentil herte" whose passion or "pite" defines a subject boundlessly aware of and inhabited by an intimate other. It is on the basis of this relation to the intimate other that *fin' amors* founds its ascetic timing and its ethics.

Chivalric discourse usually presents the relation between the subject and its intimate other as one of service or rescue. It thereby ethicizes the honorable subject's finitude, what we might call its ignoble origins, its mimetic dependence on the other. A subject founded on the image of an other is a subject that will never be full, or fully be; and because of this its ability to help or to be helped is finite.[27] For Lacan, this is so partly because the Other that structures the subject also has its limits (73, 304). The symbolic order is open, it offers no absolute guarantee of meaning or pleasure or redemption, and its import is the finitude of powers and of the subjects who take shape through their workings.

If the power of the Other is limited, then in relation to his finitude man "can expect help from no one"; nor can ultimate enjoyment be attained any more than absolute power, because desire *is* change as such (293). The subject's wish for rescue—a wish addressed to and by ethics—points to but also obscures the finitude of the subject and the Other, "the Other whose primacy of position Freud affirms in the form of something *entfremdet*, something strange to me, although it is at the heart of me, something that on the level of the unconscious only a representation can represent" (71). The dependence of the subject's "experience of satisfaction" on the Other, the other as *"Nebenmensch,"* is for Lacan the insight fundamental to any understanding of charitable practices of (self-)rescue.[28]

When we recoil from the obligation to love our neighbor, we do so, argues Lacan, because of the "evil" that dwells within the neighbor, the *"jouissance"* we don't dare go near, but of which we have an inkling because some form of unspeakable evil dwells also within us (186). Instead of love, all too readily we offer our neighbor the helping hand, whereby we recreate our neighbor according to the reassuring image of our own narcissism. Altruism thus secures the ideal image; through it

> I can avoid taking up the problem of the evil I desire, and that my neighbor desires also. That is how I spend my life, ... in my neighbor's time, where all the neighbors are maintained equally at the marginal level of reality of my own experience.
> ... What I want is the good of others in the image of my own. ...
> The whole thing deteriorates so rapidly that it becomes: provided that it depend on my efforts. (Lacan, *Ethics*, 187)[29]

This is why we are so easily turned back from the path of our *jouissance* (a question posed urgently in courtly literature, for example by the *Legend*'s repeated amatory debacles): we retreat from the danger posed by *jouissance* either to self or to other, because self and other are always mutually implicated. We retreat "from assaulting the image of the other, because it was the image on which we were formed as an ego. Here we find the convincing power of altruism . . . [and] the leveling power of a certain law of equality—that which is formulated in the notion of the general will."[30]

The transitivism of charity seeks in the specular structure of benevolence to manage the finitude implied by the founding of the subject on the image of the other; it seeks the reassurance of equivalence, as though either the mortifying or exhilarating aspects of the subject's difference from the ideal image could be dealt with by adequating an image defined as common, capable of universal possession. This is why figures of the common good, and discourses of rescue, are so often related to the figure of the intimate stranger: hence the "apotheosis of the neighbor" in Christianity as well as in *fin' amors* (in the form of the *bon vezi*, the "good neighbor," the "lady"); hence the repeatedly enjoined rescue, in treatises on chivalry, of widows, orphans, and the Eucharist—that figure of a proximate, humanized God, of God as *Nebenmensch*, who feeds us with his lifeblood while divinizing the object's capacity to endure suffering, and who thereby takes on all the evil that lies within the hearts of all the neighbors.[31]

In courtly literature, the figure of near distance, in time or space, repeatedly marks the strange intimacy of the Other, the element of the unknown in the subject's desire. In *The Legend of Good Women*, for example, Cleopatra is "another wyf" (594); between Piramus and Tysbe "ther nas but a ston-wal" (713); Dido's "pity" turns Aeneas the "straunger" into her "newe gest" and then her "dere herte" (1075, 1158, 1294); Procne finds her mutilated sister "in a litel stounde" (2374). As Lacan puts it, covetousness is addressed to the good that is our neighbor's, to an object valuable because it has "the closest possible relationship" to the field of the subject's desire, "to that in which the human being can rest"—"insofar," that is, "as it is the good in which he may find rest" (83). The phantasm of repose in "the good" (in goods and in that which is defined as the good) is thus closely linked to restlessness, insofar as the good that seems to provide it is always in the possession of the neighbor.

Thus the *brevitas* of Chaucer's legends of good women—the haste with which they are narrated—marks them as taking place in the time of the neighbor. And in the legends, as in so much other courtly literature, the rescued or rescuing lady is nearby, that is, uncannily able to be found, but also impossible to stay with. Both proximity and distance are crucial to the lady's positioning, because she is "extimate": she marks not only the intimacy of the "I's" formation through the other, but also a limit, the "I's" distance from itself, from the stranger within. She is both inaccessible and next door; in the case of Alceste, she is in the possession of, but (in a figure that doubles her neighborliness) yet not the wife of, the god of Love.[32] And when the god of Love first addresses the narrator of the Prologue to the *Legend*, it is to challenge his nearness: "What dostow her / So nygh myn oune floure, so boldely? / It were better worthy, trewely, / A worm to neghen ner my flour than thow" (315–18).

The plasticity of the figure of the *Nebenmensch* is crucial to its role in the ethical structure of courtly love. Neighborliness is not identity; next door is not unknown territory. Insofar as the spatiality of the *Nebenmensch* is "over there," in a place that can be found but never secured, the beauty of the lady likewise marks the extimacy of the structuring of the subject according to the image of the other.[33] Her most rigorous and inhuman forms reveal that she is *not* to be equated with the good; she does not offer a phantasmatic image of desire's closure but rather of its relentlessness. Her arbitrary, capricious demands express the exactions of the ideal image, the impossibility of identifying with it fully, and therefore the endless labor involved in the ethical pursuit of (self-)rescue.

It is, moreover, continuous with the logic of extimacy that the image of beauty should, in some courtly poems, decompose altogether to reveal the "vacuole" of unimaginable desire, in the form of the knight's sodomitical encounter, via the *ascesis/jouissance* of shame, with the lady's "hole."[34] The "lady" can readily point to a desire that goes beyond certain limits, where sodomy serves as a figure for the abjection/jubilation of the extimacy of the body. Or the lady might be turned into an image of the "good," her virtue chivalrously rescued, her gender secured. If the obverse of shame is the glory of beautiful form, the result of such a rescue in the Prologue to the *Legend* is Alceste, whose status as heterosexual, female, constant, and salvific is established through the metamorphosis of a daisy, the "blisful sighte" of which "softneth" the "sorwe" of the narrator (than whom "Ther loved no wight hotter in his lyve" [50, 59]), into a woman wearing a "whit corowne" (216). It could be argued that, whereas in Ovid the human body is transformed through the workings of desires that perpetually escape the confines of the ideal image, Chaucer does it to Alceste in reverse. But the Prologue's attempt to fix the mobility of desire is not entirely successful, and both the attempt and the failure are central to the Prologue's legendary beauty. The ethical poetics of *The Legend of Good Women* both assert and put into question the humanization, feminization, and heterosexualization of the indeterminate inhuman partner.

## The Legend of Good Women

A number of critics have noted the importance of queenly intercession to the Prologue of *The Legend of Good Women*.[35] Critics have also drawn attention to the *Legend*'s apotropaic handling of the power of good women.[36] Repeatedly in the *Legend*, "pite" is placed in the heart of woman and given to man: Alceste's pity saves the narrator (503); Dido's pity gives Aeneas a kingdom (1080); Hypermnestra's pity paralyzes her hands that "ben nat shapen for a knyf" (2684, 2692). "Pite" signifies the feeling of being bound to the other, as its derivation from *pietas* suggests.[37] When Alceste rescues the narrator from the anger of the god of Love, the god praises her: "pite renneth soone in gentil herte; / That maistow seen; she kytheth what she ys" (503–4). In an eagerly specular assent worthy of the *Book of the Duchess,* the narrator replies, "No moore but that I see wel she is good" (506). "Pite," crossing the line between subject and other, is linked with the specular construction of goodness and identity, and with the promise of their visibility or demonstrability ("she kytheth what she ys"); to open oneself up or pour oneself out is to show what one is and that one is.[38]

In the *Speculum dominarum* the queen's charity makes her "*praeclarissima, illustrissima,* and *excellentissima*": clear, beautiful, honorable, *manifest.*[39] *Kithen,* too, means not only to reveal, but also to prove oneself, and to give alms.[40] "Pite" rushes in and reveals itself outwardly at the moment of perfected memory and identification: Alceste's pity not only shows that she is "good," that she "is what she is"; the narrator can now remember who she is. Pity binds subject to other; one is obliged to recognize it. Like "compassioun," "bounte," "merci," the signifier "pite" promises, and promises to signify, what Butler calls "the manageability of unspeakable loss."[41]

That the phantasmatic promise of the good offered by these signifiers is unsustainable, that their promise of "semantic abundance" is unrealizable, is of course figured in the legends' repetitively failed unions, their ceaseless slippage from truth to treachery; despite the cradling framework of the "good" women's constancy, of the object's phantasmatic capacity to endure, the wind of faction and betrayal blows throughout, as cruelly in the historical events that haunt the Prologue as in the sails that blow away the faith of pious Aeneas (1365).[42] The Prologue is glorious; but its semantics speak of, and do not clearly condemn, broken faith. The birds "deffye" the "foweler" (138; *defien* can mean to disavow a pledge, to renounce one's allegiance to a lord); the god of Love accuses the narrator of having "reneyed" his "lay" (336; *reneien* means to forsake one's beliefs, retract a pledge, withdraw one's devotion).[43] In the Prologue cruelty afflicts the very earth, hurt by winter's "swerd of cold" (127), "naked made and mat" — changed into the poor and shameful obverse of the magnificent outpouring of compassionate identity that is Alceste. The birds suffer from the "foweler," "that, for his coveytise / Had hem betrayed with his sophistrye" (136–37). But the evil in the heart of the "foweler" turns up in the hearts of certain of its prey: those "that hadde doon unkyndenesse / As dooth the tydif, for newfangelnesse" (153–54).

It is consistent with the brilliant symbolicity of the Prologue, with the faith it lavishes on beautiful signifiers, that the promise, despite its springtime transience, asks for, and to some extent gets, our credence.

The pain caused by the "foweler," displaced by the pain caused by the treachery of certain "foweles," is relieved through the birds' capacity to promise and thus to renew themselves: they "sworen on the blosmes to be trewe / So that hire makes wolde upon hem rewe" (157–58). Their reward: "Pitee, thurgh his stronge gentil myght, / Forgaf, and made Mercy passen Ryght" (161–62). And this masculinizing of pity is followed by a protestation as to its ethical status: "But I ne clepe nat innocence folye, / Ne fals pitee, for vertu is the mene, / As Etik seith; in swich maner I mene" (164–66).

But despite this pious affirmation of the "mene" — which promises to settle everything through its rhyming of "I mean" with the "mean" of virtue — the text implies that all the birds, not just particular ones that have "doon unkyndenesse," may have been hateful: "And thus thise foweles, voide of al malice, / Acordeden to love, and laften vice / Of hate" (167–69). The referent of "thise foweles" is unclear — for example, does it include the pitying birds (presumably female, although pity is "stronge")? In the midst of this (re)generative pageant, the text's search for a figure of universality produces the implication of a universal capacity for betrayal and shame. Promise and pity make these birds into good neighbors; the signifier, in this case song, promises a perfection of redeemed and lawful pleasure ("Welcome, somer, oure governour and lord!" [170]), but part of the power of this much-admired passage is undeniably that, in it, we glimpse something unspeakable.

Almost without our noticing, prey turns into predator, and predators then turn into a chorus singing "alle of oon acord" (169). The poetics of the Prologue are both metamorphic (shape-shifting, but with the aim of recovering innocence) and specular (but the kind of mirroring that has something slightly different — the other — on the other side). This is why the narrator introduces his impossible vegetable love, the daisy, while introducing himself: "And as for me" (29); "Now have I thanne eek this condicioun / That, of al the floures in the mede, / Thanne love I most thise floures white and rede, / Swiche as men callen daysyes in our toun" (40–44). His "condicioun," his "mode of being," is to love "most" that which he repeatedly desires to see ("ther daweth me no day / That I nam up and walkyng in the mede / To seen this flour ayein the sonne sprede / Whan it upryseth erly by the morwe" [46–50]). He arises as she arises from the "derknesse" that she hates (63); the ritual re-creation and salvific protectiveness of his "reverence" in her "presence" involves a devotional seeing (51–52; *reverence* is respect, honor, but also specifically religious veneration).[44]

This seeing is transitivist, specularly vivifying: the "blisful sighte" of the daisy "softneth al [his] . . . sorwe," even as his "reverence" raises this "she," this "daisy," to "the dignity of the Thing." Its/her consolatory, restorative power mirrors the ritual attentiveness he provides it/her. Moreover, the ritual repetitiveness of his devotion is mirrored in her constancy *as* vision: it is "evere ilyke faire and fressh of hewe" (55); then the narrator says, "And I love it, and ever ylike new, / And evere shal" (56–57). "Ever ylike new" is indeed the ambition of the Prologue's beauty, through which the narrator constitutes both the mirage of the object's vitality and the reflected endurance of the devotional subject. The importance of visibility is emphasized even more when the narrator must run quickly not only in the morning but also in the evening "To seen this flour, how it wol go to reste, / For fere of nyght, so hateth she derknesse" (62–63). The figure of the daisy becomes a means to divinize the very conditions of visibility through which the screen of beauty may blind us, and point us, to the field of desire that lies beyond it: "Here chere is pleynly sprad in the brightnesse / Of the sonne, for ther yt wol unclose" (64–65).

Like Schreber in relation to his God, the daisy is heliotropic—fully visible, "pleynly sprad" (the fantasy is of its perfect accessibility) in response to the eye of day, the sun. The daisy's own solar identity is made even more explicit when the narrator describes himself at a subsequent moment (a moment that reiterates previous devotions) as sinking down "softely" (the word used to describe the daisy's restorative power), "And, lenynge on myn elbowe and my side" (in other words, planted), "The longe day I shoop me for t'abide / For nothing elles, and I shal nat lye, / But for to loke upon the dayesie, / That wel by reson men it calle may / The 'dayesye,' or elles the 'ye of day,' / The emperice and flour of floures alle. / I pray to God that faire mote she falle, / And alle that loven floures, for hir sake!" (178–87). The sublime object that is the daisy emerges as the day's eye under the eye of day at the moment when the narrator dedicates his day to eyeing her. And the specular nature of intercession and rescue is brought out again here when the narrator prays for the daisy's well-being ("faire mote she falle") and for "alle that loven floures," that is, for himself.

This narrator whose sorrow is softened by following the daisy's every movement, by gazing at it and at its own ocular receptivity, locates salvific power in visibility itself; visibility screens from view the hateful "derknesse" that frightens the daisy, despite her powers of resurrection. Visibility also calls attention to that darkness. The Prologue's desire for and deferral of the limit, of transformation—its pacifications of destructivity, its heteronormative pageantry, but also its passion for scoping daisies, not to mention its logophilia—are enacted in that moment of repose when the narrator "shoop" himself "for t'abide" "the longe day," in the sweetly inspired "joly month of May," in which he thought he might, "day by day, / Duellen alwey" (171–81). "Dwellen" can mean "to remain," "live, dwell," but also "to procrastinate, delay, linger." It can mean to take time to tell something, a constant problem for the narrator ("I may not al at-ones speke in ryme" [102], although his richly artificed repetitions suggest he's trying his hardest), but also "to hold back or restrain (lust)," to postpone, to desist, refrain or stay away from, to stop speaking of something—in short, "al at-ones," to linger *and* to leave, to dilate *and* to abbreviate.[45] When one dwells, one is either at home or away, or a bit of both: neighborly.

"Dwellen" epitomizes that saturated aspect of the poetic timing of the Prologue, its attempt to slow description down to the stillness of the captivating image. "Dwellen" epitomizes also the fantastic pleasure of a fullness of expectation conferred by deferral. The narrator gets up before daylight because he is "constreyned" with "gledy desir," he "thursts," he runs home swiftly at night "erly for to ryse" (103–7, 200–201). Being near, nigh, on the brink, is a matter of time as well as space, the time of the *Nebenmensch*.[46] Insofar as "dwellen" evokes both lingering and hastening away, dilating and abbreviating, the leisurely lyricism of the Prologue and the comparatively unadorned haste of the legends seem to split the verb apart; but this divide is adumbrated in the Prologue itself, in the almost comic (were it not so beautiful) dashing-about the narrator has to do in order to follow the movements of his flower, "hastening" being what passes for the *finamen*'s ordeal in the earlier, comforting stages of the Prologue, and haste and rest being, apparently, his only two gears.[47]

Thus the specularly heliotropic, "hot" narrator hastens home "To goon to reste, and erly for to ryse, / To seen this flour to sprede, as I devyse. / And in a litel herber that I have, / That benched was on turves fressh ygrave, / I bad men sholde me my couche make" (201–5). The daisy in effect puts the narrator to sleep, in an alluring image of the repose man seeks in the objects of his desire, but this image points uncannily to the potential destructivity of desire with respect to the "nothing I" of the subject, a destructivity from which the narrative then runs away. The narrator goes to bed in his "herber," with its newly dug earthern benches, but lest things get too deadly there, in the space of a few lines he wakes into a dream in daylight in the meadow, looking ("To seen this flour" [211]) instead of hiding his eyes (208).

The dream is a vision that raises the stakes of vision even further, by enhancing the daisy's solar properties; it/she is now both Alceste and a brilliant crown, a thing and a woman. There are apotropaic aspects to this transformation; an impossible object, an uncannily vivid plant, decomposes into images at once more human and more intricately insentient. Yet Alceste herself is a "relyke" (321). She signifies survival and its evanescence; she is a trace, a vestige, an aftereffect.[48] Being neighborly now means being a ghostly simulacrum, accessible even beyond the limit of life, which the narrator now comes close to facing. Her solar properties are enhanced also through her association with the god of Love, whose "face shown so bryghte / ...unnethes myghte I him beholde," who steals the "gledy" narrator's fire (the god has two fiery darts, "gleedes rede," in his hands; his "lokynge" makes the narrator's heart cold (232–

33, 167, 172). *Cold* in such a context can mean "to lose warmth (as in death)" (the *Middle English Dictionary* cites several uses of the verb *colden* in descriptions of dying), as well as "to be chilled, shocked, or overcome"; when used "of love, charity, joy," it means "to lose fervor, slacken."[49] *Colden* is thus one of the terms in the Prologue that form a rich semantic cluster around both charity (*pite, compassioun, merciable, mek, tretable, benigne, bounte, comfort, releven*) and aggressivity (*peine, reneien, agreven, defien, disteinen, colden*).

It is noteworthy that the god's solar power freezes us in our tracks. What works on one level as a sanctification of sexual difference—whereby the mortality, the changefulness, that the signifier signifies is made brilliant and merciable in the figure of Alceste, and brilliant and terrifying in the case of the god of Love—reveals a transitivist structure or, in other words, reveals the destructivity in the heart of the charitable neighbor. For Alceste's very excellence, even if what she excels in is pity, makes her as potentially lethal as the god of Love; she is *praeclarissima,* and the *Balade* confers upon her a similar power to drain the heat and light, the life and visibility, from her rivals. Other good women are sentenced to be neither seen nor heard, even at the moment of their invocation (a sentence strangely fulfilled by the comparative lifelessness of the women in the legends): "Thy faire body, lat yt nat appere, / Lavyne"; "Maketh of your trouthe neythir boost ne soun"; "My lady cometh, that al this may dysteyne" (256–57, 267, 269). *Disteinen* can mean either to color or stain something, *or* its reverse—to deprive something of color, brightness, beauty; figuratively, to dim or put in the shade.[50] Even more aggressively it can mean to sully someone's reputation or to desecrate something worthy of honor; it is thus related to *defien* and *reneien*. The semantic range of this word tracks the specular relation between the god of Love and Alceste; for all their supposed differences of gender, of temper, they share a power of alteration, a power of brightening *and* of obscuring. "Disteinen" reveals the aggressivity of Alceste's image, of her status as image, largely hidden from view but emerging in the "Balade"— as if the terrifying (shameful, abjecting) implications for the admiring subject of Alceste's superlative condition could only emerge openly in a structure even more formal, repetitive, and deliberately devotional than is the rest of the Prologue.

The doubleness of the ideal image—its promise of rescue, its rejection of everything that needs rescue—leaves its traces in a few of the Prologue's other words of praise (as well as in the abjecting of the good women of the legends). The meanings of *digne* (the word used by the god of Love to describe his ghostly "relyke" [321]) shade from "worthy of great honor or reverence" to "proud," "disdainful."[51] Alceste's "bounte," which according to the god of Love "doubleth" her "renoun" (522), is one of the terms linking Alceste's charity to the power of her identity, in the form of its capacity to manifest itself; *bounte* is "the quality of kindness, benevolence, mercy," "liberality in giving."[52] But other meanings of *bounte* hint at Alceste's participation in the aggressivity of which the god of Love is such a brilliant image: *bounte* can also mean "knightly prowess, strength, valor, chivalry." And even so benign a word as *benigne* (243) points to the brinksmanship of the Prologue: it can mean simply "gentle, kind, generous, merciful"; but, of an inferior, "meek, submissive"; of an animal, "friendly, gentle, tame," a range of meanings also registered in *meke*, that is, "gentle, quiet, unaggressive"; of a woman, "modest," "merciful," "submissive, obedient, docile, amenable"; of an animal, "tame," "lowly, poor, unimportant, abject," "weak, helpless."[53] *Benigne* tracks the transitivist crossings of the subject who helps and the subject who is helpless.

Helplessness thus haunts the Prologue, significantly in the form of poverty, described in the story of the birds who escape the fowler as one of the ills surmounted by the earth in springtime through the ability of "th' atempre sonne" to "releven" it: "Forgeten hadde the erthe his pore estat / Of wynter" (128, 125–26). The redress of poverty is one of the meanings of relief (*releven*) (hence the term "relief fund"): it can mean "to ease or mitigate, . . . to render less burdensome": to requite love, gratify; to provide for, "to help in poverty or necessity"; to feed an animal or bird, to feed the soul, to bring deliverance, rescue; to spare from death, to free a land from hardship (*OED*, s.v. "relieve"; *MED*, s.v. "releven"). *Comfort*, attributed to the "presence" of Alceste by the worried narrator (who at the same time prays for her [277–79]), can, like *releven*, refer to pleasure, gratification, invigoration; relief of poverty, illness, suffering, as when food warms and comforts the bodies of beasts or cool water comforts animals fleeing the hunt (*MED, OED*, s.v. "comfort").

If solar privilege is the obverse, adversary, and comforter of poverty, it is not surprising that the narrator's dream also intensifies the ethical stakes of vision by mortifying the "nothing I" that the narrator earlier imagines himself to be ("ye ben verraily / The maistresse of my wit, and nothing I" [87–88]). The narrator is (in the eyes of the god of Love at least) less worthy than a worm "to neghen ner my flour" (318), more negligible than the kind of creature who burrows its way through earthy recesses. In the *Parliament of Fowls* "wormes corrupcioun" is one of the insults flung at the lower-class birds who do not have "gentil hertes" and cannot "guess" what love is. The prestige of this creature who is not even a worm is very low, but insofar as shame and beauty both point to the unspeakable desire that lies beyond them, the neighborly interest Alceste takes in this not-even-worm — the way, from a distance, they mirror each other — is instructive. "Nothing" is indeed likely to be the condition of the "I" who gets too near the *Nebenmensch*, too near the nonknowing framed by the image of beauty.

In its way, the Prologue is as repetitious as the legends: daisies turn into crowns that look like daisies, "nothing I" turns into not-even-worm, the narrator runs back and forth, he prays for his daisy, she prays for him. But the Prologue has seemed beautiful to many critics, whereas the legends have often seemed merely drab. The problem of beauty and drabness is not incidental to the *Legend's* ethical concern with the evil that lies in the heart of the neighbor, but is, rather, its formal manifestation. The sheer concentration of the Prologue's sublime poetics, the very brilliance of its mirrors, points to the ethical meaning of artifice as such—the way beauty signifies symbolicity itself as that which must always emerge around the indeterminacy of desire; the way, as Lacan puts it, beauty reveals the "site of man's relationship to his own death . . . in a blinding flash," because it is "insofar as the subject articulates a signifying chain that he comes up against the fact that he may disappear from the chain of what he is" (Lacan, *Ethics*, 295); the way there emerges, from and through the specularity of the Prologue, the transitivism that blocks but cannot be without mobility; in other words, the way metonymy takes over (the daisy becomes Alceste), the "change as such" that is desire (293).[54]

It is precisely the vitalization of the object's transience—the claim made on our desire by something we know to be a fabrication—that powers the beauty of the Prologue and makes Alceste not just a remembered image of the power of rescue, but also an image that "disteynes." Because she is supremely illustrious and fatal to any figure that seeks to resemble her, she is displaced; although she revives the figure of sexual difference after the wonderful weirdness of the indeterminate it/she daisy, her position is equivocal—she goes to hell for her husband but appears to us as the consort of another man. And in keeping with the brinksmanship of the Prologue, her beauty courts disaster; some of the most awkward poetry of the Prologue is to be found in the lines that describe her crown, almost ready to topple from the weight of accumulated resemblance:

> For al the world, ryght as a dayesye
> Ycorouned ys with white leves lyte,
> So were the flowrouns of hire coroune white.
> For of o perle fyn, oriental,
> Hire white coroune was ymaked al;
> For which the white coroune above the grene
> Made hire lyke a daysie for to sene,
> Considered eke hir fret of gold above. (218–25)

And the visual center of this crowning accumulation of resemblance ("ryght as," "So were," "lyke," "for to sene") is the "o perle fyn," which almost stops our gaze by taking the "vacuole" one step further and revisioning it as that for which emptiness is so often itself a screen: the pearl of *jouissance*, the site of the *bon vezi*'s enjoyment. This is to put something in the place of nothing, which indeed has the same destabilizing effect on sexual difference as putting nothing in the place of something. Something of the uncanniness of the daisy's opaque floral eye is transferred here, rarefied, but equally captivating.

The comparative drabness of the legends is not of a different aesthetic order from the beauty of the Prologue. Rather, the legends enact the failure of metamorphic promise, the loss of expectancy and *jouissance,* the weariness of the object condemned phantasmatically to charitable endurance. It is this "power to support a form of suffering," this re-creation of the *Nebenmensch* as a "double" "made inaccessible to destruction," that makes the legends suffer by comparison.[55] The legends fail to be beautiful because they figure the exhaustion of the enduring form of the image. The depressed value of the signifier in the legends is the result of a certain decathexis of the signifier as such, that is, of its changefulness; the legends try to retain the signifier while stripping it of its power to escape.

It could be argued that Sade makes, as it were, much more vivid work of the image of suffering than do the legends; what bars this in Chaucer's poem is its unwillingness to relinquish the figure of rescue, so that the "good" stops us short of confronting the unbearable suffering of the image when we demand that it live on despite our attempts to destroy it. *The Legend of Good Women* fantasizes that good women, despite their suffering, have really been rescued, worthy of their textual resurrection because of their capacity for sacrifice. The narrator is their redeemer; although chivalric rescue fails within the legends, the legends are produced by a chivalrous rescuer of the reputations of women—at no small cost to himself, as the narrator repeatedly reminds us, since writing the legends is hard work. No wonder he wants to get through them as quickly as possible, since they are for him precisely a sacrificial payment, the loss of *jouissance* in the neighbor's time.

The legends gender as feminine the suffering but never obliterated "good" object, the loss of *jouissance* at stake in charitable donation. The women of the legends often begin their stories with substantial resources of affection, wealth, and secret knowledge; by the end of their stories they have usually been robbed, emptied, and eviscerated. They are "benigne": rescuers so imperiled by the extent of their power to give themselves away that they cannot rescue themselves or be rescued by others. It is noteworthy that, despite what they do for others, good women seem helpless largely because they cannot help themselves; it is also noteworthy that, despite their goodness, their acts of pity can seem ethically equivocal.[56] But these facts only underscore the endlessness of the demand that impels charity. Help will always be flawed and disappointing; no power of wealth, rule, or love can redress the outrage of lost *jouissance.* And in the legends, the mortal creature's failure to secure rescue from the image of the other on whom it is founded, is — it's an old story — given to the woman in her figure *as* helper.

In the legends the impossibility of absolute rescue is represented as the frustration of heterosexual love. The difference that separates "men" from "women" and makes heterosexual union so charged, delicate, and desperate a matter stands in for finitude, turning limit into exploit, impossibility into irony, and producing thereby the truth of the genders that seem unable to enter into relation with one another no matter how hard they try. Thus we might address the mystery of the poem's repetitively failed transactions, exchanges, and unions by proposing that these very failures, these breaches of contract, these endings of love in betrayal, of life in death, reinscribe the certainty of gender by insisting on the depth, variety, and intractability of the walls, oceans, fathers, gods, passions, and errors that keep men and women apart — and make their attempts to unite, however futile, so heroic and so tragic.

In other words, the legends try to make it look as though it's the walls, and not the emptiness between them, that pose the problem for good loving. The genders on which heterosexuality depends, and the ideologies of conception that deploy these categories, have as their central goal the explanation of why *jouissance* is never perfect and why the subject has its limits. This is why "prohibitions" seem to mandate that we must join with those who bear our *proximate* image (i.e., again, the prohibition screens the impossibility of full coincidence), and this is why sexual difference so often becomes a question for ethics.

But of course to the extent that the gender divisions thus ontologized on behalf of conceptive certitude in fact cannot merge absolutely (although only because absolute merger is impossible), the displacement and displaceability of desire emerges as an irony within the apotropaic figure of irony. If "women" are to be constituted as such in relation to goodness, that is, in relation to a certain capacity for evisceration, "women" emerge precisely for that reason as displaced. In other words, they emerge as such, as a category, most strongly when they are displaced from their male counterparts, as in the "Balade," where they are represented in a transitivist, invidious relation among themselves, along the axis of superlative visibility and invisibility, as the signifier itself — the mark that cannot be effaced and that nonetheless is never what it seems to be ("My lady cometh"; "Thy faire body, lat yt nat appere").

The comparative structure of the "Balade" acknowledges that appearing and disappearing, the power of illustration and its privation, are both at stake in acts of making. At the heart of the figure of union ("alle yfere," 263) is envy, the evil that lies in the heart of my neighbor; and concomitant with this disclosure of extimacy is the disclosure of the fact that "woman" is a signifier — an artifact whose finitude has everything to do with its ethical implications for gendered subjects. It's an ar-

tifact that reveals something also exposed by the *Legend's* distinction
between the adventuring men of the legends and the chastised and rescuing narrator: honor's biggest lie is its restyling, in the form of freedom,
risk, and adventure, of the finitude that reappears elsewhere in the equally
reassuring guise of rituals of submission to the law. The folly of honor is
not its sacrifice of the "good" but rather its sacrifice of *jouissance.*

## Notes

1. D. W. Robertson Jr., *A Preface to Chaucer: Studies in Medieval Perspectives* (Princeton: Princeton University Press, 1962), 25; citing his translation of Augustine, *On Christian Doctrine* (New York: Liberal Arts Press, 1958), 3.10.16.

2. Michel Foucault, *The Care of the Self*, vol. 3 of *The History of Sexuality*, trans.
Robert Hurley (New York: Vintage, 1988), 41–42. On medieval hygiene as "ethical activ-
ity," see Glending Olson, *Literature as Recreation in the Later Middle Ages* (Ithaca, N.Y.:
Cornell University Press, 1982), 54.

3. Lacan uses "creationism" to refer to ethical traditions that explain (and mytholo-
gize) the emergence of humanity and of the signifier; see *The Seminar of Jacques Lacan:
Book VII: The Ethics of Psychoanalysis, 1959–1960*, ed. Jacques-Alain Miller, trans. Dennis Porter (New York: Norton, 1992), esp. 3, 120–25, hereinafter cited in the text. Other
important contemporary readings of creationist discourse include Elaine Scarry, *The Body
in Pain: The Making and Unmaking of the World* (New York: Oxford University Press,
1985); Judith Butler, *Bodies That Matter: On the Discursive Limits of "Sex"* (New York:
Routledge, 1993), esp. 27–55; Jean-Joseph Goux, *Symbolic Economies* (Ithaca, N.Y.: Cornell University Press, 1990), esp. 213–43; and Kenneth Burke, *The Rhetoric of Religion:
Studies in Logology* (Berkeley: University of California Press, 1970).

4. F-Prologue, *Legend of Good Women*, line 166, hereinafter cited by line numbers in
the text; all citations to Chaucer's poetry are from *The Riverside Chaucer*, ed. Larry D.
Benson (Boston: Houghton Mifflin, 1987).

5. Saint Thomas Aquinas, *Commentary on the Nicomachean Ethics*, trans. C. I.
Litzinger, O.P. (Chicago: Henry Regnery, 1964), 7.50.5, c. 1374–75, pp. 641–42.

6. Aquinas, ibid., c. 1376, p. 642.

7. See Butler, *Bodies That Matter*, 50–51, on resemblance.

8. Saint Thomas Aquinas, *Summa theologica* [*ST*], trans. Fathers of the English Dominican Province, 5 vols. (Westminster, Md.: Christian Classics, 1981), vol. 1, part 1, question 92, article 1; hereinafter cited in the text.

9. Ockham, Holkot, and other fourteenth-century philosophers questioned whether
enjoyment (*fruitio*, the act of inhering in love with something for its own sake) could be
distinguished from the pleasure the self takes in enjoyment; see Arthur Stephen McGrade,
"Enjoyment at Oxford after Ockham: Philosophy, Psychology, and the Love of God," in
*From Ockham to Wyclif*, eds. Anne Hudson and Michael Wilks (Oxford: Ecclesiastical
History Society, Basil Blackwell, 1987), 63–88. On the common good, see Paul Strohm, *Social Chaucer* (Cambridge, Mass.: Harvard University Press, 1989), 145–47; on the pleasures
of the ruler in mirrors for princes, see Olson, *Literature as Recreation*, 53–83. The best
current treatment of medieval theories of charity is Michel Mollat's *The Poor in the Middle Ages*, trans. Arthur Goldhammer (New Haven, Conn.: Yale University Press, 1986).

10. Sigmund Freud, "Psycho-analytic Notes on an Autobiographical Account of a Case
of Paranoia (Dementia Paranoides)," in *The Standard Edition of the Complete Psychological Works of Sigmund Freud*, trans. James Strachey, vol. 12 (1911–13) (London: Hogarth
Press, 1958; reprint, 1981) (*SE*), 21; hereinafter cited in the text. Freud cites Schreber's
*Denkwurdigkeiten eines Nervenkranken* (Leipzig: Oswald Mutze, 1903) (*DN*), 409; the
translations from *DN* are Strachey's and are hereinafter cited in the text.

11. Freud, *SE* 65, 72. See Butler, *Bodies That Matter*, 64–65, on how prohibitions structure the form of the body as "an allegory of prohibited love, the *incorporation* of loss"; see ibid., 98–99, on disidentification with libidinal positions that seem "too saturated with injury or aggression."

12. Elaine Scarry uses the term "power of alteration" in *The Body in Pain*, 189.

13. Schreber, Introduction to *DN* 4; *SE* 32 n. 1. Freud notes that Schreber's identification with Jesus Christ appears only at a very late stage (*DN* 338, 431; *SE* 28). On Schreber's association of femaleness with disgrace, see Freud's citation of Dr. Weber's report, *SE* 16–17, and *DN* 127, *SE* 20.

14. Schreber is supported throughout his ordeal by the belief that until his transformation into a woman is complete, his personality will "remain indestructible" (*SE* 7, 48).

15. Schreber explains in a footnote to the words *"contrary to the Order of Things"* that he hopes to show that "emasculation for quite another purpose," a "purpose *in consonance with the Order of Things*," "is within the bounds of possibility" (*SE* 19–20).

16. *DN* 283, *SE* 34; *DN* 188, *SE* 52 n. 3; *DN* 333, *SE* 27. On the miseducation of the miracled birds, see *DN* 208–14, *SE* 35–36.

17. Prudence Allen, *The Concept of Woman: The Aristotelian Revolution, 750 BC–AD 1250* (Montreal: Eden Press, 1985), 415, 470–71.

18. Paul Strohm, *Hochon's Arrow: The Social Imagination of Fourteenth-Century Texts* (Princeton, N.J.: Princeton University Press, 1992), 95; Pauline Stafford, *Queens, Concubines, and Dowagers: The King's Wife in the Early Middle Ages* (Athens: University of Georgia Press, 1983), 196.

19. Diane Bornstein, *The Lady in the Tower: Medieval Courtesy Literature for Women* (Hamden, Conn.: Archon Books, 1983), 81–82. The *Speculum dominarum* (Bibliothèque Nationale, manuscrits latins 6784) was written for Jeanne de Navarre by her confessor, Durand de Champagne, early in the fourteenth century; it was translated into French with the title *Miroir des dames* (Bibliothèque Nationale, f. fr. 610). Stafford's work makes clear that patronage was also a very important aspect of early queenship (*Queens, Concubines, and Dowagers*, 99, 101, 108–9).

20. Bornstein, *The Lady in the Tower*, 120; she notes that Christine de Pisan's *Livre de trois vertus* is the only mirror for the princess to give serious consideration to the queen's economic and political activities.

21. Lacan defines sublimation as raising "an object . . . to the dignity of the Thing," i.e., to the place of the impossibility of the subject's desire (112); see also Slavoj Žižek on *The Sublime Object of Ideology* (New York: Verso, 1989), 194.

22. Ian Maclean, *The Renaissance Notion of Woman: A Study in the Fortunes of Scholasticism and Medieval Science in European Intellectual Life* (Cambridge: Cambridge University Press, 1980), 60, 66.

23. See Judson Boyce Allen, *The Ethical Poetic of the Later Middle Ages: A Decorum of Convenient Distinction* (Toronto: University of Toronto Press, 1982), 28; and Olson, *Literature as Recreation*, 210.

24. On the indeterminacy of queenship, see Louise O. Fradenburg, *City, Marriage, Tournament: Arts of Rule in Late Medieval Scotland* (Madison: University of Wisconsin Press, 1991), 75–90. On the role of virtue in rendering "invisible" the "traumatic, intolerable dimension" of "the Lady," see Slavoj Žižek, "From the Courtly Game to *The Crying Game*," *re: Post* 1 (1993): 5–9; and Lacan, *Ethics*, 194.

25. See John Carmi Parsons, "Ritual and Symbol in the English Medieval Queenship to 1500," in Louise O. Fradenburg, ed., *Women and Sovereignty, Cosmos* 7 (Edinburgh: Edinburgh University Press, 1992), 60–77, for a discussion of how medieval queenship rituals both acknowledge and limit queenly power.

26. See Lacan, *Ethics*, 152, on the "ethical function of eroticism" as displayed in courtly love's "sexual valorization of the preliminary stages of the act of love." Mary Wack theorizes the medicalization of *amor hereos* as an effort to substantiate the reality of the condition of passionate love among the nobility (see Mary Frances Wack, *Lovesickness in the*

*Middle Ages: The* Viaticum *and Its Commentaries* [Philadelphia: University of Pennsylvania Press, 1990]; and see John Livingston Lowes, "The Loveres Maladye of Hereos," *Modern Philology* 11 [1913–14]: 1–56/491–546].

27. Lacan's notion of the formation of the subject according to the image of the other in "The Mirror Stage" (see *Ecrits: A Selection*, trans. Alan Sheridan [New York: Norton, 1977], 2) is central to his analysis of charity in the *Ethics of Psychoanalysis*.

28. See Lacan, *Ethics*, 139, on "the intimate exteriority or 'extimacy,' that is the Thing."

29. Butler discusses "the ambivalence at the heart of political forms of altruism" in *Bodies That Matter*, 99.

30. The "general will" promotes the "respect for certain rights," but Lacan's concern is that "it can also take the form of excluding from its boundaries, and therefore from its protection, everything that is not integrated into its various registers" (195).

31. See Lacan, *Ethics*, 152, on the "apotheosis of the neighbor" in Christianity and on the *bon vezi*, Guillaume de Poitiers's term for his beloved; see 261–62 on sadism's construction of a double of the self made phantasmatically inaccessible to destruction, and the crucifixion as the "apotheosis of sadism," the "divinization" of that "limit in which a being remains in a state of suffering."

32. The notion that when the "lady" is a married spouse something astonishing has occurred in the annals of courtly love is an overreaction; although the distinction between the wife and the neighbor's wife—and the neighbor's wife is herself a neighbor—is important insofar as it figures the proximity/distance involved in coveting what lies in the field of the other, the crucial element is the "extimacy" of the lady, and the wife can figure that, too, by a number of different ruses, for example Blanche's deadness in *The Book of the Duchess*.

33. For Lacan, beauty and "the good" both block our access to *jouissance*, but only beauty also points our way to it (*Ethics*, 216–17; see also 298 on beauty as a function of temporality).

34. Like its obverse, beauty, shame marks the limit of the ideal image and points, comically or punitively, to what lies beyond it (Lacan, *Ethics*, 298). Lacan remarks of a poem by Arnaut Daniel in which the lover is asked to "put his mouth to [the lady's] trumpet" that "the idealized woman...finds herself suddenly and brutally positing, in a place knowingly constructed out of the most refined of signifiers, the emptiness of a thing in all its crudity,...the one that is to be found at her very heart in its cruel emptiness" (162, 163). See also Fradenburg, *City, Marriage, Tournament*, 260–62, for a related reading of Dunbar's poem "Ane Blake Moir."

35. Strohm, *Hochon's Arrow*, 113–17, discusses Alceste's role as intercessor and her relation to Queen Anne. David Wallace, in *Chaucerian Polity* (Stanford, Calif.: Stanford University Press, 1997), reads Alceste as part of Chaucer's broad concern with wifely eloquence and its power to subdue masculine violence. See also Robert Burlin, *Chaucerian Fictions* (Princeton, N.J.: Princeton University Press, 1977), 40–41, and Allen, *Ethical Poetic*, 268.

36. Dinshaw's reading of *The Legend of Good Women* emphasizes Chaucer's "excising of the women's acts of honor and virtue, or recrimination and revenge" (*Chaucer's Sexual Poetics* [Madison: University of Wisconsin Press, 1989], 86). Elaine Hansen stresses the *Legend*'s preoccupation with the instability of gender roles in *Chaucer and the Fictions of Gender* (Berkeley: University of California Press, 1992), 1–10; see also Jill Mann's discussion of gender and pity in the *Legend* in *Geoffrey Chaucer* (Atlantic Highlands, N.J.: Humanities Press International, 1991), 39–48, and Sheila Delany, *The Naked Text: Chaucer's Legend of Good Women* (Berkeley: University of California Press, 1994), 153–64.

37. *Pietas* is "dutiful conduct toward the gods, one's parents, relatives, benefactors, country, etc., *sense of duty*," "love"; in later Latin, "Gentleness, kindness, tenderness, pity, compassion" (Charlton L. Lewis [Lewis and Short], *A Latin Dictionary*... [Oxford: Clarendon Press, 1879, 1984], s.v. "pietas"). Although often linked to "charite," "pitee" appears more often in Chaucer's poetry (122 times) and in a wider range of contexts (legal, petitionary,

amorous, devotional) than does "charite" (26 occurrences). See Larry D. Benson, ed., *A Glossarial Concordance to the Riverside Chaucer*, 2 vols. (New York: Garland, 1993), s.v. "pite."

38. Mann notes that "Alceste's 'pitee' is the very mark of her identity" (*Geoffrey Chaucer*, 41).

39. Lewis and Short, s.v. "praeclarus," "illustris," "excellens"; Bornstein, *The Lady in the Tower*, 81.

40. *Middle English Dictionary* (*MED*), s.v. "kithen."

41. Butler, *Bodies That Matter*, 209.

42. See Butler, *Bodies That Matter*, on Žižek's notion of "political signifiers," their posturing as a "site of radical semantic abundance," and the inevitable "disappointment or disidentification" that follows in their wake (208–9).

43. *MED*, s.v. "defien," "reneien."

44. *MED*, s.v. "reverence."

45. *MED*, s.v. "dwellen."

46. *MED*, s.v. "neigh"; as an adjective *neigh* can mean "near by kinship, friendship, or allegiance," "reconciled," as well as spatially proximate; as an adverb, "almost," "closely"; as a preposition, "close to, near to," as in the senses of "close to the political rank of (sb.)," "in the confidence of (sb.)," "on the brink of."

47. The Prologue is full of what Freud called "primal words" ("words with two meanings, one of which says the exact opposite of the other") (" 'The Antithetical Sense of Primal Words': A Review of a Pamphlet by Karl Abel, *Uber den Gegensinn der Urworte*, 1884," in Sigmund Freud, *On Creativity and the Unconscious: Papers on the Psychology of Art, Literature, Love, Religion*, ed. Benjamin Nelson [New York: Harper, 1958], 55–62).

48. *MED*, s.v. "relik."

49. *MED*, s.v. "colden."

50. *MED*, s.v. "disteinen."

51. *MED*, s.v. "digne."

52. *MED*, s.v. "bounte."

53. *MED*, s.v. "benigne," "mek."

54. Lisa Kiser gives a finely detailed reading of the figurative transformations in the Prologue, in *Telling Classical Tales: Chaucer and the* Legend of Good Women (Ithaca: Cornell University Press, 1983); see esp. 28–49 and 58.

55. See Lacan, *Ethics*, 261, on Sade: "the object of . . . torture is to retain the capacity of being an indestructible support"; "Suffering is conceived of as a stasis which affirms that that which is cannot return to the void from which it emerged"; that is, suffering reassures the subject that it cannot die absolutely.

56. See Delany, *The Naked Text*, 231–32, on the legends' "Pauline-Augustinian orthodoxy."

CHAPTER 8

❖

# Conversion and Medieval Sexual, Religious, and Racial Categories

*Steven F. Kruger*

Work in feminist theory has taught us that to take an identity category like gender and treat it in isolation from such other categories as race, ethnicity, class, and sexuality—failing to consider the ways in which the meaning of "woman" or "man" differs as these other aspects of identity vary—is to risk universalizing one possible (usually privileged or dominant) experience of gender. As Elizabeth V. Spelman suggests:

> [D]ominant feminist theory locates a woman's true identity in a metaphysical space where gender is supposed to be able to roam free from race and class. I have tried to explain why though doing this appears to be necessary for feminism, it has the effect of making certain women rather than others paradigmatic examples of "woman"—namely, those women who seem to have a gender identity untainted (I use the word advisedly) by racial or class identity, those women referred to in newspapers, magazines, and feminist journals simply as "women," without the qualifier "Black" or "Hispanic" or "Asian-American" or "poor." What is in fact a function of the privilege of white middle-class women is being passed off as a metaphysical truth: that is, that we can talk about a woman "as a woman" without explicitly or implicitly alluding to her race or class.[1]

For medieval studies, which has often tended to project a vision of the Middle Ages as a monolithically unified era, such a caveat is particularly crucial. Consider, as metonymic for an enormous body of medievalist work, the title of Rosalind Brooke and Christopher Brooke's *Popular Religion in the Middle Ages: Western Europe 1000–1300.*[2] Although this title specifies a time period and geographic location, it leaves "religion" unspecified; as it turns out, "religion" is Christianity (although, to the authors' credit, "heretical" movements within Christianity are treated alongside "orthodox" ones). Jews merit four entries in the book's index, Muslims five, but always at the center of inquiry are Christians. My point is not that there is necessarily a problem in focusing attention solely on Christianity. As bell hooks argues, "While it is in no way racist for any author to write a book exclusively about white women, it is fundamentally racist for books to be published that focus solely on the American white woman's experience in which that experience is assumed to be *the* American woman's experience."[3] Work in medieval studies too often assumes that "religion" means simply Christianity; that "society" means a European Christian society that, despite attempts to isolate itself from non-Christian and non-European contacts and influences, was rarely if ever able to do so; that "woman" means a Christian woman, and often a woman of a particular class status. As Kathleen Biddick has powerfully suggested, even in a complex and sophisticated work of scholarship like Caroline Walker Bynum's *Holy Feast and Holy Fast: The Religious Significance of Food to Medieval Women,* "the foundational category of medieval Christendom [is] invisibly at work," facilitating a reinscription of "the very exclusions in relation to which medieval genders were maintained."[4]

Of course, Christianity was part of a dominant medieval construction, and it has continued to be central to European and Western cultural formations; the texts that have survived to become the basis for both scholarly and popular images of "the Middle Ages" are mostly texts that reflect this Christian dominance. But medieval studies, and in particular a "new" medieval studies that employs oppositional critical practices like feminism, gay and lesbian studies, and queer studies, needs to attend to both the dominant construction and those entities against which it defined itself. As we "construct medieval sexuality," reading sexual otherness back into texts where it has been obscured, pushed aside, or made to speak only as that which must be disavowed, we need to be careful not to (re)construct a sexual system that leaves unquestioned and in place other systems of (often violent) differentiation and opposition. In exploring the boundaries of "normal" sexual behavior and positioning, in excavating oppositional or resistant medieval sexualities, we need to think about how both norms and possible means of opposing these are not universal; how medieval thinking about the sexuality of Christians is crucially different from, and yet intimately intertwined with, medieval constructions of the sexuality of Jews, Muslims, "heretics"; how excluded sexualities are constructed in relation to other excluded or disfavored identity positions—femaleness, religious and class difference, and disease (most notably "leprosy"). We need to ask, for the Middle Ages, the kinds of complex question that Judith Butler raises about modern and contemporary constructions of sexuality:

[T]he reproduction of the species will be articulated as the reproduction *of* relations of reproduction, that is, as the cathected site of a racialized version of the species in pursuit of hegemony through perpetuity, that requires and produces a normative heterosexuality in its service. Conversely, the reproduction of heterosexuality will take different forms depending on how race and the reproduction of race are understood. And though there are clearly good historical reasons for keeping "race" and "sexuality" and "sexual difference" as separate analytic spheres, there are also quite pressing and significant historical reasons for asking how and where we might read not only their convergence, but the sites at which one cannot be constituted save through the other. This is something other than juxtaposing distinct spheres of power, subordination, agency, historicity, and something other than a list of attributes separated by those proverbial commas (gender, sexuality, race, class), that usually mean that we have not yet figured out how to think the relations we seek to mark. Is there a way, then, ... to articulate the convergent modalities of power by which sexual difference is articulated and assumed?[5]

As recent historical work has emphasized, medieval categories of sexuality, religion, and race are deeply interimplicated. The very naming of certain sexual acts and (perhaps) a loosely defined sexual identity after the "egregious cities"[6] of Sodom and Gomorrah suggests an attempt to make sexual difference ethnic or racial, to fortify the casting out of sexual "perversity" by conflation with a morally charged geopolitical differentiation. Conversely, religious divergence — schism, "heresy," the "infidelities" of Islam and Judaism — and racial or ethnic difference are often associated with sexual "crimes": adultery, rape, promiscuity, incest, sodomy, bestiality. John Boswell has suggested in a sweeping but not inaccurate formulation that "the fate of Jews and gay people has been almost identical throughout European history, from early Christian hostility to extermination in concentration camps":

> The same laws which oppressed Jews oppressed gay people; the same groups bent on eliminating Jews tried to wipe out homosexuality; the same periods of European history which could not make room for Jewish distinctiveness reacted violently against sexual nonconformity; the same countries which insisted on religious uniformity imposed majority standards of sexual conduct; and even the same methods of propaganda were used against Jews and gay people — picturing them as animals, bent on the destruction of the children of the majority.[7]

R. I. Moore has traced the parallel ways in which, beginning in the eleventh and twelfth centuries, male homosexuals, female prostitutes, "heretics," "lepers," and Jews were all "identified ... as source[s] of social contamination, ... excluded from Christian society and, as its enemies, held liable to pursuit, denunciation and interrogation, to exclusion from the community, deprivation of civil rights and the loss of property, liberty and on occasion life itself."[8] Indeed, as I have suggested previously, medieval sexual, religious, and racial "queernesses" were all constructed along certain similar lines.[9] First, they were all seen as involving "gender insubordination," most often the transformation of the male into the female. Thus, male homosexuality was often depicted as "feminization,"[10] and Jewish men were "feminized" in the common belief that they menstruated[11] and in their frequent association with female prostitutes: brothels were often located alongside the Jewish quarter, and legislation sometimes treated Jews and prostitutes as similarly polluting presences—"the Avignon municipality, for example, provided that, if a Jew touched fruit on a stand, he, like a prostitute, had to purchase it because he had defiled it."[12] The "gender insubordination" associated with various sorts of "queerness" might also, although more rarely, involve the turning of the "properly" female into the male, as in Chaucer's depiction of villainous Islamic and pagan women as "mannysh" viragos[13] and in the "masculinizing" representations of lesbians noted by Susan Schibanoff:

> One of the few extant medieval medical discussions of female homosexuality, by William of Saliceto in 1285, characterizes the lesbian as a figure of anatomical excess: some women, William explains, experience a growth called *ragadia,* which begins in the uterus and can protrude beyond the vagina in the form of a penis. Thus, William concludes, woman may take man's place in sexual intercourse with another woman.[14]

Sexual, religious, and racial "others" were also consistently constructed as marked by both bodily and intellectual degeneracy and perversity. Jews were proverbially literal readers of Scripture, unable to penetrate the spiritual truth of their own texts, and this literal bent was closely associated with supposed Jewish bodily exorbitancies and disintegrations.[15] Muslims were similarly thought to distort the truth of revelation, "heretically" claiming spiritual status for what was merely corporeal. Thus, for instance, the Christian chronicler of the First Crusade, Guibert of Nogent, depicts Islam as illegitimately claiming that Muhammad's epilepsy (concocted by his medieval Christian "biographers") was not a bodily weakness but rather a spiritual gift; Islamic tradition, in Guibert's account, also conceals the (again invented) grotesque mode of Muhammad's death—dismembered and eaten by a herd of pigs during an epileptic seizure—with the claim that the prophet was in fact assumed into heaven.[16] The construction of "sodomy," too, depended upon an association with both intellectual and bodily corruption—particularly in the close linkage of homosexual behavior to a "heresy" understood not just as doctrinal error but as a corruption of the body inseparably linked to such error.[17]

While I believe that it is important to recognize such parallels in the construction of medieval sexual, racial, and religious categories, and while I would argue that such a recognition suggests much about the ways in which a dominant cultural identity is secured through its differentiation from gendered, racialized, and sexualized "others," the danger in stressing the analogies and congruences among different identity categories is that these will simply be collapsed into each other, conflated as some singular, monolithic "otherness" or "queerness." As Boswell recognizes, having made his strong case for the parallels of Jewish and gay history, there are also important differences between how gay people and Jews are positioned within broader communities: "Jewish family life flourished as the main social outlet for a group cut off from the majority at many points in its history, imparting to individual Jews a sense not only of community in the present but of belonging to the long and hallowed traditions of those who went before"; "gay people," on the other hand, "are for the most part not born into gay families," and "[t]hey suffer oppression individually and alone, without benefit of advice or frequently even emotional support from relatives or friends."[18] To make the point more generally, sexual, racial, and religious categories each have their own complex histories — and these are histories not just of interconnection and similarity but of mutual differentiation.

Here I want to suggest that conversion experience, because it explicitly foregrounds the possibility of, as well as the limits to, a movement between opposed identity positions and opposed positions of cultural inclusion and exclusion, provides particularly fertile ground for testing the complex ways in which sexual, racial, and religious "queernesses" interact, reinforcing but also diverging from each other. If, for instance, we consider how late-twentieth-century Western constructions of race, religion, and sexuality are related to the idea that identity might be converted or convertible, we begin to see important differences among these categories despite their shared capacity for generating excluded or abjected identity positions. At the current moment, religion and race stand largely opposed to each other when it comes to their imagined susceptibility to conversion. Indeed, conversion experience is thought of primarily *as* religious (moral) change, while racial "otherness" (in the American context, most often "Blackness") is biologized and geneticized, and hence defined as stable, unchangeable. This is made particularly clear in ideas about the phenomenon of "passing," where the person who can "pass" as "white" is thought of not as having achieved a racial conversion but rather as concealing his or her "true (racial) self." Certain fantasies of racial convertibility — *Black Like Me,* Michael Jackson — are powerful, but these remain largely confined to a phantasmatic realm and perhaps operate most strikingly to reconfirm the "proper" boundaries of racial distinctiveness. Jackson's changes in skin color and facial features, for instance, are most often depicted as "perverse," "artificial" attempts to transform the self; they represent a conversion that exceeds what is "natural" and that is significantly linked to a suspect, "perverse" sexuality, itself understood as transgressive and "unnatural."

While contemporary views of religion and race are strongly differentiated by their differing relations to the experience of conversion, the two continue to be conflated in many ways—for instance, in the mixing of ethnic/racial and religious identifications in the construction of "Bosnian Muslims." Most striking in our century has been the Nazi racialization of Judaism and the concomitant denial of religious conversion as enabling a "true" conversion of identity. Religious conversion may provide a route toward assimilation into a dominant culture; but insofar as race remains intractable to conversion, and insofar as a "stable" racial identity is made to override religious "choice" in definitions of "true" identity—with race understood as a biological category more determinate of the "essential" self than is a culturally determined religious identity—religious conversion does not finally guarantee a full transformation of self.

The category of sexuality, in this same period, is made to stand somewhere between race and religion in its convertibility. Conceived, simultaneously and contradictorily, as biological difference, as social construction, as (unconscious) psychological effect, and as (conscious) choice, sexuality is, as Eve Kosofsky Sedgwick has suggested, caught between "minoritizing" models that posit distinct and relatively stable subpopulations of lesbians and gay men and "universalizing" models that envision homosexuality as a possibility for anyone.[19] Even with the current strong tendency to biologize (homo)sexuality, as in the work of Simon LeVay and Dean H. Hamer,[20] the possibility of radical sexual conversion maintains a powerful hold on contemporary thinking. This is, of course, true in recent attention to transgender/transsexual experience,[21] as it is in thinking about the relations between the categories of hetero- and homosexuality. Homophobic discourses emphasize, on the one hand, the feared possibility of "straight" subjects being "recruited" to gayness and, on the other, the hoped-for possibility of "curing" lesbians and gay men (sometimes, indeed, by means of an actual religious conversion). While gay men and lesbians ourselves most often deny both these homophobic fantasies, we still maintain certain ideas of sexual convertibility—the belief, for instance, that "straight"-identified women and men may discover at some point in their lives a homosexual identity "buried" inside. The heterosexually married person who "comes out" relatively late in life is, in fact, a common and important figure in lesbian and gay communities. And in the realm of sexual fantasy, an equally central figure is the "straight" person who gives in to an irresistible homosexual desire.

In sum, while Blackness, Jewishness, and sexual queerness are all, in the contemporary American context, relegated to a certain realm of exclusion, the strong *differences* in construction of such categories can be at least partly recognized through a consideration of how susceptible they are thought to be to the phenomenon of conversion.

For the Middle Ages, sexuality, race, and religion are all constructed at least partly in moral terms—as choices that might be changed—and partly as biological difference, which would suggest perhaps a more determinate and unchangeable (sexual, racial, or religious) "nature." Insofar as homosexual behavior is conflated with hermaphroditism and eunuchry, as much of the material uncovered in Boswell's *Christianity, Social Tolerance, and Homosexuality* would suggest, medieval sexuality seems to be constructed as irreducible biological difference. But of course "sodomy" is also importantly seen as a reversible moral choice, a vice or crime that might be avoided or abandoned. Its complex nature—susceptible, but also resistant, to change—is captured, for instance, in the address to Pope Leo IX with which Peter Damian opens his *Liber Gomorrhianus*. Here, homosexual acts are constructed both as a vice demanding moral attention and as physical plague:

Heu! pudet dicere, pudet tam turpe flagitium sacris auribus intimare; sed si medicus horret virus plagarum, quis curabit adhibere cauterium? Si is, qui curaturus est, nauseat, quis ad incolumitatis statum pectora aegrota reducat? Vitium igitur contra naturam velut cancer ita serpit, ut sacrorum hominum ordinem attingat.[22]

[Alas! it is a disgrace to speak, it is a disgrace to intimate such a foul crime to the holy ears [of the Pope]; but if the doctor dreads the poison of plagues [or wounds], who will attend to applying the cauterizing brand? If the one who is to attend to this is nauseated, who can lead sick breasts back to a state of safety? The vice against nature thus creeps as a cancer [or crab] so that it touches the order of holy men.]

Peter's biologizing of sexual "crime" bespeaks a strong sense of the deep intractability of the "vitium contra naturam," which, he predicts, may not be able to be stopped "from the impetus of its course"; he also, however, recognizes the possibility of intervention (cure) by "the vigor of the apostolic seat."[23]

A similar complexity marks medieval ideas of the convertibility of racial and religious identity. Depictions of "Saracens" as "dogs," or the distant "monstrous races" as only partly human, or Jews as having tails and horns, present ontological distinctions that would seem difficult to overcome through a process of conversion. Still, there are accounts that depict even such biological differences as disappearing with moral change. In the king of Tars romances, when a Saracen sultan who has married a

Christian princess converts and is baptized, "he changes color from black to white."[24] And in some Eastern versions of the Saint Christopher story, in which Christopher is depicted as originally from a "dog-headed" race, his conversion to Christianity also effects a transformation of physical form.[25] Such examples of striking racial conversion, however, are relatively rare, and Jews and Saracens, thought of as both religiously and racially different and as possessing bodies somehow essentially other than Christian bodies, are often depicted as strongly resistant to conversion, with Jewish "stubbornness" becoming a platitude in medieval Christian depictions of Jews.[26] More abstractly, at least in a certain strain of Christian thinking about the Jews as a people or race rather than as individual moral agents, strong arguments are presented for why the *gens Judaica* has not been, and should not be, wholly converted (or destroyed). The reasoning here is pointedly incoherent, maintaining the importance of individual conversion at the same time that it perpetuates the idea of a perverse race largely intractable to conversion. The Jewish people must survive in order to continue to be punished and to continue as an example of "infidelity," but also, in the words of the Jewish convert to Christianity Petrus Alphonsi, "God did not wish to destroy the Jewish people" because "he saw truly that some of [their] seed at some time would believe in him and be saved, and therefore, for them, he did not wish totally to ruin [their] stock."[27]

While medieval categories of race, religion, and sexuality thus share with each other a certain simultaneous susceptibility and resistance to conversion, the separate identity categories often do not function in parallel ways within conversion narratives. Conversion to Christianity is not necessarily accompanied by a sexual conversion, and a change in sexual state, a movement, for instance, into normative heterosexuality, is not necessarily correlated with moral or religious correction. In part this lack of parallelism results from a certain complexity in medieval conceptions of sexuality that is obscured by the modern tendency to construct sexuality primarily around a homo/hetero divide. Homo- and heterosexual acts *are* opposed to each other in the Middle Ages, but both are also opposed to the "higher" state of chastity. Movements from a not fully heterosexual position toward heterosexuality, while reflecting a sense of what is accepted and normative in the sexual realm, do not necessarily participate in the "moral" reform of the individual. Insofar as such movements may represent an increasing awareness of and dedication to the corporeal, they may indeed be suspect from a Christian "moral" perspective. Thus, for instance, the conversion of Marie de France's Guigemar from a state of sexual indifference, defined explicitly as an error of nature, to heterosexual and courtly love involves a movement into adultery that runs counter to Christian precepts as well as to the social structures of vassalage, knighthood, marriage, and family (although all of these are ultimately recuperated in the *lai*).[28] In Chaucer's

*Clerk's Tale,* Walter's conversion to a married state allows for his family to continue as rulers of his people—it conforms to a particular sociopolitical agenda—and it represents a movement toward containing and reordering Walter's desires (his "lust present"),[29] but at the same time it releases a certain perverse and violent energy.

On the other hand, religious conversions are likely to be accompanied not by an embracing of normative heterosexuality, but rather by a movement from uncontrolled "luxury" into a more chaste and "ordered" state. Hermann of Cologne, as he prepares to make the leap from Judaism to Christianity, is held back from that move by a (hetero)sexual temptation orchestrated, according to Hermann's own postconversion account, by the devil and the Jewish community: "ipse [diabolus] mihi in meam ruinam mulierem matrimonio copulavit" (he himself [the devil] united a woman to me in matrimony to my ruin).[30] Hermann's Christian "familiars," who had previously brought him to the brink of conversion, lament this marriage as a fall back into the carnality of Judaism, a retreat from the spiritual (Christian) position he had earlier begun to approach: "Nos tibi semper monita salutis dabamus, quibus te aliquando consensurum et in Christum nostre salutis auctorem crediturum sperabamus; et ecce contra spem nostram tuas potius sequi concupiscentias elegisti ac desperata salute perditioni te ad integrum tradidisti" (We often gave to you prophecies of salvation, to which we hoped you would at some time assent and believe in Christ the author of our salvation; and behold against our hope you have chosen rather to follow your concupiscence and have surrendered yourself completely to perdition, without hope of salvation [101]). For a postconversion Hermann reflecting on his former life, as for these Christian friends, giving in to sexual pleasure is closely linked to the retreat from Christianity: "cepi cum summa illic carnis voluptate iacere, quo me ante timueram precipitare" (I began with the greatest pleasure of the flesh to lie there where before I had feared that I would fall [102]); "propter modicam carnis delectationem in tantam me perditionis voraginem precipitassem" (because of the limited delight of the flesh I had fallen into so great an abyss of perdition [103]). Ultimately Hermann regains his desire for spiritual truth—that is, in the terms of his account, he resumes his interest in Christian teaching—and he is converted in part through the prayers of two religious women: "meritis ipsarum et precibus tanta repente cordi meo christiane fidei claritas infulsit, ut ab eo totius pristine dubietatis et ignorantie tenebras penitus effugaverit, congrua nimirum vicissitudine, ut per feminam lapsum femine precibus sublevarent" (by the merits and prayers of those same women, so great a brightness of Christian faith suddenly shone into my heart that it completely drove away from [my heart] the shadows of all previous doubt and ignorance—with this alteration truly appropriate, that they lifted up one who had fallen through a woman with the prayers of a woman [108]). As Hermann makes explicit, the "fall" back into hereditary Judaism, identified with a "fall" into heterosexual "concupiscence," is compensated for by a chaste spiritual involvement with women. As Christianity replaces Judaism, prayer replaces sex.

The medieval privileging of chastity over either hetero- or homosexual commitments, existing alongside a hierarchy of "straight" and "queer" sexualities, might be enabling for some marginalized members of Christian society—for instance, giving some women a way out of some kinds of subjugation to men. As Dyan Elliott suggests, in the practice of "spiritual marriage," there might be "a collapse in the husband's authority and...a relative suspension of the gender hierarchy" that enabled women at least "a limited and situationally defined...agency."[31] And religious communities may have provided at least some women and men, whose affective attachments were somehow queer, a place to escape compulsory heterosexuality. The same sexual system that might thus have "liberated" (however partially) certain individuals from certain kinds of oppression could, however, be deeply constrictive for others, including the new convert to Christianity. For him or her, the construction of ideal sexuality as chastity meant that religious conversion, conceived as moral transformation, was likely to entail not integration into Christian family and kinship structures but rather a movement into a delimited space beyond both "straight" and "queer" sexual expression.

Such a delimitation would be supported by Christian anxieties about Jewish and Muslim bodies and by uncertainty about whether religious conversion truly transformed those bodies, cleansing them of their impurities, repairing their imperfections, and removing the tinges of animality that clung to them in Christian fantasies. Christianity had a long history of legislation against intermarriage and interfaith sex,[32] legislation that was importantly involved in the (never wholly successful) effort to maintain a strict segregation of Jewish, Christian, and Muslim communities. Thus, one rationale often given for insisting that Jews and "Saracens" wear distinctive clothing was a specifically sexual one; the Fourth Lateran Council (1215) decreed:

In nonnullis ecclesie provinciis a Christianis Judeos, seu Saracenos habitus distinguit diversitas; sed in quibusdam sic quedam inolevit confusio, ut nulla differentia discernantur. Unde contingit interdum quod per errorem Christiani, Judeorum, seu Saracenorum, et Judei seu Saraceni Christianorum mulieribus commisceantur. Ne igitur tam damnate commixtionis excessus per velamen (-tum) hujusmodi erroris, (ulterius) excusationis possint habere diffugium, statuimus, ut tales utriusque sexus in omni Christianorum provincia, et omni tempore qualitate habitus publice ab aliis populis distinguantur cum et per Moysen hoc ipsum eis legatur iniunctum.[33]

Whereas in certain provinces of the Church the difference in their clothes sets the Jews and Saracens apart from the Christians, in certain other lands there has arisen such confusion that no differences are noticeable. Thus it sometimes happens that by mistake Christians have intercourse with Jewish or Saracen women, and Jews or Saracens with Christian women. Therefore, lest these people, under the cover of an error, find an excuse for the grave sin of such intercourse, we decree that these people (Jews and Saracens) of either sex, and in all Christian lands, and at all times, shall easily be distinguishable from the rest of the populations by the quality of their clothes; especially since such legislation is imposed upon them also by Moses.[34]

Similarly, the often renewed injunction against Jews owning Christian slaves or employing Christian servants—particularly women servants and wet-nurses—had a clear sexual component, as is evident in a papal bull of 1205 addressed to the king of France:

[C]um in Lateranensi concilio sit statutum, ut Judei, nec sub alendorum puerorum obtentu, nec pro servitio, nec alia qualibet causa, in domibus suis habere permittantur mancipia christiana, sed excommunicentur qui cum eis presumpserint habitare, ipsi et servos Christianos habere non dubitant, et nutrices, cum quibus eas interdum abominationes exercent, quas te potius punire convenit quam nos deceat explicare.[35]

[A]though it was enacted in the [Third] Lateran Council that Jews are not permitted to have Christian servants in their homes either under pretext of rearing their children, nor for domestic service, nor for any other reason whatever, but that those who presume to live with them shall be excommunicate, yet they do not hesitate to have Christian servants and nurses, with whom, at times, they work such abominations as are more fitting that you should punish than proper that we should specify.[36]

And a similar letter some forty years later (1244) declares: "faciunt Christianas filiorum suorum nutrices in contumeliam fidei Christiane, cum quibus turpia multa committunt" (they make Christian women nurses for their children, in insult to the Christian Faith, and with these women they commit many shameful actions).[37]

Although such measures were certainly directed toward "obviat[ing] the kind of contact that might result in untoward religious influence,"[38] they also reflected, as the language they employ—"abominationes," "turpia"—suggests, a certain visceral repugnance at the bodies that they sought to rope off from Christendom. Intermarriage was classed as a sexual crime equivalent to adultery and hence subject to capital punishment, and sex that transgressed the lines of religious distinction was associated with both "bestiality" and "sodomy."[39]

Presumably efforts at keeping religious communities segregated did not apply directly to those who had converted to Christianity. It is indeed clear that converts sometimes married and entered into the social life of Christian communities. The early church Council of Chalcedon declared that "even clerics and their sons could marry converted Jewesses."[40] Innocent III ruled in 1199 that if a married person converted to Christianity but his or her spouse did not, the new Christian could remarry.[41] A Jewish woman who had converted to Christianity along with her husband petitioned Pope Martin V to allow her to marry a Christian after her first husband reverted to Judaism; the Pope granted the petition in 1427.[42]

It is equally clear, however, that the anxious establishment of boundaries between religious communities that partly expressed itself in the condemnation of interfaith sexual contacts translated into uncertainty about the licitness of sexual and family relations with new converts to Christianity. The differences between Jewish and Christian rules concerning legitimate marriages—with Jews both accepting marriages that fell within the prohibited degrees of relationship for Christian marriage and legislating levirate marriages unacceptable to Christianity—raised the problem for Christianity of whether Jewish marriages that would have been disallowed to Christians could continue after a married couple's conversion. Innocent III's ruling that those marriages could indeed continue on the one hand displayed tolerance toward converts.[43] On the other hand, however, it reinscribed the Christian belief in the "perversity" of Jewish sexual mores that permitted "incest" and furthered inbreeding, and it suggested that Jewish converts, despite having embraced Christianity, might not be able to move out of such suspect practices. Furthermore, in an action that less ambiguously expressed a distrust of incorporating converts into the Christian community, Pope Clement IV in 1268 rebuked Alfonso III of Portugal for allowing marriages of Christian men to women of Saracen and Jewish *origin*—"quae de Sarracenis aut Judaeis *traxerunt originem.*"[44] In at least one instance, in late-fourteenth-century Aragon, "the death penalty for all sex relations between Jews and Christians" was reiterated in such a way as to "includ[e] new converts."[45] And in 1459, Pope Pius II granted the annulment of the unconsummated marriage between a Christian man and a woman of Jewish heritage who was accused of "Judaizing" and "heretical" behavior; the Pope's treatment of the connection between the woman's unorthodox behavior, her ancestry, and the possible Jewishness of her future progeny expresses a strong suspicion of the insincerity and incompleteness of Jewish conversion and some sense of a hereditary aspect of Judaism that might not easily be overcome—perhaps especially when female converts are involved:

Sane, pro parte dilecti filii Petri dela Cavalleria, minoris dierum, civitatis Cesaraugustane, nobis nuper oblata petitio continebat, quod dudum ipse cum Blancha Palau, civitatis Valencie, que habita erat et reputata Christiana, matrimonium per verba legittime de presenti contraxit, carnali copula minime subsecuta; verum, quia manifeste deprehendit, quod dicta Blancha Iudaice insanie et Iudeorum ritibus et cerimonialibus heretica est et heretice vivit, et ita relatu fidedignorum perhibetur, quod mater ipsius Blanche de gente Iudeorum veniens, eadem heretica pravitate laborans, ipsam dictam Blancham instruxit et imbuit, prefatus Petrus, verus Catolicus, potius perpetue carceris erumptiam [*sic*] et omne mortis periculum subire paratus est, quam velit huiusmodi matrimonium consumare, ne forsan sua procreanda proles matris insaniam prosequeretur, et ex Christiano Iudeus crearetur, pro parte dicti Petri nobis fuit humiliter supplicatum, ut matrimonium ipsum nullum fuisse et esse declarari, vel si forsan matrimonium dici potest, ut et illud ex premissis causis dissolvere, prefatoque Petro, ut alteri nubere possit, concedere, aliasque sibi et statui suo in premissis opportune providere, de benignitate apostolica dignaremur.[46]

[Surely, on the part of [our] beloved son Petrus dela Cavalleria, a minor in age, of the city of Saragossa, a petition presented to us not long ago included [the following claims]: That some time ago he himself in the legitimate verbal form of the present contracted marriage with Blancha Palau, of the city of Valencia, who was held and reputed a Christian, [but] a carnal joining [of the two] did not at all follow. Truly, since he manifestly detected that the said Blancha is a heretic in [participating in] the rites and ceremonies of Jewish insanity and of the Jews, and lives heretically, and [since] it was thus brought forward in the account of trustworthy men that the mother of this same Blancha, coming from the people of the Jews [and] toiling in this same heretical depravity, instructed and initiated the said Blancha herself—[because of all this] the aforesaid Petrus, a true Catholic, [is] prepared to submit to <the breaking out of>[47] perpetual imprisonment and every peril of death rather than be willing to consummate a marriage of this sort, lest perhaps his offspring that would be begotten might follow the insanity of the mother, and a Jew would [thus] be created out of a Christian. On the part of the said Petrus it was to us humbly besought, that the marriage itself should be declared to have been and to be nothing, even if it could perhaps be called a marriage, [and] that we should consider it worthy, out of [our] apostolic benignity, both to dissolve that [marriage] for the preceding causes and to grant the aforesaid Petrus that he be able to wed another, and fitly to provide otherwise for himself and for his situation.]

Distrust of converts was not limited to the realm of sexuality. The Fourth Toledan Council (633) forbade the appointment to public office of the baptized second generation of Jewish converts.[48] In the dispute over the papacy between Innocent II and the "antipope" Anacletus II (1130–38), the greatgrandson of a converted Jew, Anacletus's heredity became an issue, with Bernard of Clairvaux remarking that "it is well known that Jewish offspring now occupies the see of St. Peter to the injury of Christ."[49] Converted Jews in Catalonia and Valencia in 1437 had to petition the pope for relief against discrimination practiced by the established Christian community.[50] While conversion to Christianity was repeatedly encouraged, and indeed often coerced, converts clearly occupied an uncomfortable position in relation to both their old and their new religions, and perhaps particularly when it came to the possibility of being integrated into Christian sexual and familial structures. As Jeremy Cohen suggests, "Spurned by their former coreligionists, never fully assimilated into the rank and file of the European laity, and often deprived of their property by secular princes, many [Jewish apostates] must have remained on the margins of medieval society, frequently finding their only secure haven in the ranks of the Christian clergy, or hovering indecisively between two hostile religious communities."[51] Hermann of Cologne, after his conversion, became a priest in the Premonstratensian order. Pablo Christiani ended up a Dominican preacher dedicated to attacking Judaism in Spain, Provence, and France. Petrus Alphonsi, whose intellectual and medical career seems to have continued relatively uninterrupted by his conversion, positioned himself, in his *Dialogue*, as distant from sexual expression.[52]

Conversion to Christianity leads to a kind of inclusion in Christian society, but that inclusion is by no means complete or unambivalent, and what remains unassimilated or unassimilable to the dominant is often involved in the sexual realm. Consider the fictional instance of Sir Palomides the Saracen in Malory's "Book of Sir Tristram de Lyones." In this romance, Palomides hovers consistently on the edge of Christendom and on the edge of Tristram's court, his love for Isode simultaneously pulling him into the main action of the book and threatening his full alienation from knightly society as he becomes Tristram's rival. At one point, his alienation is expressed as a marking of the body that suggests racial difference: "in the watir he sawe his owne vysayge, how he was discolowred and defaded, a nothynge lyke as he was. / 'Lorde Jesu, what may this meane?' seyde sir Palomydes. And thus he seyde to hymselff: 'A, Palomydes, Palomydes! Why arte thou thus defaded, and ever was wonte to be called one of the fayrest knyghtes of [the] worlde?'"[53] Of course, that Palomides sees his "discoloration" here as a *change* in his identity suggests—at least to a modern understanding of racial characteristics as unchangeable—that something other than racial marking is here at work. But, recalling medieval accounts in which race (indicated by skin color and other physical characteristics) is depicted as changing quite radically, perhaps we should consider whether this depiction and others like it (Arcite's physical changes in the *Knight's Tale*, Orfeo's becoming "lene, rowe, and blac" in *Sir Orfeo*)[54] might suggest that a transformation of a loosely conceived racial identity can accompany a radical change in romantic/sexual status. In Malory, might the point be that Palomides overcomes a certain racial difference in attaining true knightly prowess but that, as he falls into the realm of sexual desire, such difference reasserts itself?

In any case, the action of the story suggests that Palomides' desire for Isode must be "conquered" if he is to move fully into the Christian world: in the story's final movement, Palomides and Tristram engage in a battle that simultaneously allows Palomides' conversion (508) and leads him to abandon any claim to Isode's love (510). Baptized, with Tristram and another knight as "godfadyrs" (510), Palomides enters Christianity, but only as he abandons any hope of fulfilling his love. And while the story concludes with Tristram returning to "Joyus Garde" and Isode, it shows Palomides, although Christianized, still relegated to a place of marginality: he takes up again his never-ending search for "the questynge beste," a search that largely keeps him outside social structures (510).

The closing off to the convert of certain sexual possibilities that are accepted and even legislated for nonclerical Christians is one way to maintain the queerness of even the converted Saracen or Jewish body. The convert remains somehow different, still of an other people, *gens*, race than the Christian society to which he is assimilated. The naming of former Jews in medieval texts—Petrus Alphonsi "ex Judeo Christiani," "Hermannus quondam Judaeus," Pablo Christiani—asserts simultaneously the saliency of their conversion and their Jewish origin. Larger groups of Jews converting to Christianity (often under duress) were themselves often given separate names and social status. Visigothic legislation referred to "Jews, baptized and non-baptized,"[55] suggesting that baptism did not truly transform a Jewish to a Christian identity. In other locations and at other historical moments, converts formed a class of *conversos*, or "New Christians," that continued to be distinguished from the more established Christian community; even in legislation intended to argue for equal treatment of "New Christians," use of such a distinguishing designation suggests the real obstacles to achieving equal treatment.[56] While the move to convert represented a certain impulse toward amalgamation on the part of both Jewish converts and the Christian communities that encouraged or forced their conversion, such an impulse was often not allowed to reach fruition. The consistent Christian anxiety that converted Jews would "relapse" to their original religion—the fear that converts had not "truly" become Christian, that they were always on the verge of reverting to a prior state—suggests how fully problematic was their integration into Christendom.[57] Texts that describe Jewish conversions, even as they suggest a unidirectional movement out of Jewish "darkness" into Christian "light," from "caecitas" to lucid vision, often also preserve the dark point of origin from which the convert emerges. Hermann's *Opusculum de conversione sua* operates circularly to return us, in its conclusion, to a moment prior to Hermann's interest in Christianity. This conclusion, while it reiterates the truth of Christianity, also reminds us of Hermann's initial Jewishness and its materially implicated errors.

In Petrus Alphonsi's *Dialogue,* the Jew whom Peter once was is conjured up in an even more striking way. Peter indicates explicitly that the names chosen for the interlocutors of his dialogue are autobiographically significant: "In tutandis etiam Christianorum rationibus, nomen quod modo Christianus hebeo [habeo?], posui: rationibus vero adversarii confutandis, nomen quod ante baptismum habueram, id est Moysen" (For the Christian arguments that are to be defended, I have put forward the name that I now have as a Christian, but for the arguments to be confuted, [I have put forward] the name that I had before baptism, that is Moses).[58] For the purposes of argument, Peter recreates his former Jewish self, the self cast off through conversion, and when the dialogue proper begins, Moses takes on a life of his own, fully personified as an individual distinct from Peter:

A tenera igitur pueritiae aetate quidam mihi perfectissimus adhaeserat amicus, nomine Moyses, qui a primaeva aetate meus consocius fuerat et condiscipulus. Ad hunc cum pervenisset sermo quod ego paterna lege relicta Christianam delegissem fidem, relicto suae stationis loco, ad me festinus pervenit, in ipso adventu quemdam vultum ferens hominis indignantis, et increpans salutavit me more non amici, sed quasi alieni. (537)

[From the tender age of boyhood a certain most perfect friend adhered to me, by the name of Moses, who from my youthful age was my companion and costudent. When the word came to him that I had chosen the Christian faith, having relinquished the paternal law, he came hastening to me, having relinquished the place of his abode, in his advent making the face of an offended man, and greeted me speaking angrily in the manner not of a friend but of a stranger.]

The conversion has resulted in a certain alienation of current and former selves that Peter chooses not to cover over—not to treat as though the old Moses were irrecoverably thrown out—but rather to dramatize, posing the old self, angry at Peter's self-desertion, against the new one, seemingly confident in its new positioning, but still, in the very writing of the *Dialogue*, recognizing a conflict between old and new. Moses comes to Peter to bring him back to Judaism. And while Peter's dialogue itself operates in an inverse manner, transforming Moses' angry movement against Peter into a "relinquishing" of Jewish positions, it never fully overcomes the splitting of self dramatized in the opening scene.

Moses shows himself an apt student of Peter's anti-Jewish arguments, ultimately acceding to all of Peter's positions, concluding "[h]actenus Judaicae gentis fides quam inanis et inconstans in omnibus esset" (how empty and inconstant in all things the faith of the Jewish people has hitherto been), and admitting "in quanto permanserim hactenus...errore" (in how great an error I [myself] have hitherto persisted [597]). At the same time, however, Moses shows himself obtuse: convinced of the "inanity" and "inconstancy" of Jewish faith, he nonetheless at first sees *Islam*, and not Christianity, as the most attractive alternative to Judaism: "Sed cum paternam reliqueris fidem, miror cur Christianorum et non potius Sarracenorum cum quibus semper conversatus atque nutritus es delegeris fidem" (I am amazed at why you have chosen the faith of the Christians and not rather that of the Saracens, with whom you have always lived and [by whom] you have been nourished [597]). The turn toward Islam here demonstrates on Moses' part, and from Peter's perspective, a continuing materialism, an inability to grasp spiritual truth. Indeed, the Islam that Moses depicts is consistently a religion of bodily (and particularly sexual) pleasures—multiple wives and concubines, easy divorce, incestuous alliances:

> Licet...eis eodem tempore quatuor legitimas habere uxores, et qualibet repudiata aliam semper accipere, ita tamen, ut nunquam quaternarium transeat numerum....Emptitias vero atque captivas quotcunque voluerit habere licitum erit....Conceditur insuper eis de propria cognatione habere uxores ut sanguinis proles accrescat, et fortius inter eos amicitiae vinculum vigeat. (598)

> [It is permitted...to them to have, at the same time, four legitimate wives, and if one is repudiated [divorced] another always can be taken, as long as the limit of four [wives] is never transgressed.... However many bought or captive women one wishes to have will be legal.... Furthermore they are permitted to have wives from their own kin, so that the offspring of their blood may increase, and the bond of friendship among them be vigorous.]

Where Moses sees real attractions, however, the already Christianized Peter identifies dangers:

Quod de uxoribus dixisti licere quatuor accipere et qualibet repudi-
ata aliam accipere, hoc nulla quidem praecipitur ratione, neque enim
nisi causa filios procreandi, praeceptum est uxorem accipere (*Lev.*
xviii). Quod autem emptitias et captivas quotlibet possunt habere,
hoc quidem quantum ad nos adulterium est, quia multoties pater
emit aliquam stupratam a filio, et contra filius vel frater a patre
corruptam. (604)

[That which you have said concerning wives, that it is allowed to
take four and, when any of them has been repudiated [divorced], [it
is allowed] to take another, this certainly is commanded by no reason, nor truly except for the cause of begetting sons was it commanded to take a wife (Leviticus 18). That moreover they are able
to have however many purchased wives and captives, this certainly,
as far as we are concerned, is adultery, since oftentimes a father
buys a woman defiled by his son, and conversely a son or brother
one corrupted by his father.]

Peter indeed suggests that the Islamic law that would allow such practices represents no real law but rather Muhammad's personal expression
of inordinate sexual desire: "Mahomethus valde feminas diligebat, et
pernimium luxuriosus erat, et sicuti ipsemet professus est, vis luxuriae
quadraginta hominum in eo manebat" (Muhammad very much loved
women, and was far too lustful; as he himself acknowledged, the
strength of lust in him was that of forty men [604–5]).

At the center of Peter's *Dialogue*, then, is a movement that suggests
that the Jew, even after having been persuaded of the errors of Judaism,
is impelled (naturally?) toward the even more debased religious alternative of Islam rather than toward Christian spirituality. Peter ultimately
helps Moses past this impasse. The last words of the *Dialogue* urge Moses
toward a conversion that Peter himself has already undergone:

Hoc procul dubio donum sancti Spiritus baptismi gratia contulit,
quae corda nostra ita illuminat, ne falsi aliquid credere praesuma-
mus. Quod si tu quod credimus, ipse etiam crederes, et baptizari te
faceres, eamdem Spiritus sancti illuminationem haberes, ut et quae
vera sunt agnosceres, et quae falsa respueres. Nunc autem, quoniam
super te pietatem habeo, Dei misericordiam imploro, ut Spiritus
sui plenitudine te illustret, et finem meliorem quam principium
tibi praestet. (671–72)

[This gift of the Holy Spirit, without doubt, the grace of baptism
conferred, which [grace] thus illuminates our hearts so that we do
not presume to believe anything false. And if you yourself also believed that which we believe and had yourself baptized, you would
have the same illumination of the Holy Spirit, so that you would

recognize those things that are true and reject those that are false. Now, moreover, since I have compassion for you, I implore God's mercy that he enlighten you with the fullness of his Spirit, and show to you an end better than your beginning.]

The *Dialogue*, however, never takes the final step of re-merging Peter and Moses; still inscribed in the text is the sense of a perverse Jewish countermovement to the (proper) movement of conversion. Moses' transformation through the spirit remains wished for rather than completed; the preconversion Jew still stands alongside his postconversion self. A residue of Jewish identity is thus ineffacably inscribed within Peter's celebration of his own embracing of Christianity. That residue, with its stubborn attachment to the flesh, remains resistant to full incorporation into the body of Christian society. It is a certain queer residue that maintains the converted Jew as still (racially and sexually) different from those whom he has joined through conversion.

## Notes

1. Elizabeth V. Spelman, *Inessential Woman: Problems of Exclusion in Feminist Thought* (Boston: Beacon Press, 1988), 186.

2. Rosalind Brooke and Christopher Brooke, *Popular Religion in the Middle Ages: Western Europe 1000–1300* (London: Thames and Hudson, 1984).

3. Bell hooks, *Ain't I a Woman: Black Women and Feminism* (Boston: South End Press, 1981), 137.

4. Kathleen Biddick, "Genders, Bodies, Borders: Technologies of the Visible," *Speculum* 68 (1993): 389–418; the citations are at 400 and 417.

5. Judith Butler, *Bodies That Matter: On the Discursive Limits of "Sex"* (New York and London: Routledge, 1993), 167–68.

6. Petrus Damianus, *Liber Gomorrhianus*, *Patrologia Latina* (hereafter *PL*), ed. J.-P. Migne, vol. 145 (Paris, 1874), 162.

7. John Boswell, *Christianity, Social Tolerance, and Homosexuality: Gay People in Western Europe from the Beginning of the Christian Era to the Fourteenth Century* (Chicago: University of Chicago Press, 1980), 15–16. Boswell's work has been widely criticized as "essentialist," and the passage quoted does participate in a certain leveling of historical difference—in relation to both "gay people" and "Jews." Boswell elsewhere in his book, however, specifies complexities and changes that occur in such categories, and, in "Revolutions, Universals, and Sexual Categories," in *Hidden from History: Reclaiming the Gay and Lesbian Past*, ed. Martin Bauml Duberman, Martha Vicinus, and George Chauncey Jr. (New York: Meridian, 1989), he reflects explicitly on the problem of "essentialism": "Merely cataloguing references to 'Jews' or to 'Blacks' may distort more than it reveals of human history if due attention is not paid to the meaning, in their historical setting, of such words and the concepts to which they apply. Do such reservations, on the other hand, uphold the claim that categories such as 'Jew,' 'black,' or 'gay' are not diachronic and can not, even with apposite qualification, be applied to ages and times other than those in which the terms themselves were used in precisely their modern sense?" (21). Also see the "constructionist" essays printed in *Hidden from History* alongside Boswell's "Revolutions": David M. Halperin, "Sex before Sexuality: Pederasty, Politics, and Power in Classical Athens," 37–53, and Robert Padgug, "Sexual Matters: Rethinking Sexuality in History," 54–64.

8. R. I. Moore, *The Formation of a Persecuting Society: Power and Deviance in West-ern Europe, 950–1250* (Oxford: Blackwell, 1987), 99.

9. Steven F. Kruger, "Racial/Religious and Sexual Queerness in the Middle Ages," *Medieval Feminist Newsletter* 16 (Fall 1993): 32–36.

10. See, for instance, the twelfth-century "Ganymede and Helen," in Boswell, *Chris-tianity,* 381–89.

11. See Joshua Trachtenberg, *The Devil and the Jews: The Medieval Conception of the Jew and Its Relation to Modern Anti-Semitism* (Philadelphia: Jewish Publication Society of America, 1983 [1943]), 149; Sander Gilman, *Jewish Self-Hatred: Anti-Semitism and the Hidden Language of the Jews* (Baltimore: Johns Hopkins University Press, 1986), 75; and Kruger, "Racial/Religious," 33–34.

12. Salo Wittmeyer Baron, *A Social and Religious History of the Jews,* 2d ed., 18 vols. (New York: Columbia University Press, 1952–1983), 11:85–86. Also see Shlomo Simonsohn, *The Apostolic See and the Jews,* vols. 1–2, *Documents: 492–1404* and *Documents: 1394–1464* (Toronto: Pontifical Institute of Mediaeval Studies, 1988–89), doc. 319 (334–35).

13. Geoffrey Chaucer, *Man of Law's Tale,* in *The Riverside Chaucer,* 3d ed., ed. Larry D. Benson (Boston: Houghton Mifflin, 1987), II.359, II.782.

14. Susan Schibanoff, "Chaucer's Lesbians: Drawing Blanks?" *Medieval Feminist News-letter* 13 (Spring 1992): 12. Also see Helen Rodnite Lemay, "Human Sexuality in Twelfth-through Fifteenth-Century Scientific Writings," in *Sexual Practices and the Medieval Church,* ed. Vern L. Bullough and James Brundage (Buffalo: Prometheus Books, 1982), 196.

15. For a fuller discussion, see Steven F. Kruger, "The Bodies of Jews in the Late Mid-dle Ages," in *The Idea of Medieval Literature: New Essays on Chaucer and Medieval Cul-ture in Honor of Donald R. Howard,* ed. James M. Dean and Christian K. Zacher (Newark: University of Delaware Press; London and Toronto: Associated University Presses, 1992), 301–23.

16. Guibert of Nogent, *Gesta Dei per Francos,* in *Receuils des historiens des croisades, Historiens occidentaux,* vol. 4, L'Académie des Inscriptions et Belles-Lettres (Paris: Im-primerie Nationale, 1879), 128–30. On medieval Christian misrepresentation of Muham-mad's life, see R. W. Southern, *Western Views of Islam in the Middle Ages* (Cambridge, Mass.: Harvard University Press, 1962), 29–31; Norman Daniel, *The Arabs and Mediaeval Europe,* 2d ed. (London: Longman, 1979 [1975]), 235–40, and Daniel, *Islam and the West: The Making of an Image,* rev. ed. (Oxford: Oneworld, 1993 [1960]), 125–29.

17. On the linkage of "sodomy" and "heresy," see Boswell, *Christianity,* 283–86; and on the bodily corruptions associated with homosexuality, ibid., 210–13, 359–63, 375–78, among other passages.

18. Ibid., 16.

19. Eve Kosofsky Sedgwick, *Epistemology of the Closet* (Berkeley and Los Angeles: University of California Press, 1990), especially the "axiomatic" introduction and chap. 1.

20. Simon LeVay, "A Difference in Hypothalamic Structure between Heterosexual and Homosexual Men," *Science* 253 (August 30, 1991): 1034–37; LeVay, *The Sexual Brain* (Cam-bridge: MIT Press, 1993); Dean H. Hamer, Stella Hu, Victoria L. Magnuson, Nan Hu, and Angela M. L. Pattatucci, "A Linkage between DNA Markers on the X Chromosome and Male Sexual Orientation," *Science* 261 (July 16, 1993): 321–27; Hamer and Peter Copeland, *The Science of Desire: The Search for the Gay Gene and the Biology of Behavior* (New York: Simon and Schuster, 1994).

21. See, for instance, Kate Bornstein, *Gender Outlaw: On Men, Women, and the Rest of Us* (New York: Routledge, 1994), and Leslie Feinberg, *Transgender Warriors: Making History from Joan of Arc to Dennis Rodman* (Boston: Beacon Press, 1996).

22. Petrus Damianus, *Liber Gomorrhianus, PL* 145:161.

23. Ibid.: "Et nisi quantocius sedis apostolicae vigor occurrat, non est dubium, quin ef-frenata nequitia cum restringi voluerit, a cursus sui impetu desistere nequeat."

24. John Block Friedman, *The Monstrous Races in Medieval Art and Thought* (Cam-bridge, Mass.: Harvard University Press, 1981), 65.

25. Ibid., 72–73.

26. See, for instance, Baron, *Social and Religious History*, 4:92.

27. Petrus Alphonsi, *Dialogi, PL* 157:575: "Quod si in ipso tempore quo peccatum a vobis est commissum, totam Judaicam progeniem funditus delevisset, multis temporum circulis transactis, culpa oblivione deleta, a nullo mortalium sciretur, sicque et infamiae opprobrium, et malorum evitaretis periculum, sicut et de multis contigit gentibus et reg-ibus, quorum gesta temporum sunt vetustate deleta. Est et alia causa, propter quam Deus Judaicam noluit perdere gentem. Videbat enim quosdam de semine vestro quandoque in se credituros, atque salvandos, et ideo propter eos noluit omnino vestram disperdere stirpem."

28. Marie de France, *Guigemar*, in *The Lais of Marie de France*, trans. Robert Hanning and Joan Ferrante (Durham, N.C.: Labyrinth Press, 1982 [1978]).

29. Chaucer, *Clerk's Tale*, in *Riverside Chaucer*, IV.80.

30. Hermann of Cologne, *Opusculum de vita sua*, ed. Gerlinde Niemeyer, Monumenta Germaniae Historica: Quellen zur Geistesgeschichte des Mittelalters, 4 (Weimar: Böhlaus, 1963), 98; subsequent references to Hermann's *Opusculum* are given parenthetically in the text.

31. Dyan Elliott, *Spiritual Marriage: Sexual Abstinence in Medieval Wedlock* (Prince-ton: Princeton University Press, 1993), 298.

32. On Christian injunctions against intermarriage and sex with Jews or Muslims, see Solomon Grayzel, *The Church and the Jews in the Thirteenth Century: A Study of Their Relations during the Years 1198–1254, Based on the Papal Letters and the Conciliar De-crees of the Period*, rev. ed. (New York: Hermon Press, 1966 [1933]), 184–85, 198–99, 204–5, 208–9, 210; Jacob R. Marcus, ed., *The Jew in the Medieval World: A Source Book: 315–1791* (New York: Atheneum, 1981 [1938]), 39, 102; Baron, *Social and Religious His-tory*, 3:50, 3:142–43, 3:189, 4:9, 5:133, 11:77–87; Simonsohn, *Apostolic See*, docs. 126 (130–32), 138 (147–49), 489 (527–28), 490 (529), 881 (1089); and Mark R. Cohen, *Under Crescent and Cross: The Jews in the Middle Ages* (Princeton: Princeton University Press, 1994), 34–35, 129–30. There were also, of course, Jewish injunctions against intermarriage and interfaith sex; see Baron, *Social and Religious History*, 3:142–43, 5:100, and Cohen, *Crescent*, 109. Muslim law was more lenient toward intermarriage with *dhimmis* ("peo-ple of the Book," including both Jews and Christians); see Cohen, *Crescent*, 133.

33. Grayzel, *The Church and the Jews*, 308.

34. Ibid., 309. For more on legislation concerning distinctive clothing, including the badge, see ibid., 61–62, 156–57, 166–67, 168–69, 206–7, 258–59, 282–83, 294–95, 314–15; Marcus, *The Jew in the Medieval World*, 138; Simonsohn, *Apostolic See*, docs. 94 (99), 96 (101), 99 (103), 102 (105), 108 (111), 113 (117), 115 (118), 127 (132–34), 134 (141–43), 136 (145), 137 (145–47), 166 (174–75), 175 (185–86), 189 (199), 192 (200–201), 203 (209), 223 (227–29), 261 (268–70), 366 (388–89), 406 (431–32), 419 (445–46), 434 (460), 487 (518–24), 492 (530–31), 497 (536–38), 507 (555–56), 508 (556), 538 (593–602), 563 (624–27), 567 (629–30), 568 (630–34), 569 (635–36), 571 (637), 591 (669–71), 599 (685), 619 (719), 629 (730–31), 630 (731–34), 636 (739–40), 687 (809–10), 689 (811), 697 (819), 733 (858–59), 801 (977–98), 804 (983), 805 (984–85), 851 (1043–44), 859 (1055–56), 860 (1057–58), 863 (1060–61), 871 (1071–73), 896 (1106–7); and Cohen, *Crescent*, 64, 129–30.

35. Grayzel, *The Church and the Jews*, 106.

36. Ibid., 107.

37. Ibid., 252–53. On the injunctions against Jewish ownership or employment of Chris-tians, see ibid., 296–97, 314–15; Baron, *Social and Religious History*, 4:11, 4:16–17, 5:133, 11:86–87; and Simonsohn, *Apostolic See*, docs. 48 (50), 57 (60), 80 (84), 82 (86–88), 134 (141–43), 137 (145–47), 171 (180–82), 221 (225–26), 232 (239–40), 235 (243–44), 255 (262–64).

38. Robert Chazan, *Daggers of Faith: Thirteenth-Century Christian Missionizing and Jewish Response* (Berkeley and Los Angeles: University of California Press, 1989), 31.

39. See Trachtenberg, *Devil*, 187; Baron, *Social and Religious History*, 3:189, 11:78, 11:80, 11:82; and Chazan, *Daggers*, 35. Trachtenberg notes that "in 1222 a deacon, after standing trial before Archbishop Langton, was burned at Oxford on a charge of bestiality:

he had embraced Judaism in order to marry a Jewess" (187). But Baron interprets the event differently: "The romantic interest was not the compelling motive in his conversion. Even at his trial before the Council of Oxford in 1222 no one stressed the fact that he had a Jewish consort; according to contemporary chroniclers, he was prosecuted only for apostasy, the desecration of the host, defilement of the crucifix, and blasphemies against the Virgin" (11:84). Both Trachtenberg and Baron also discuss the postmedieval case of Jean Alard, "who kept a Jewess in his house in Paris and had several children by her": "he was convicted of sodomy on account of this relation and burned, together with his paramour, 'since coition with a Jewess is precisely the same as if a man should copulate with a dog' " (Trachtenberg, *Devil*, 187; see Baron, *Social and Religious History*, 11:80, 11:82).

40. Baron, *Social and Religious History*, 3:10.

41. Grayzel, *The Church and the Jews*, 88–91. Also see Simonsohn, *Apostolic See*, doc. 69 (72–73). In the inverse situation, where one of two married Christians apostasized, the spouse who remained Christian was *not* allowed to remarry.

42. Simonsohn, *Apostolic See*, doc. 647a (755–56).

43. Grayzel, *The Church and the Jews*, 18–19, 88–89, 100–101; and Simonsohn, *Apostolic See*, docs. 62 (65), 68 (72), 76 (79).

44. Simonsohn, *Apostolic See*, doc. 233 (241); emphasis mine.

45. Baron, *Social and Religious History*, 11:79.

46. Simonsohn, *Apostolic See*, doc. 856 (1051).

47. The sense here seems to demand the opposite of the Latin *erumptiam*, which I have translated as "breaking out." The point is that Petrus would prefer to undergo perpetual imprisonment and death rather than consummate a marriage with the "heretical" Blancha.

48. Baron, *Social and Religious History*, 3:248.

49. Ibid., 4:10–11.

50. Simonsohn, *Apostolic See*, doc. 721 (845–47).

51. Jeremy Cohen, "The Mentality of the Medieval Jewish Apostate," in *Jewish Apostasy in the Modern World*, ed. Todd M. Endelman (New York and London: Holmes and Meier, 1987), 23.

52. For a comparison of the motives behind these three conversions, see ibid.

53. Sir Thomas Malory, *Works*, ed. Eugène Vinaver (Oxford: Oxford University Press, 1971), 473; subsequent references are given parenthetically in the text.

54. *Sir Orfeo*, ed. A. J. Bliss (London: Oxford University Press, 1954), 459.

55. Baron, *Social and Religious History*, 3:39.

56. See ibid., 3:176; and Simonsohn, *Apostolic See*, docs. 775 (935–37), 802 (979–80).

57. On the "relapse" of converts, see Baron, *Social and Religious History*, 3:39, 3:247, 4:5; and Simonsohn, *Apostolic See*, docs. 42 (42), 77 (80–81), 236 (244–45), 241 (248–49), 258 (266), 260 (267–68), 263 (271–72), 264 (273–74), 266 (275–76), 278 (285–86), 295 (303–4), 318 (334), 353 (371), 362 (384–85), 371 (394–96), 379 (405–6), 380 (406–7), 383 (408–10), 397 (422–23), 408 (433–36), 467 (497–98), 705 (824–27), 815 (999–1001).

58. Petrus Alphonsi, *Dialogi*, PL 157:538; subsequent references are given parenthetically in the text.

## CHAPTER 9

# Mystical Acts, Queer Tendencies
## *Karma Lochrie*

"Queering" is a project of contestation, in Judith Butler's words, "a contestation of the terms of sexual legitimacy." It works through the hyperbolic appropriation and reversal of the delegitimization signified by the term "queer," transforming it into a site of opposition. "The hyperbolic gesture is crucial to the exposure of the homophobic 'law' that can no longer control the terms of its own abjecting strategies," according to Butler.[1] For Butler, as for Eve Kosofsky Sedgwick, queering is a performance that exploits and exposes "the open mesh of possibilities, gaps, overlaps, dissonances and resonances, lapses and excesses of meaning when the constituent elements of anyone's gender, of anyone's sexuality aren't made (or *can't be* made) to signify monolithically."[2]

The historical reach of the queering project, according to these two definitions, seems to be confined to the modern regimes of sexuality that it presupposes — homophobic laws and monolithic sexualities. Yet as Jonathan Goldberg, Louise O. Fradenburg and Carla Freccero, Simon Gaunt, and others have argued, queering risks the anachronism of speaking of sexuality in the Middle Ages and Renaissance in order to challenge and disrupt historicist and literary assumptions and practices. Queer readings, like queer histories, seek out those dissonances, gaps, and excesses of meaning that signal heteronormative protocols of representation and that enable a disruption of those same protocols.[3] The risk involved in queering premodern histories and texts derives from the lack of organizing terminology — heterosexual, homosexual, and bisexual — and from the identity politics invested in these categories. Queering does not seek to discover or install lesbian and gay identities in premodern subjects or histories; rather, it risks the anachronism of speaking of sexuality in the first place to unsettle the heterosexual paradigms of scholarship; to contest medieval representational practices across sexual, gender, and class lines; and to produce readings of medieval texts that trouble our assumptions about medieval culture and textual practices.

The venture of queering medieval mystical sex runs two risks, of finding sex where it is not (or where it is only "convention") and of anachronism — of lodging sex at the center of the mystical experience and sexuality at the core of the mystic's identity. Queering, however, is not simply an inversion of the not-sexual, or conventional, into the sexual. If it were, it would amount to no more than a "reverse-discourse" that reinstates the very terms and categories it seeks to overcome.[4] Not only does the translation of the previously conventional or metaphorical language into the sexual merely reverse the terms of heteronormative paradigms without changing them, it implicitly deploys a repression model of the history of sexuality.[5]

The "queer tendencies" of my title is deliberately vague in its reference—to mystical acts, to the slippage between acts and tendencies exploited by the "Don't ask, don't tell" military policy, to the territory that is opposed to those acts (as in the acts/identities paradigm), to the mystic's desire, to the trajectory of this essay. My purpose is to emphasize that "queer" is not simply a reconstructed term for homosexual or homoerotic, but a category marking the sexual as the site for a variety of cultural struggles.

To queer late medieval female mysticism is to posit one such site of cultural struggle and to endeavor to unsettle our current ways of understanding it. Constructions of feminine desire and sexuality, religious paradigms of devotion, and modern medieval scholarship are all implicated and cast into doubt through this queering. At the end of this essay, I will consider whether the queer tendencies in female mystical practice signify opposition or transgression.

## Mystical Love *Noir*

Women's spirituality during the late Middle Ages is usually considered to be marked by erotic, nuptial, and maternal themes, along with an increased attention to Christ's humanity.[6] Medieval scholars have positioned this spirituality in a patrilineage extending back to the language of the biblical Song of Songs and its commentaries, the secular tradition of courtly love, and Cistercian and Franciscan influences on late medieval piety.[7] What emerges from most accounts of women's spirituality of the late Middle Ages is a highly romanticized or, alternatively, allegorized vision of their practices of mystical sex and a rigidly heterosexualized version of their sexuality.

There is, in effect, a master narrative of medieval mystical devotion that remains unquestioned in spite of the evidence of women's mystical texts. This master narrative works in a variety of ways to preserve its own heterosexual framework and to restrict the domain of what we regard as sexual in mystical texts. As with most master narratives, there is some truth in this one—that is, that much of mystical sex is both heterosexual and reflective of the Song of Songs tradition. However, I want to argue that mystical sex is not always so conveniently located in the *locus deliciarum* of the Song of Songs and that mystical sexuality is not limited to a heterosexual model. Medieval scholars usually "find"

181

mystical sex within the "place of delights," the garden of the Song of Songs, and the format of the *sponsa Christi*, the Bride of Christ.[8] A virtual bower of bliss inhabited by the mystical lover, this place of delights seduces her with its voluptuousness. Here, the lover becomes enflamed with desire and awaits the kiss of her beloved and his entrance into her voluptuous but sealed garden (Song of Songs 5:1–4). The conventions of courtly love lend themselves to this location and scenario of mystical devotion by emphasizing the lover's suffering and languishing for the absent beloved.[9]

Yet these two traditions of the allegorization of the Song of Songs and its sentimentalization in the "place of delights" are not the only provinces in which mystical sex occurs. These traditions help us to understand some — but not all — of the various kinds of sexual experiences found in mystical texts. By adhering too closely to these alternative constructs, we miss other equally important aspects of mystical eroticism. I want to focus on one that rarely gets discussed, and that is the violence and disturbing darkness of mystical love and sex in women's texts. This kind of mystical love — what might be called love *noir* — cannot be safely "fit" into the courtly love tradition, since it is women, and not men, who are the subjects of its sexual violence and despair. Queering occurs through a reversal of secular and mystical love conventions, which in turn dislodges and disperses the gender categories they support.

This potential of mystical discourse to exceed and collapse modern categories of gender and sexuality is observed by the important scholar of medieval female mysticism, Caroline Walker Bynum. In her early work, *Jesus as Mother*, Bynum issues a warning against our tendency as scholars to make clear delineations between sexual and affective mystical experiences and, at the same time, against our desire to preserve gender boundaries and the implicitly heterosexual paradigm we bring to medieval mysticism. Bynum acknowledges that she, too, is guilty of trying to preserve these boundaries, and she cautions against this inclination to separate sex from other kinds of mystical ecstasy and masculine from feminine:

> Medieval authors do not seem to have drawn as sharp a line as we do between sexual responses and affective responses or between male and female. Throughout the Middle Ages, authors found it far easier than we seem to find it to apply characteristics stereotyped as male or female to the opposite sex. Moreover, they were clearly not embarrassed to speak of all kinds of ecstasy in language *we* find physical and sexual and therefore inappropriate to God.[10]

Bynum's concern in this passage is that she is perhaps applying too rigorously modern notions of sex and sexual categories to her own account of Cistercian maternal and nuptial imagery in the twelfth century. What

Bynum seems to allow for here is the mystical transgression of categories of sexual difference and social identities and a queering of the language of ecstasy.

Yet Bynum's virtual acknowledgment that mystical sex may not be separable from other kinds of affective mystical experiences contradicts most of the argument of her book, *Holy Feast and Holy Fast*. In this work she steadfastly denies or ignores the sexual and erotic as categories of investigation, while in her other work, she explicitly calls for a "wiping away" of modern constructions of the sexualized body in order to historicize the medieval body. In her view the medieval body has "less to do with sexuality than with fertility and decay."[11] It is only fair to recognize that this dismissal is part of an overall strategy in much of her work of rehabilitating the study of women's mysticism from some admittedly reductive views of sex and sexual repression. She reveals this agenda in her discussion of mystical union with Christ:

> Physical union with Christ is thus described not only in images of disease and torment but also in images of marriage and sexual consummation; it sometimes culminates in what appears to be orgasm.... Although scholars have, of course, suggested that such reactions are sublimated sexual desire, it seems inappropriate to speak of "sublimation." In the eucharist and in ecstasy, a male Christ was handled and loved; sexual feelings were, as certain contemporary commentators (like David of Augsburg) clearly realized, not so much translated into another medium as simply set free.[12]

It is interesting in this passage that Bynum translates mystical sex into something not worth investigating. She does not acknowledge the possibility that sex, like the body, as she so convincingly shows, might also be constructed. She hints at such a construction when she links the nuptial imagery and sexual imagery with disease and torment, yet she is too quick to eliminate sex and eroticism from her analysis. Where Bynum discusses eroticism in her book *Holy Feast and Holy Fast*, it is always ad hoc, that is, it is linked with specific images of fertility and decay. She devotes only one sustained discussion to eroticism in her entire book. What she comes so close to saying—that eroticism and sex in the religious experiences of medieval women were constructed in terms of violence, suffering, and decay—is what makes mystical sex unrecognizable to modern sensibilities, both religious and secular, and what makes it capable of transforming the mystic's body and soul. Mystical sex is not just "sex as we know it," but that more troubling field of experience that strays into the realms of violence, suffering, and torture. Bynum succeeds in deromanticizing mystical sex by insisting on removing it from the *locus deliciarum*, the masculine idealizing gaze of courtly love, and the domestic bliss of the Bride and Bridegroom. Yet once she removes sex from these contexts, it seems to disappear entirely from her works, as though it were no longer "sex" without these conventions.

Bynum shows us that aggression, violence, masochism, and dark despair are as fundamental to the visions of some women mystics as the tropes of marriage and the languorous desire that we usually think of in connection with mystical sex. Eroticism and sex inhabit more perverse and polymorphous regions than is usually acknowledged, whether through the imagery of hunger and voraciousness so abundantly documented in Bynum's work or in the extremes of suffering found in many late medieval mystical texts. This kind of mystical desire is queer in its effects — exceeding and hyperbolizing its own conventionality and fracturing the discourses of mystical love and sex.

The poems and letters of Hadewijch, the thirteenth-century Flemish mystic and beguine, contain some of the most erotic and, at the same time, disturbing images of mystical sex there are. In her writings, love is not a tasting of the sweet apples of the beloved Bridegroom but a never-satiated hunger and a hell of suffering, even of disgust:

> As Hell turns everything to ruin,
> In Love nothing else is acquired
> But disgust and torture without pity;
> Forever to be in unrest,
> Forever assault and new persecution;
> To be wholly devoured and engulfed
> In her unfathomable essence,
> To founder unceasingly in heat and cold,
> In the deep insurmountable darkness of Love.
> This outdoes the torments of hell.[13]

The torment of desire is a frequent theme of Hadewijch's poetry, and it is not simply the absence of the Beloved that creates this torment. Holy love itself is a hell of persecution, unrest, and disgust, as well as a voraciousness. It is wanton, ferocious, and implacable.

If Hadewijch's poetry and visions remind us of the medical treatises on lovesickness or the symptoms of courtly love, it is because of the consistent emphasis in both on love's violence and its narcissism. The narcissism of courtly love discourse, enacted in the linguistic display of much secular poetry, is displaced in mystical discourse by the violence done to the lover's violated body. Angela of Foligno's (1248–1309) experience of Love's visitation is similar to those described by Hadewijch:

> And then at once she was filled with love and inestimable satiety, which, although it satiated, generated at the same time inestimable hunger [*famem inextimabilem*], so that all her members were unstrung and her soul languished and desired to fly away [*omnia mem-*

*bra tunc disjungebantur et anima languebat et desiderabat per-
venire].* And she wished neither to see nor to feel any creature.
And she did not speak and did not know whether she could speak,
but within she spoke, clamoring that God not let her languish in
such a death, for she thought life to be death.[14]

Sexual consummation is achieved with a violence which she mistakes
for death itself. There is no mistaking the narcissism of this experience,
nor its connection with violence. At the same time, it marks a liminal
experience for Angela by which she crosses over the boundaries of speech
and the body into death.

Finally, the analogy between female mystical discourse of sex and
courtly love simply ignores entirely the role that gender plays. Although
the violence of lovesickness can affect both men and women, it is most
often conceived of in the Middle Ages as a masculine affliction. The discourse of courtly love, too, is a violent one that is more often directed at
women than at the frustrated lover.[15] The terms of courtly love are simply not adaptable to the discourse of women mystics because they are
gendered, and we must be careful not to subsume the violence of the sexual language in their writings to masculine uses of the language of courtly
love. By reversing this convention, the women mystics sometimes contest the idealizing strategies of male abjection and the spiritualized mythos
of courtly love.

Violence, enslavement, demonic desire, torture, and even death become
defining "negative experiences" of mystical love and sex—experiences
that lead to a dissociation of speech and thought from human subjectivity.[16] Bernard of Clairvaux and Richard of Saint Victor both emphasize
the extremes of violence that characterize the limit experiences of mystical eros. For Bernard, holy love is both violent and narcissistic:

> What a violent, consuming, impetuous love this is! It thinks only of
> itself, disregards everything else, despises everything, is satisfied with
> itself! It confuses stations, disregards manners, knows no bounds.
> Proprieties, reason, decency, prudence, judgment are defeated and
> reduced to slavery.[17]

This experience of love bears an uncanny resemblance to Hadewijch's
experience of Love in her poetry—as violent, disgusting, indecent, irrational, unmannered, transgressive, and narcissistic.

Richard of Saint Victor (d. 1173) describes the insatiability, violence,
and persecution of this mystical love in his treatise, the *Four Degrees of
Violent Charity*. Each of the four degrees of love—wounding, binding,
languishing, and, finally, disintegration of mind and soul in its unifica-
tion with Christ—is characterized by a form of violence, and, in fact,
Richard views this violence as one of the main distinguishing features

185

of holy love from other kinds of love—familial, marital, or parental.[18] That these mystical transports are also sexual is no secret in Richard of Saint Victor's work, for he draws analogies between each of the four degrees of spiritual and human love.[19]

For many female mystics, as for Bernard and Richard, mystical sex was not a courtship of lover and beloved, nor was it a nuptial metaphor: it was a frightening, violating, and debilitating experience, as the examples of Angela and Hadewijch suggest it was. Neither the voluptuous, seductive imagery of the Song of Songs nor the convention of courtly love really explains the darkness of this version of mystical sex, although the darker zones of mystical sex are often contained within these discourses. Nor does the tradition represented by the works of Bernard of Clairvaux and Richard of Saint Victor explain what it meant for women to engage in this violent sex with the figure of Love or with Christ.

The queering of mystical tropes for love and desire occurs at the sites of these conventions through the dislodging of the particular masculinist fantasies associated with each. In the words of Bernard of Clairvaux, this queer love "confuses stations, disregards manners, knows no bounds," and it precipitates a crisis in the conventions through the dissonance it enacts. Since cultural models of courtly love were based on the impossibility of female desire, the assumption and expression of mystical desire in courtly terms already exposes the heterosexual laws it usurps. Mystical and courtly notions of love are based, too, on the idea of masculine heterosexual suffering for the Beloved, a suffering that is constructed upon the repression of the feminine. By confusing the "stations" of suffering, female mystics could queer the heterosexual and masculinist strictures governing mystical desire and love. With the reversal and crossing of gender boundaries comes a loss of the idealizing effects of the courtly and mystical love tropes, leaving, in Hadewijch's words, "nothing else . . . but disgust and torture without pity." What has always been "there" in courtly conventions—the suffering and ennoblement it produces—is removed from this idealizing ideological framework and becomes . . . strange, queer.

The troubling of these medieval idioms of mystical love represents only one kind of queering that occurs in female mysticism. In addition to stripping away the idealizing and masculinist fantasizing effects of mystical love rhetoric, the desire of the female mystic often strays from the heterosexual realm she is assumed to inhabit as Bride of Christ. Because of the presumptive heterosexuality of most mystical scholarship, the question has never been asked, What does it signify when a female mystic desires and adores the feminized body of Christ?[20] In addition to addressing this question, I want to examine how scholarship has worked hard not to ask it in the first place and, finally, to offer some directions for future queering.

## Mystical Sexuality

The feminization of the body of Christ is usually considered to be one of the most distinctive features of late medieval piety and the devotion of female mystics in particular. This feminization is regarded as part of a cluster of shifts in devotional belief and practice emphasizing Christ's humanity, physical access to the sacred, and the deployment of social roles to define Christ's relationship to the mystic as mother, husband, lover, and child. Yet scholars almost never explore the feminized body of Christ *as lover* to female mystics. In Caroline Walker Bynum's important study of food imagery in women's religious discourse, *Holy Feast and Holy Fast*, the feminized body of Christ is made legible almost exclusively (and safely) as a nonsexual *maternal* body. The maternal Christ offers his breasts to suckle the female mystic; he gives birth through the wound in his side; and he feeds the suffering, sinful soul with his body, as a mother does. In its generative and nurturing capacity alone the feminized body of Christ is made to signify. Not only does her understanding of the maternal cancel out the sexual but it requires interventionist gender correction to avoid any queer tendencies. In spite of the gender dislocation that occurs when the female mystic identifies with the feminized Christ, Bynum argues, she always made the necessary gender—and by implication, sexuality—adjustments in her mystical intercourse: "Female *imitatio Christi* mingled the genders in its most profound metaphors and its most profound experiences. Women could fuse with Christ's body because they *were* in some sense body, yet women never forgot the maleness of Christ."[21] It is ironic that Bynum, who indulges in the brief self-criticism quoted earlier in this essay, continues nevertheless to deploy a heterosexual model for understanding the feminized body of Christ in relation to male mysticism and an asexual model in the case of female mysticism. In the quotation above she desexes the feminized aspects of Christ and renders his gender entirely masculine, and the sexuality of female mystic, safely heterosexual.

Women were not the only ones to correct ambiguous sexuality in their relationships with Christ, according to Bynum. Twelfth-century Cistercian monks, in particular, "had a problem," says Bynum: "For if the God with whom they wished to unite was spoken of in male language, it was hard to use the metaphor of sexual union unless they saw themselves as female.... [One] solution ... was of course to seek God as female parent, with whom union could be quite physical (in the womb or at the breast." The problem that is never explicitly named is homosexuality. The ever-vigilant Cistercian, on his guard against the heterosexual crisis, makes the necessary adjustment by assuming the role of child to parent and eliminating sexuality altogether from his affective relationship with Christ. As she notes, this solved the "problem" of the metaphorical sexual union with a male Christ.[22] It is as though the mystics were engaged in a gender-correction process during their ecstatic transports in order to avoid the embarrassment of a homosexual union.[23]

In order for the heterosexuality of female mysticism to remain intact, an awful lot of adjustments need to be made, forcing us to wonder whose paradigm this is anyway: Bynum's (and that of most scholars of mysticism) or the female mystic's? The instability of the heterosexual paradigm of mystical desire requires constant vigilance and correction on the part of the scholar to maintain it and to occlude the queer tendencies. When the devotee is male, he desires (but never identifies with) Christ's feminized body, while the female devotee identifies with the feminized body, ever reminding herself in her more erotic transports that Christ is male.

There is no evidence in the mystical writings usually cited of such gender and sexuality policing by female or male mystics; however, there is evidence of scholarly intervention when mystical genders and sexualities stray from heterosexual paradigms. The queer desire of female mystics for the feminized body of Christ is excluded by Bynum's interpretation of that feminization in terms of his maternity. Christ's feminization is chiefly expressed through his maternal physical and spiritual qualities, and his maternity, in turn, is assumed to be asexual. The queer crisis posed by female mystical desire is thus averted by the assumption that the maternal disavows the sexual.

The mystical maternal body of Christ, however, does not enact such repudiation of the sexual but "opens a mesh of possibilities" for the queering of categories—of mystical devotion, the body of Christ, female desire, and the medieval construction of maternity. Bynum frequently cites Catherine of Siena to exemplify the maternity of Christ and the mystic's infantilized relationship to his body, but I would insist upon the conjunction of the erotic with the maternal, and of mystical pleasure with nurturing:

> With that, he tenderly placed his right hand on her neck, and drew her towards the wound in his side. "Drink, daughter, from my side," he said, "and by that draught your soul shall become enraptured with such delight that your very body, which for my sake you have denied, shall be inundated with its overflowing goodness." Drawn close in this way to the outlet of the Fountain of Life, she fastened her lips upon that sacred wound, and still more eagerly the mouth of her soul, and there she slaked her thirst.[24]

Bynum consistently interprets such accounts as "nursing metaphors" in which Catherine of Siena merges her own suffering with Christ's. Her desire here is tantamount to a "eucharistic craving" that suspends all other appetites, according to Bynum's analysis. The explicitly sexual nature of Christ's gesture and the erotic desire expressed in Catherine's slaking of her thirst is disallowed by the nursing metaphor and a modern asexual construction of maternal nurturance.[25]

Queering Christ's gesture and the mystic's desire requires that the reader entertain an open mesh of possibilities, including not only the maternal's potential to function erotically here but the sacred wound's polysemy. When the wound is not *made* to signify monolithically—when excluded meanings are (re)introduced into the domain of cultural legibility—queer possibilities begin to signify as dissonant sites in heteronormative mystical discourse. The queer already inhabits Christ's gesture and Catherine's response at the site of his wound once the heterosexual matrix is suspended. Another cultural reference point becomes visible: Christ's wound as vulva/vagina—and an ulterior form of mystical desire becomes possible.

The sexual nature of the mystic's devotion to Christ's wound is made explicit in one of the most important texts of Franciscan mysticism, the *Stimulus Amoris* by James of Milan. Mystical union between soul and God is figured as a joining of wounds in a mystical act of copulation. In fact, Wolfgang Riehle argues for a "typical and quite consciously intended analogy between this wound of Christ and the female pudenda." Furthermore, Riehle suggests a kind of punning on words, vulva and *vulnus*. The "copulation" of mystical soul with Christ thus occurs at the site of his wound (*vulnus*), which is transformed into the female vulva when *vulnus vulneri copulatur*, "wound is joined to wound."[26] The key to the idea of the joining of wounds is that the lover's soul becomes wounded with love, and this wounding in turn allows him to join in Christ's suffering. In James of Milan's text the speaker is enflamed with desire for entrance into the wound. Elsewhere in the *Stimulus Amoris*, the wound is an object of the speaker's desire for union (*copulo, copulari*).[27]

James of Milan even uses the metaphor of the wound as a "gate of Paradise," invoking that famous garden of delights, the paradise enclosed, which is usually reserved for the female Bride and the allegorical figure of the Church in Song of Songs 4:12: "My sister, my spouse, is a garden enclosed, a garden enclosed, a fountain sealed up." Christ's wound is the open garden through which the *locus deliciarum* is achieved. The physical union of Christ and lover in the Song of Songs occurs at the "hole in the wall" where Christ "put his hand" and "my bowels were moved at his touch." In the *Stimulus Amoris* text, this image is reversed so that Christ invites penetration through the hole in his side and offers consolation and rest as well as inebriation and innumerable delights. There, the lover/speaker drinks, eats, meditates, and experiences "such an abundance of delight that it is impossible for [him] to describe."[28]

This reversal of the Song of Songs tradition in which Christ becomes the feminized lover has never been commented on, as far as I know. In the *Stimulus Amoris* and elsewhere, gender and sexuality are transitive, rather than binary and monolithic. Christ's wound becomes the site of the "garden enclosed" usually occupied by the intact vagina of the feminine lover, and thus becomes queer.[29] Whether or not there is a specific pun on vulva and *vulnus*, as Riehle suggests, the *Stimulus Amoris* text provides a cultural template for making such an identification of vulva/vagina and wound.

This transitivity of wound to vulva/vagina, of masculine to feminine bodies, and of sexualities is most vividly rendered in late medieval devotional imagery.[30] In one fourteenth-century illustration of the Man of Sorrows, the wound is detached from Christ's side and dramatically enlarged to life-size, somewhere in excess of two inches (Figure 9.1). Here, it is the focus of the viewer's devotion, rather than one among many devotional objects associated with the crucifixion. Inscribed around its edge is the claim that this image is the exact size of the wound of our Lord, who suffered death for us. Such inscription is a fairly common invocation to devotional practice among wound images by providing a vivid, quantifiable measure of Christ's suffering and hence his love. At the same time, the sexual connotation of this image is unmistakable. The visual conjunction of wound and vagina provides a visual pun of vulva and *vulnus*, such as Riehle finds in the *Stimulus Amoris*.

In the Psalter and Hours of Bonne of Luxembourg, the wound stands alone (Figure 9.2). The text states that this wound measures the distress and the bounty of Christ's suffering for us. It also represents the wounding that is meant to take place in the viewer's heart, as in the Song of Songs, so that he or she is "wounded with desire." An object of adoration and love, this wound is also the object of violence, suggested in the surrounding implements of torture. Suffering and love are conjoined in acts of violence inflicted not only on the body of Christ, but also, by implication, against the feminized wound/vulva.

This last image is part of a devotional book of hours designed for a female patron, Bonne of Luxembourg, a wealthy woman who would later become the mother of Charles V. Not all these images were designed explicitly for women, but there is evidence in devotional texts for and by women that the wound was a focus for sexual experiences of mystical union. Religious instruction and devotional texts for women explicitly invite them to touch, kiss, suck, and enter the wound of Christ.[31]

A key to the gendered inscription of Christ's wound in medieval devotional texts for women is obliquely alluded to in the thirteenth-century devotional manual for religious women, *Holy Maidenhead*. This text is a defense of virginity by means of a harsh polemic against the horrors of marriage. In it the virgin is warned against losing that which joins her to Christ: "And you, blessed maiden, assigned to him with the mark of maidenhood, break not that seal which seals you together."[32] The writer alludes to the unbroken hymen, the unruptured seal that guarantees her relationship to Christ and that is lost irrevocably in mar-

Figure 9.1. Man of Sorrows and Wound (ca. 1375). The Pierpont Morgan Library, New York, M.90, fol.130. By permission.

riage. There is another reference embedded in this imperative. When the author says, "Break not that seal which seals you together," he uses for "you" the word *inc*, the dual second personal pronoun meaning "the two of you." The mark of maidenhead, the virgin's intact vagina, is joined in yet another seal to Christ.

This sealing of Christ and devotional lover through the vulvic (or vaginal) wound, the mark of Christ's love and the virgin's virginity, is translated into contractual language. Christ's body becomes the charter of

Figure 9.2. Wound of Christ, Psalter and Prayer book of Bonne de Luxembourg (1345). Metropolitan Museum of Art, New York, Cloisters Collection, 69.86, fol. 331r. By permission.

his love, by which he binds us to him and guarantees through his suffering the promise of divine bliss. He authenticates this charter with his wound as a seal (Figure 9.3). Christ appends the "wound in my heart" as a seal to the charter of his body in this image, and in others, he provides the names of his witnesses and the imprint of a notary public.[33] In this image, Christ's wound is both seal and vagina, the broken seal and the open vagina to which the virgin in *Holy Maidenhead* offers her own unbroken, intact genital seal. While this image is later than the *Maidenhead* text, the latter invokes the same kind of association between the wedding vows that the female religious and Christ exchange and the joining of "wounds," vulva/vagina and vulnus, that we found in the *Stimulus Amoris*.

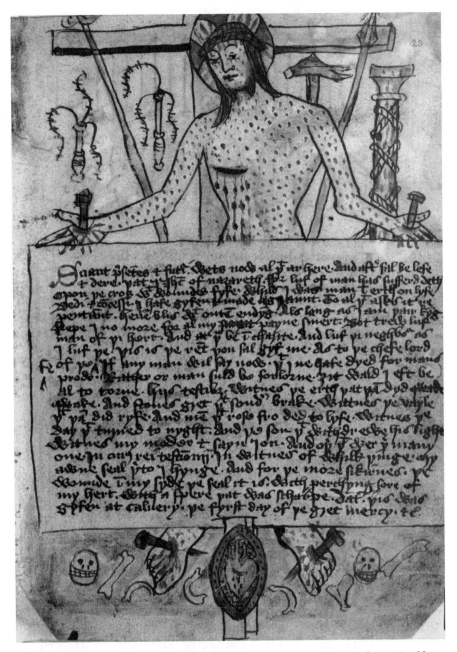

Figure 9.3. The Charter of Christ (fifteenth century). British Library, London, MS Add. 37049, fol. 23. By permission of the British Library.

The wound of Christ is one aspect of the feminization of Christ's body, and it exists in a representational nexus of a woman's vulva and vagina and documentary imagery of institutional seals. By bringing this nexus to the reading of medieval mystical texts by women, we are forced to confront the "problem," as Bynum calls it, of mystical sexuality and of the feminization of Christ's body. The queering of Christ's body and of mystical desire is more common in female mystical discourse than has yet been considered by medieval scholarship.[34] Efforts to queer mystical desire and sexuality, including this one, should not seek merely to uncover or activate the sexual dissonances in mystical discourse; they must also interrogate the queer-effects of such phenomena. In this case, what is signified by the queer tendencies of female mystical discourse?

By destabilizing gender and sexuality categories that deeply structure mystical experience and religious devotion, queer mystical rapture seems to offer a cultural site of resistance, opposition, or transgression for medieval women mystics. Valerie Traub's work, however, cautions us to examine not only the representation of "other" sexualities and desires, but also their capacity to signify. For example, she argues that Renaissance discourse about female tribadism and sodomy was possible precisely because feminine homoerotic desire "did not signify."[35] Her conclusion raises a question for this study of female mystical discourse, namely, are the queer tendencies documented here finally illegible for medieval culture because of the very gender and sexuality imperatives they appropriate? At stake in this question is that potential for the "contestation of sexual legitimacy" cited by Butler as central to the project of queering.

As both Judith Butler and Jonathan Dollimore point out, all such contestation occurs within the dominant cultural codes of legibility and ideologies.[36] The case of female mystical erotics is further complicated by the fact that medieval mystical discourse exists apart from—and often as an alternative to—the social order of women mystics and the medieval church. Mystical discourse insists upon a position both outside the institutional regime of the church and inside its foundation through the Word of God.[37] The regulatory economies of medieval society and religious systems inform mystical discourse and circumvent it. This problematic position of mysticism in medieval society casts in doubt its capacity for a contestation of sexual and gender codes, for a "transgressive reinscription" of those codes.[38]

Within the context of language, however, mystical discourse is able to queer, disrupt, and expose the normative surfaces of language and the conventions language sponsors.[39] The polymorphousness of Christ's body, with its feminine genital wound and its simultaneous masculine properties, introduces confusion at a very foundational level of religious language and, therefore, of religious devotion. The confounding of courtly love tropes in configurations of mystical love by female mystics exposes those "abjecting strategies" of courtly love conventions and the fantasies of masculinity they support. Assessing the queer-effects of female mystical desire — that is, its power to signify — is more difficult.

In Bynum's work and in most medieval scholarship on the subject, female mystical desire signifies only when it is heterosexual, when it confirms the masculine conventions of mysticism. When it becomes queer, it fails to signify, or it is corrected to signify monolithically. Heterosexuality is an imperative in scholarship of medieval mysticism, resolving the more radical discontinuities of female mystical discourse within the dominant tradition even as it blunts the operations of female desire and pleasure. From Hadewijch's fierce inversion of the courtly love tropes of mystical desire to Catherine of Siena's erotic coarticulation of the erotic and the sexual, female mystical discourse confounds gender and the heteronormative categories it inhabits, queering them, causing them to lapse, balk, and swerve.

Such a possibility for queering exists in the feminizing of Christ's body, in the genitalizing of his wound in representational art, and in the discursive expressions of feminine desire. This desire is potentially oppositional in that it seeks to disturb these same categories, and in the process, it exposes the heteronormative laws governing most mystical discourse. The transpositioning of vulva to Christ's wound, the partial feminizing of Christ's body, and Catherine's pleasure contest our own categories for understanding the cultural archives available to medieval mysticism — categories of feminine and masculine, typologies of love, sexualities, and desire. These possibilities for the queer are not foreclosed by the conventions deployed in medieval mysticism, nor are they rendered harmless by the fact that female mysticism occupied a narrow and problematic position within medieval culture.

Both male and female medieval mysticism are desperately in need of more such queering, and both medieval scholarship and modern theorizing about sexuality are equally in need of new "meshes of possibility," to borrow Sedgwick's words. Neither the acts/identity distinction nor the focus on same-sex desire is adequate or desirable as a framework for queering medieval mysticism.[40] The medieval queer offers us an opportunity to "queer" contemporary discourse about the history of sexuality and contemporary queer theory, opening up a mesh of possibilities within it and challenging its categories of understanding. This particular example of the medieval queer invites us to rethink the "queer" in ways that are less exclusive of female sexualities and desires and less assuming of modern identity categories. Finally, as Judith Butler has argued, queering as an oppositional strategy needs to theorize the complex interrelationship between gender and sexuality:

One deciding issue will be whether social strategies of regulation, abjection, and normalization will not continue to relink gender and sexuality such that the oppositional analysis will continue to be under pressure to theorize their interrelations. This will not be the same as reducing gender to prevailing forms of sexual relations such that one "is" the effect of the sexual position one is said to occupy. Resisting such a reduction, it ought to be possible to assert a set of non-causal and non-reductive relations between gender and sexuality, not only to link feminism and queer theory, as one might link two separate enterprises, but to establish their constitutive interrelationship.[41]

The pressure to theorize the interrelations of gender and sexuality comes not only from contemporary social strategies of oppression but from historicizing strategies as well. Scholars of queer theory and medieval studies ought to seek out that mesh of possibilities between gender and sexuality, between medieval and modern structures of oppression, and *among* the queer of different historical periods. Female mystical discourse offers one such pressure point for theorizing the queer in the Middle Ages and the twentieth century.

## Notes

1. Judith Butler, *Bodies That Matter: On the Discursive Limits of "Sex"* (New York and London: Routledge, 1993), 232.

2. Eve Kosofsky Sedgwick, *Tendencies* (Durham, N.C.: Duke University Press, 1993), 8. For a discussion of the parameters and stakes of queer theory, see Teresa de Lauretis, "Queer Theory: Lesbian and Gay Sexualities: An Introduction," *differences: A Journal of Feminist Cultural Studies* 3, no. 2 (1991): iii–xviii. David M. Halperin defines the noun "queer" as a positionality rather than a positivity, describing "a horizon of possibility" in *Saint Foucault: Towards a Gay Hagiography* (New York and Oxford: Oxford University Press, 1995), 62. Halperin also warns of the political liabilities and potential for appropriation in the use of the term, but maintains that it is nevertheless useful for "a radical reversal in the logic of homophobic discourses" (66). For his full discussion of the term, see 62–67.

3. I am paraphrasing Jonathan Goldberg, who calls for risking anachronism in his introduction to *Queering the Renaissance*, ed. Goldberg (Durham, N.C.: Duke University Press, 1994), 5–6. Louise O. Fradenburg and Carla Freccero call for "dislodging and indeed queering the truth-effects of certain historicist practices — especially historicist practices that repudiate the roles of fantasy and pleasure in the production of historiography," in *GLQ: A Journal of Lesbian and Gay Studies*, 1, no. 4 (1995), *Premodern Sexualities in Europe*, ed. Fradenburg and Freccero, 375; see also 377. Simon Gaunt regards queer reading as a way of "examining how representations of transgressive sexualities define and produce the limits of heterosexual norms and of 'troubling' heteronormative paradigms"; "Straight Minds/'Queer Wishes,'" *GLQ* 1, no. 4 (1995): 441. See also these essays revised and reprinted: Fradenburg and Freccero, eds. *Premodern Sexualities* (New York: Routledge, 1996), xiii–xxiv, 153–174.

4. I am using Butler's term "reverse-discourse," "in which the defiant affirmation of queer dialectically reinstalls the version it seeks to overcome," in *Bodies That Matter*, 21.

5. This is a problem with Richard Rambuss's otherwise interesting work on seventeenth-century devotional poetry, "Pleasure and Devotion: The Body of Jesus and Seventeenth-Century Religious Lyric," in *Queering the Renaissance*, ed. Goldberg, 253–79. While

Rambuss succeeds in revising the conventional view of Christ's body by emphasizing its permeability and penetrability, he ends up merely reinstalling this Christ and homo-erotics for the previously heterosexual model without examining the gender and religious ideologies entailed. See also Karma Lochrie, "Desiring Foucault," *Journal of Medieval and Early Modern Studies* 27(Winter 1997): 3–16.

6. See, for example, Caroline Walker Bynum's definitions of affective spirituality, *Holy Feast and Holy Fast: The Religious Significance of Food to Medieval Women* (Berkeley: University of California Press, 1987), 26, 28, 153–61. Bynum locates a "feminization of religious language" in late medieval spirituality, in *Jesus as Mother: Studies in the Spirituality of the High Middle Ages* (Berkeley: University of California Press, 1982), 129–69. For other overviews of affective spirituality, see Clarissa W. Atkinson, *Mystic and Pilgrim: The* Book *and the World of Margery Kempe* (Ithaca, N.Y.: Cornell University Press, 1983), 129–31, 136–38, 147–49, 154–58, and André Vauchez, *Les laïcs au Moyen Age: Pratiques et expériences religieuses* (Paris: Editions du Cerf, 1987).

7. For a discussion of the secular contribution to mystical language of love, see Mary F. Wack, *Lovesickness in the Middle Ages: The Viaticum and Its Commentaries* (Philadelphia: University of Pennsylvania Press, 1990), 24–27.

8. See John Bugge's analysis of sexualized virginity, as an example, *Virginitas: An Essay in the History of a Medieval Idea*, Archives internationales d'histoire des idées, series minor 17 (The Hague: Martinus Nijhoff, 1975), 59–96.

9. See Wack's brief discussion of the overlapping of the discourses of lovesickness and spiritual eroticism in *Lovesickness in the Middle Ages*, 18–27.

10. Bynum, *Jesus As Mother*, 162.

11. Carolyne Walker Bynum, "The Female Body and Religious Practice in the Later Middle Ages," in *Fragments for a History of the Human Body*, ed. Michel Feher, Ramona Naddaff, and Nadia Tazi (New York: Urzone, 1989), 162, reprinted in Bynum, *Fragmentation and Redemption: Essays on Gender and the Human Body in Medieval Religion* (New York: Urzone, 1991), 182.

12. Bynum, "Women Mystics and Eucharistic Devotion in the Thirteenth Century," in *Fragmentation and Redemption*, 133–34. See also Bynum, *Holy Feast and Holy Fast*, 248.

13. *Hadewijch: The Complete Works*, trans. Columbia Hart (New York: Paulist Press, 1980), 356.

14. "Et tunc post hoc statim repleta fuit amore et satietate inextimabili, que quamvis satiet, generat tamen maximam famem tantum inextimabilem, quod omnia membra tunc disjungebantur et anima languebat et desiderabat pervenire. Et volebat nec sentire nec videre aliquam creaturam. Et ipsa non loquebatur et nescit quod potuerit loqui extra; set intus loquebatur, intus clamans quod non faceret eam tantam mortem languere, quia vitam extimabat mortem"; Angela of Foligno, *Le Livre de l'expérience des vrais fidèles: Texte latin publié d'après le manuscrit d'Assise*, ed. and trans. M.-J. Ferré and L. Baudry, (Paris: Droz, 1927), par. 75, pp. 156–58; trans. in Bynum, *Holy Feast and Holy Fast*, 248. Compare this vision with Vision 7 of Hadewijch, in *Hadewijch: The Complete Works*, 280.

15. For a discussion of the aggression in this type of discourse, see Toril Moi, "Desire in Language: Andreas Capellanus and the Controversy of Courtly Love," in *Medieval Literature: Criticism, Ideology and History*, ed. David Aers (New York: St. Martin's Press, 1986), 11–57.

16. I am borrowing the term from Foucault, who borrows it from Georges Bataille, to characterize eroticism that is transgressive and that seeks the absence of limitations, leading to a "veritable destruction of [the] subject, in its dissociation, in its upheaval into something radically 'other'"; quoted in James Miller, *The Passion of Michel Foucault* (New York: Simon and Schuster, 1993), 93.

17. Trans. in Julia Kristeva, *Tales of Love*, by Leon S. Roudiez (New York: Columbia University Press, 1987), 166: "O amor praeceps, vehemens, flagrans, impetuose, qui praeter

te aliud cogitare non sinis, fastidis cetera, contemnis omnia praete, te contentus! Confundis ordines, dissimulas usum, modum ignoras; totum quod opportunitatis, quod rationis, quod pudoris, quod consilii iudiciive esse videtur, triumphas in temetipso et redigis in captivitatem"; *Sermones super Cantica Canticorum*, ed. J. Leclercq, C. H. Talbot, and H. M. Rochais, in *S. Bernardi Opera*, vol. 2 (Rome: Editiones Cistercienses, 1957), 79, 1, p. 272. See Kristeva's discussion of Bernard's theory of violence in connection with his commentary on the Song of Songs in *Tales of Love*, 151–69.

18. Gervais Dumeige, ed., *Les quatre degrés de la violente charité*, Textes philosophiques du moyen âge, 3 (Paris: J. Vrin, 1955), par. 3, pp. 127–29.

19. See especially Dumeige, *Les quatre degrés*, pars. 18–20, pp. 145–47.

20. Rambuss raises the possibility of a "same-sex erotic fusion" between Catherine of Siena and Christ, but he focuses his discussion on male devotion to Christ's body in seventeenth-century poetry, in "Pleasure and Devotion," 267–68. Simon Gaunt raises a close parallel to my question in his study of saints' lives: "Is there any room in hagiography, amidst the celibacy or alongside the implicitly heterosexual 'bride of Christ' metaphor, for non-heterosexual sexualities?"; "Straight Minds/'Queer' Wishes," 441.

21. Bynum, "The Female Body and Religious Practice," 186 and 187–88.

22. Bynum, *Jesus As Mother*, 161. Bynum raises the example of Rupert of Deutz, who embraced and kissed Christ without making any gender adjustments, as one of those "occasional examples of monks describing what appears to us to be a sexual union with a male God" (161). For further discussion of this example, see Wack, *Lovesickness in the Middle Ages*, 24–25.

23. My critique of Bynum's work is not intended to diminish its brilliance or my own indebtedness to it. It merely calls attention to the embeddedness of our views about sexuality in our work. Besides, as I have shown, there are at least two "Bynumisms" in Bynum's work—two Bynums, in effect: the Bynum who recognizes the ambiguated sexuality of medieval mystical discourse and the Bynum who insists on subsuming that sexuality to other foundational categories, such as fertility and decay, for studying women's mysticism. I would like to think that I am taking the cautionary voice of Bynum 1 as my lead and running with it, even though my conclusions diverge significantly from hers.

24. Raymond of Capua, *The Life of Catherine of Siena*, trans. Conleth Kearns (Wilmington, Del.: Michael Glazier, 1980), 156. Also quoted in Bynum, *Holy Feast and Holy Fast*, 172.

25. Bynum further develops this argument in *Fragmentation and Redemption*, 79–238.

26. Wolfgang Riehle, *The Middle English Mystics*, trans. Bernard Standring (London: Routledge and Kegan Paul, 1981), 46. Riehle quotes this phrase, *vulnus vulneri copulatur*, from the Digby 58 manuscript version of the Franciscan text, rather than the standard edition of it. I have not been able to consult this text, but I have checked with the standard edition of the *Stimulus Amoris*, ed. Quaracchi, Bibliotheca franciscana ascetica medii aevi, 4 (N.p.: Quaracchi, 1905). There is no exact correspondence to the above quotation in Riehle's text in the Quaracchi edition, but there are many that are close in general meaning. The frequent reference and invocation to the side wound of Christ testifies to the erotic theme. The joining of wounds—of lover wounded by love and of Christ—is frequently alluded to. See Riehle, *Middle English Mystics*, 13, 20–21, and chaps. 5 and 14.

27. Quaracchi, *Stimulus Amoris*, 71–76.

28. Quaracchi, *Stimulus Amoris*, 73–74; and 71: "Ideoque ibi habito et, quibus vescitur, cibis vescor ac ibi inebrior suo potu; ibi tanta abundo dulcedine, ut tibi non valeam enarrare."

29. I am borrowing the term of gender transitivity from Eve Kosofsky Sedgwick, *The Epistemology of the Closet* (Berkeley: University of California Press, 1990), 1–2, 87–90. Sedgwick contrasts models for viewing homosexual desire in terms of essentialist and transitivist approaches to gender. According to essentialist definitions, gender is constituted by natural and essential features, while the transitive definitions view gender as so-

cially constructed and therefore occupying a liminal position. Although I am adopting Sedgwick's term here, I am not so convinced of the discreteness of her categories.

30. Caroline Walker Bynum includes one example of the *Arma Christi* from the fourteenth century in *Fragmentation and Redemption*, 278, fig. 7.6. She concedes that "the sexual overtones modern viewers find in such depictions may have been apparent also to medieval viewers." One wonders what Bynum actually means by her comment: whether medieval viewers may have been slower to apprehend "sexual overtones," or whether they had different images of the vulva than we do. Of course, the possibility that the female genitals might have been viewed differently in medieval culture is a real one. Thomas Laqueur suggests as much in his study of medical imagery, but he does not provide images from the medieval period; see *Making Sex: Body and Gender from the Greeks to Freud* (Cambridge: Harvard University Press, 1990), 1–62. Even if medical imagery of vulva and/or vagina was significantly different than the wound imagery, we cannot necessarily assume that medical imagery was the standard cultural construction of the female sexual anatomy.

31. For examples, see *The Ancrene Riwle*, trans. M. B. Salu (London: Burns and Oates, 1955), 130, or for the Middle English, *The English Text of the Ancrene Riwle: Ancrene Wisse* (Corpus Christi College, Cambridge, 402), ed. J. R. R. Tolkien, EETS 249 (London: Oxford University Press, 1962), 151; also Bonaventure's *De perfectione vitae ad sorores*, quoted in Jeffrey F. Hamburger, *The Rothschild Canticles: Art and Mysticism in Flanders and the Rhineland circa 1300* (New Haven: Yale University Press, 1990), 72–73; and *Aelred of Rievaulx's De Institutione Inclusarum*, ed. John Ayto and Alexandra Barratt, EETS 287 (London: Oxford University Press, 1987), 49.

32. *Hali Meiðhad*, ed. Bella Millett, EETS 284 (London: Oxford University Press, 1982), 5: "Ant tu þenne, eadi meiden, þet art iloten to him wiþ mei[þ]hades merke, ne brec ðu nawt ðet seil ðet seileþ inc togederes."

33. For a discussion of the "charter of Christ" image, see Douglas Gray, *Themes and Images in the Medieval English Religious Lyric* (London: Routledge and Kegan Paul), 129–31. See also M. C. Spalding, *The Middle English Charters of Christ* (Bryn Mawr, 1914), and Rosemary Woolf, *The English Religious Lyric in the Middle Ages* (Oxford: Clarendon Press, 1968), 213–14.

34. For a few specific examples of possibly queer female desire for Christ's wounds, see *Julian of Norwich: Showings*, trans. Edmund Colledge and James Walsh (New York: Paulist Press, 1978), 220; Angela of Foligno, *Le livre de l'expérience des vrais fidèles: Texte Latin publié d'après le manuscrit d'Assise*, ed. and trans. M.-J. Ferré and L. Baudry (Paris: Droz, 1927), 138; Mechtild of Hackeborn, *The Booke of Gostly Grace of Mechtild of Hackeborn*, ed. Theresa A. Halligan, Studies and Texts, 49 (Toronto: Pontifical Institute of Medieval Studies, 1979), 175–76, 321–22, 335, 352; and Catherine of Siena quoted in Bynum, *Holy Feast and Holy Fast*, 173. For devotion to the wounds in medieval lyrics, see Douglas Gray, *Themes and Images in the Medieval English Religious Lyric* (London: Routledge and Kegan Paul, 1972), 52–54, 129–34; and Rosemary Woolf, *The English Lyric in the Middle Ages* (Oxford: Clarendon Press, 1968), 183–248. For the Mass of the Five Wounds in English liturgy, see R. W. Pfaff, *New Liturgical Feasts in Later Medieval England* (Oxford: Clarendon Press, 1970), 84–91.

35. Valerie Traub, "The (In)Significance of 'Lesbian' Desire," in *Queering the Renaissance*, ed. Goldberg, 80. See also my discussion of Traub in "Desiring Foucault."

36. See Judith Butler, *Gender Trouble: Feminism and the Subversion of Identity* (New York: Routledge, 1990), 1–38, 134–41; and Jonathan Dollimore, *Sexual Dissidence: Augustine to Wilde, Freud to Foucault* (Oxford: Clarendon Press, 1991), 33–35.

37. See Michel de Certeau, *Heterologies: Discourse on the Other*, trans. Brian Massumi (Minneapolis: University of Minnesota Press, 1986), 92–93, and my discussion of mystical discourse, *Margery Kempe and Translations of the Flesh* (Philadelphia: University of Pennsylvania Press, 1991), chap. 2, esp. 63–64.

38. Dollimore uses this term to mean the generating of "internal instabilities within repressive norms" and the contestation that results from this; *Sexual Dissidence*, 33.

39. I am borrowing Butler's remarks on "queering" as an "exposure within language" in her analysis of Nella Larsen's *Passing,* in *Bodies That Matter,* 176.

40. For the acts/identity debate, see David M. Halperin, *One Hundred Years of Homosexuality and Other Essays on Greek Love* (New York: Routledge, 1990), 1–53; John Boswell, *Christianity, Social Tolerance, and Homosexuality: Gay People in Western Europe from the Beginning of the Christian Era to the Fourteenth Century* (Chicago: Chicago University Press, 1980); and "Revolutions, Universals, and Sexual Categories," in *Hidden from History: Reclaiming the Gay and Lesbian Past,* ed. Martin Duberman, Martha Vicinus, and George Chauncey Jr. (New York: Penguin, 1991), 17–36; Robert Padgug, "Sexual Matters: Rethinking Sexuality in History," in *Hidden from History,* ed. Duberman et al., 54–64. For critiques of this model, see Fradenburg and Freccero, "Introduction: The Pleasures of History," *GLQ* 1, no. 4 (1995): 378–79; Gaunt, "Straight Minds/'Queer' Wishes," 441–43; and Lochrie, "Don't Ask, Don't Tell: Murderous Plots and Medieval Secrets," *GLQ* 1, no. 4 (1995): 406–7, 415.

41. Judith Butler, "Critically Queer," in *Bodies That Matter,* 240. For further discussion of the debate between feminism and queer theory, see "More Gender Trouble: Feminism Meets Queer Theory," ed. Judith Butler, *differences: A Journal of Feminist Cultural Studies* 6, nos. 2–3 (Summer–Fall 1994); Judith Butler and Biddy Martin, eds., "Critical Crossings," *diacritics* 24, nos. 2–3 (Summer-Fall 1994); and Sally Driscoll, "Outlaw Readings: Beyond Queer Theory," *Signs* 22, no. 1 (Autumn 1996): 30–51.

# Contributors

**E. Jane Burns** is professor of women's studies at the University of North Carolina, Chapel Hill. She has published widely on medieval French literature, including *Bodytalk: When Women Speak in Old French Literature* and *Arthurian Fictions: Rereading the Vulgate Cycle*. She has also co-edited with Roberta L. Krueger a collection of essays, *Courtly Ideology and Woman's Place in Medieval French Literature*, and served as one of the founding editors of the *Medieval Feminist Newsletter* from 1985–95.

**Joan Cadden** is professor of history at the University of California, Davis. Her book *Meanings of Sex Difference in the Middle Ages: Medicine, Science, and Culture* was awarded the History of Science Society's 1994 Pfizer Prize for best book in the history of science. Her current projects include a textual and manuscript study of Peter of Abano's chapter on the causes of homosexual desire.

**Michael Camille,** author of *Image on the Edge: The Margins of Medieval Art* and, most recently, *Master of Death: The Lifeless Art of Pierre Remiet, Illuminator,* continues to be fascinated by the intersection of the verbal and the visual in medieval culture and is currently working on a new book, *The Medieval Art of Love*. He is professor of art history at the University of Chicago.

**Dyan Elliott,** associate professor of history at Indiana University, is the author of *Spiritual Marriage: Sexual Abstinence in Medieval Wedlock*. She is currently working on two projects. The first is a study exploring the instability of the boundaries between female sanctity and heresy in the later Middle Ages. The second is a collection of essays examining the way pollution taboos interact with medieval conceptions of gender and religion.

**Louise O. Fradenburg** is professor of English at the University of California, Santa Barbara. She is the author of essays on Chaucer and on Middle Scots Poetry and of *City, Marriage, Tournament: Arts of Rule in Late Medieval Scotland*. She is also the editor of *Women and Sovereignty* and, with Carla Freccero, of *Premodern Sexualities*.

**Mark D. Jordan,** author of *Ordering Wisdom: The Hierarchy of Philo-sophical Discourses in Aquinas* and *The Invention of Sodomy in Chris-tian Theology,* as well as of numerous articles on medieval philosophy, theology, and medicine, is currently at work on "Divine Eloquence: The Rhetorical Forms of Scholastic Theology." He is professor in the Medieval Institute at the University of Notre Dame.

**Steven F. Kruger** teaches medieval studies and lesbian and gay studies at Queens College and the Graduate School and University Center of the City University of New York. He is author of *Dreaming in the Middle Ages* and *AIDS Narratives: Gender and Sexuality, Fiction and Science.* Currently he is coediting, with Deborah R. Geis, *Approaching the Mil-lennium: Essays on "Angels in America."*

**Karma Lochrie** is associate professor of English at Loyola University, Chicago. She is the author of *Margery Kempe and Translations of the Flesh,* as well as of articles on Foucault, mysticism, and medieval sex. She is currently working on a book about the medieval uses of secrecy entitled *Covert Operations.*

**Peggy McCracken** is assistant professor of French at the University of Illinois at Chicago. She has published articles on medieval French liter-ature and is the author of *The Romance of Adultery: Queenship and Sexual Transgression in Old French Liiterature* (forthcoming).

**James A. Schultz** is professor of German and director of the Lesbian, Gay, and Bisexual Studies Program at the University of California, Los Angeles. He has published articles on medieval German literature, nar-rative theory, and the history of childhood, as well as two books, *The Shape of the Round Table: Structures of Middle High German Arthurian Romance* and *The Knowledge of Childhood in the German Middle Ages, 1100–1350.*

# Index

❖

# MEDIEVAL CULTURES

**VOLUME 3**
Edited by Marilyn J. Chiat and Kathryn L. Reyerson
*The Medieval Mediterranean: Cross-Cultural Contacts*

**VOLUME 2**
Edited by Andrew MacLeish
*The Medieval Monastery*

**VOLUME 1**
Edited by Kathryn Reyerson and Faye Powe
*The Medieval Castle*